GERMAN

PHRASE BOOK
& DICTIONARY

AVALON
TRAVEL

ii

Avalon Travel
a member of the
Perseus Books Group
1700 Fourth Street
Berkeley, CA 94710, USA

Printed in the United States of America by Worzalla.
Sixth edition. First printing November 2008.

For the latest on Rick's lectures, guidebooks, tours, and public television
series, contact Europe Through the Back Door, P.O. Box 2009, Edmonds,
WA 98020, tel. 425/771-8303, fax 425/771-0833, www.ricksteves.com,
rick@ricksteves.com.

ISBN-10: 1-59880-193-7
ISBN-13: 978-1-59880-193-4

Europe Through the Back Door Managing Editor: Risa Laib
Europe Through the Back Door Editors: Cameron Hewitt,
  Gretchen Strauch
Avalon Travel Editor: Jamie Andrade
Translation: Julia Klimek, Martin Minich, Niels Kuchenbuch
Phonetics: Risa Laib, Cameron Hewitt
Production: Darren Alessi
Cover Design: Kimberly Glyder Design
Maps & Graphics: David C. Hoerlein, Zoey Platt
Photography: Rick Steves, Dominic Bonuccelli,
  Andrea Johnson
Front Cover Photo: Heidelberg, Baden-Wuerttemberg, Germany
  © Konrad Wothe/Getty Images

Distributed to the book trade by
Publishers Group West, Berkeley, California

Rick Steves' Guidebook Series

Country Guides

Rick Steves' Best of Europe
Rick Steves' Croatia & Slovenia
Rick Steves' Eastern Europe
Rick Steves' England
Rick Steves' France
Rick Steves' Germany
Rick Steves' Great Britain
Rick Steves' Ireland
Rick Steves' Italy
Rick Steves' Portugal
Rick Steves' Scandinavia
Rick Steves' Spain
Rick Steves' Switzerland

City and Regional Guides

Rick Steves' Amsterdam, Bruges & Brussels
Rick Steves' Athens & the Peloponnese (new in 2009)
Rick Steves' Budapest (new in 2009)
Rick Steves' Florence & Tuscany
Rick Steves' Istanbul
Rick Steves' London
Rick Steves' Paris
Rick Steves' Prague & the Czech Republic
Rick Steves' Provence & the French Riviera
Rick Steves' Rome
Rick Steves' Venice
Rick Steves' Vienna, Salzburg & Tirol (new in 2009)

Rick Steves' Phrase Books

French
French/Italian/German
German
Italian
Portuguese
Spanish

Other Books

Rick Steves' Europe Through the Back Door
Rick Steves' Europe 101: History and Art for the Traveler
Rick Steves' European Christmas
Rick Steves' Postcards from Europe

(Avalon Travel)

CONTENTS

Getting Started 1–3

German Basics 4–13
   Meeting and Greeting 4   Struggling with German . . . 7
   Essentials 5   Handy Questions 8
   Where? 6   Das Yin und Yang 10
   How Much? 6   Big Little Words 11
   How Many? 6   Very German Expressions . 12
   When? 7

Counting 14–23
  Numbers 14
  Money 16
   Money Words 18
  Time 18
   Timely Expressions 19   The Month 22
   About Time 20   The Year 22
   The Day 21   Holidays and
   The Week 21   Happy Days 22

  Key Phrases: Money 16
  Key Phrases: Time 19

Traveling 24–50
  Flights 24
   Making a Reservation 24   Getting to/
   At the Airport 25   from the Airport 25
  Trains 26
   The Train Station 26   On the Platform 32
   Getting a Ticket 27   On the Train 32
   Reservations, Supplements,   Reading Train and Bus
     and Discounts 29   Schedules 33
   Ticket Talk 30   Going Places 35
   Changing Trains 31
  Buses and Subways 36
   At the Bus Station or   Taking Buses and
     Metro Stop 36   Subways 37
  Taxis 39
   Getting a Taxi 39   In the Taxi 40

Driving 41
    Rental Wheels 41   Car Trouble 44
    At the Gas Station 42   Parking 44

Finding your Way 45
    Route-Finding Words 46   Reading Road Signs 48
    The Police 48   Other Signs You May See 50

Key Phrases: Trains 29

Key Phrases: Buses and Subways 37

Key Phrases: Taxis 41

Key Phrases: Driving 43

Sleeping 51–65
    Places to Stay 51   Confirming, Changing, and
    Reserving a Room 51   Canceling Reservations . .59
    Using a Credit Card 53   Nailing Down the Price . . 60
    Das Alphabet 55   Choosing a Room 60
    Just the Fax, Ma'am 56   Breakfast 61
    Getting Specific 56   Hotel Help 62
    Families 57   Hotel Hassles 63
    Mobility Issues 58   Checking Out 64
                                Camping 65

Key Phrases: Sleeping 52

Eating 66–106
  Restaurants 66
    Types of Restaurants 66   Tableware and
    Finding a Restaurant 66   Condiments 72
    Getting a Table 67   The Food Arrives 72
    The Menu 69   Complaints 73
    Ordering 70   Compliments 73
                                 Paying for Your Meal 74

  Special Concerns 75
    In a Hurry 75   Children 76
    Dietary Restrictions 75

  What's Cooking? 78
    Breakfast 78   If You Knead Bread 83
    Snacks, Quick Lunches,   Soups and Salads 84
      and Appetizers 80   Seafood 85
    Say Cheese 81   Poultry 86
    Cheese Specialties 82   Meat 86
    Sandwichess 82   Main Course Specialties . .87

TABLE OF CONTENTS

Eating Italian. 88
How Food is Prepared . . . 88
Side Dishes. 90
Veggies 90
Fruits. 91
Nuts 92
Teutonic Treats. 92
Ice Cream. 93
Dessert Specialties 94

Drinking. 95
Water and Juice 95
Milk 97
Coffee and Tea 97
Wine 98
Wine Words 99
Wine Labels. 100
Beer. 101
Bar Talk. 102
Spirits 103

Picnicking. 104
At the Grocery 104
Tasty Picnic Words. 105

Key Phrases: Restaurants. 68

Key Phrases: What's Cooking? 79

Best of the Wurst 80-81

Avoiding Mis-Steaks 87

Styles of Cooking 89

Key Phrases: Drinking 96

Austrian Coffee Lingo 98

Menu Decoder 107-128
German / English 107
English / German 119

Activities. 129-147
Sightseeing. 129
Where?. 129
At the Sight 130
Please. 130
Tours. 131
Entrance Signs 132
Discounts. 132
In the Museum 132
Art and Architecture 133
Castles and Palaces 134
Religious Words. 135

Shopping. 136
German Shops. 136
Shop Till You Drop. 138
Street Markets. 139
Clothes. 140
Colors 141
Materials. 142
Jewelry. 142

Sports. 143
Bicycling 143
Swimming and Boating . 144
Sports Talk. 145

Entertainment 146
  Entertaining Words 146

Key Phrases: Sightseeing 130

Key Phrases: Shopping 137

Connect 148–155
  Phoning 148
    Telephone Words 149   Cell Phones 150
  Email and the Web 151
    Web Words 152   On Screen 152
  Mailing 153
    Licking the Postal Code . 154

Key Phrases: Email and the Web 151

Key Phrases: Mailing 154

Help! 156–159
    Theft and Loss 156   Help for Women 158
    Helpful Words 158

Key Phrases: Help! 157

Services 160–163
    Laundry 160   Repair 162
    Clean Words 161   Filling Out Forms 163
    Haircuts 161

Health 164–176
    Ailments 166   Contacts and Glasses . . . 173
    Women's Health 167   Toiletries 174
    Parts of the Body 168   Makeup 175
    Healthy Words 169   For Babies 175
    First-Aid Kit 173   More Baby Things 176

Key Phrases: Health 164

Chatting 177–201
    Nothing More   Map Musings 184
      Than Feelings 178   Favorite Things 184
    Who's Who 178   Weather 189
    Family 179   Thanks a Million 191
    Work 179   Smoking 191
    Chatting with Children . . . 181   Responses for
    Travel Talk 182   All Occasions 192

TABLE OF CONTENTS

Conversing with
 Animals 193
Create Your Own Conversation
Who 194
What. 195
Why. 196
A German Romance. 198
Words of Love. 198

Profanity. 193
Sweet Curses 194
. . . . 194
You Be the Judge 197
Beginnings and
 Endings. 197

Ah, Liebe 199

Key Phrases: Chatting 178

Dictionary 202–249
 German / English. 202
 English / German. 225

Tips for Hurdling the Language Barrier 250–259
Don't Be Afraid to
 Communicate 250
International Words. 251
German Verbs 252
German Tongue Twisters . 255

English Tongue
 Twisters 256
German Songs 257
Numbers and
 Stumblers. 259

Appendix 260–265
 Let's Talk Telephones 260
Country Codes 261
Directory Assistance. 261

US Embassies. 261
 Tear-Out Cheat Sheet 263
 Making Your Hotel Reservation. 265

Illustrations
Standard Road Signs 49
Parts of the Body. 170–171
Human Temp Thermometer. 172
Weather Thermometer. 190

Maps
Major Transportation Lines in Germany,
Austria, and Switzerland 34
Germany 185
Austria 186
Switzerland. 186
Europe 187
The United States. 188
The World. 188

Hi, I'm Rick Steves.

I'm the only monolingual speaker I know who's had the nerve to design a series of European phrase books. But that's one of the things that makes them better. You see, after 30 summers of travel through Europe, I've learned first-hand (1) what's essential for communication in another country and (2) what's not. I've assembled these most important words and phrases in a logical, no-frills format, and I've worked with native Europeans and seasoned travelers to give you the simplest, clearest translations possible.

But this book is more than just a pocket translator. The words and phrases have been carefully selected to make you a happier, more effective budget traveler. The key to getting more out of every travel dollar is to get closer to the local people, and to rely less on entertainment, restaurants, and hotels that cater only to foreign tourists. This book will give you the linguistic four-wheel drive to navigate through German, Austrian, and Swiss culture—from ordering a meal at a locals-only Tirolean restaurant to discussing social issues, travel dreams, and your wurst memories with the family that runs the place. Long after your memories of castles and museums have faded, you'll still treasure the close encounters you had with your new European friends.

A good phrase book should help you enjoy your linguistic adventure—not just survive it—so I've added a healthy dose of humor. But please use these phrases carefully, in a self-effacing spirit. Remember that one ugly American can undo the goodwill built by dozens of culturally sensitive ones.

To get the most out of this book, take the time to internalize and put into practice my German pronunciation tips. I've spelled out the pronunciations as if you were reading English. Don't worry too much about memorizing grammatical rules, like which gender a particular noun is—toss sex out the window, and communicate!

German is the closest thing I'll ever have to a "second language." It takes only a few words to feel like I'm part of the greater Germanic family, greeting hikers in the Alps, commiserating over the crowds in Rothenburg, prosting in the beerhalls of Munich, and slap-dancing in Tirol.

You'll notice that this book has a dictionary and a nifty menu decoder. You'll also find German tongue twisters, international words, telephone tips, and a handy tear-out cheat sheet. Tear it out and tuck it into your *dirndl* or *lederhosen* so you can easily use it to memorize key phrases during otherwise idle moments. As you prepare for your trip, you may want to take advantage of the most recent editions of my *Rick Steves' Germany, Rick Steves' Switzerland* and *Rick Steves' Vienna, Salzburg & Tirol* guidebooks.

My goal is to help you become a more confident, extroverted traveler. If this phrase book helps make that happen, or if you have suggestions for making it better, I'd love to hear from you. I personally read and value all feedback. My address is Europe Through the Back Door, P.O. Box 2009, Edmonds, WA 98020, tel. 425/771-8303, fax 425/771-0833, rick@ricksteves.com.

Happy travels, and *Viel Glück* (good luck) as you hurdle the language barrier!

Rick Steves

GETTING STARTED

Versatile, Entertaining German

...is spoken throughout Germany, Austria, and most of Switzerland. In addition, German rivals English as the handiest second language in Scandinavia, the Netherlands, Eastern Europe, and Turkey.

German is kind of a "lego language." Be on the look-out for fun combination words. A *Fingerhut* (finger hat) is a thimble, a *Halbinsel* (half island) is a peninsula, a *Stinktier* (stinky animal) is a skunk, and a *Dummkopf* (dumb head) is... um... uh...

German pronunciation differs from English in some key ways:

CH sounds like the guttural CH in Scottish loch.
J sounds like Y in yes.
K is never silent.
S can sound like S in sun or Z in zoo.
SCH sounds like SH in shine.
TH sounds like T in top.
V sounds like F in fun.
W sounds like V in volt.
Z sounds like TS in hits.
AU and **EU** sounds like OY in joy.
E sounds like A in cake.
O always sounds like O in note (never like O in not).

U always sounds like U in flute (never like U in hut).
EI sounds like I in light.
I and **IE** sound like EE in seed.

German has a few unusual signs and sounds. The letter *ß* is not a letter B at all–it's interchangeable with "ss." Some of the German vowels are double-dotted with an umlaut. The *ä* has a sound like E in "men." The *ö* has a sound uncommon in English. To make the *ö* sound, round your lips to say "o," but say "ee." To say *ü*, pucker your lips to make an "oo" sound, but say "e." The German *ch* has a clearing-your-throat sound. Say *Achtung!*

Here's a guide to the phonetics in this book:

ah	like A in father.
ar	like AR in far.
ay	like AY in play.
ee	like EE in seed.
eh	like E in get.
ehr	sounds like "air."
er	like ER in mother.
ew	pucker your lips and say "ee."
g	like G in go.
kh	like the guttural CH in Achtung.
i	like I in hit.
ī	like I in light.
o	like O in cost.
oh	like O in note.
or	like OR in core.
oo	like OO in moon.
ow	like OW in now.
oy	like OY in toy.
s	like S in sun.
u	like U in put.
uh	like U in but.
ur	like UR in purr.
ts	like TS in hits. It's a small explosive sound.

In German, the verb is often at the end of the sentence—it's where the action is. Germans capitalize all nouns. Each noun has a gender, which determines which "the" you'll use (*der* man, *die* woman, and *das* neuter). No traveler is expected to remember which is which. It's O.K. to just grab whichever "the" (*der, die, das*) comes to mind. In the interest of simplicity, we've occasionally left out the articles. Also for simplicity, we often drop the all-important "please." Please use "please" (*bitte,* pronounced **bit**-teh) liberally.

Each German-speaking country has a distinct dialect. The Swiss speak a lilting Swiss-German around the home, but in schools and at work they speak and write in the same standard German used in Germany and Austria (called "High" German, or *Hochdeutsch*). The multilingual Swiss greet you with a cheery *"Grüetzi,"* (pron. **grewt**-see), thank you by saying *"Merci,"* (pron. **mehr**-see), and bid goodbye with *"Ciao"* (pron. chow). Both Austrians and Bavarians speak in a sing-song dialect, and greet one another with *"Grüss Gott"* (pron. grews goht) which means "May God greet you."

GERMAN BASICS

While he used a tank instead of a Eurailpass, General Patton made it all the way to Berlin using only these phrases.

Meeting and Greeting

Good day.	*Guten Tag.*	**goo**-tehn tahg
Good morning.	*Guten Morgen.*	**goo**-tehn **mor**-gehn
Good evening.	*Guten Abend.*	**goo**-tehn **ah**-behnt
Good night.	*Gute Nacht.*	**goo**-teh nahkht
Hi. (informal)	*Hallo.*	**hah**-loh
Welcome!	*Willkommen!*	vil-**koh**-mehn
Mr.	*Herr*	hehr
Ms.	*Frau*	frow
Miss (under 18)	*Fräulein*	**froy**-līn
How are you?	*Wie geht's?*	vee gayts
Very well, thanks.	*Sehr gut, danke.*	zehr goot **dahng**-keh
And you?	*Und Ihnen?*	oont **ee**-nehn
My name is ___.	*Ich heiße ___.*	ikh **hī**-seh
What's your name?	*Wie heißen Sie?*	vee **hī**-sehn zee
Pleased to meet you.	*Sehr erfreut.*	zehr ehr-**froyt**
Where are you from?	*Woher kommen Sie?*	voh-her **koh**-mehn zee
I am / We are...	*Ich bin / Wir sind...*	ikh bin / veer zint
Are you...?	*Sind Sie...?*	zint zee
...on vacation	*...auf Urlaub*	...owf **oor**-lowp

4

...on business	...auf Geschäftsreise	...owf geh-**shehfts**-rī-zeh
See you later!	Bis später!	bis **shpay**-ter
So long! (informal)	Tschüss!	chewss
Goodbye.	Auf Wiedersehen.	owf **vee**-der-zayn
Good luck!	Viel Glück!	feel glewk
Have a good trip!	Gute Reise!	**goo**-teh **rī**-zeh

People use the greeting *"Guten Morgen"* (Good morning) until noon, and *"Guten Tag"* (Good day) switches to *"Guten Abend"* (Good evening) around 6 P.M.

Essentials

Good day.	Guten Tag.	**goo**-tehn tahg
Do you speak English?	Sprechen Sie Englisch?	**shprehkh**-ehn zee **ehng**-lish
Yes. / No.	Ja. / Nein.	yah / nīn
I don't speak German.	Ich spreche nicht Deutsch.	ikh **shprehkh**-eh nikht doych
I'm sorry.	Es tut mir leid.	ehs toot meer līt
Please.	Bitte.	**bit**-teh
Thank you.	Danke.	**dahng**-keh
Thank you very much.	Vielen Dank.	**fee**-lehn dahngk
No problem.	Kein Problem.	kīn proh-**blaym**
Good.	Gut.	goot
Very good.	Sehr gut.	zehr goot
Excellent.	Ausgezeichnet.	ows-geht-**sīkh**-neht
You are very kind.	Sie sind sehr freundlich.	zee zint zehr **froynd**-likh
Excuse me. (to pass or get attention)	Entschuldigung.	ehnt-**shool**-dig-oong
It doesn't matter.	Macht's nichts.	mahkhts nikhts
You're welcome.	Bitte.	**bit**-teh
Sure.	Sicher.	**zikh**-er
O.K.	In Ordnung.	in **ord**-noong
Let's go.	Auf geht's.	owf gayts
Goodbye.	Auf Wiedersehen.	owf **vee**-der-zayn

GERMAN BASICS

Where?

Where is...?	*Wo ist...?*	voh ist
...the tourist information office	*...das Touristen-informations-büro*	dahs too-**ris**-tehn-in-for-maht-see-**ohns** **bew**-roh
...a cash machine	*...ein Bankomat*	**īn** bahnk-oh-maht
...the train station	*...der Bahnhof*	dehr **bahn**-hohf
...the bus station	*...der Busbahnhof*	dehr **boos**-bahn-hohf
...the toilet	*...die Toilette*	dee toh-**leh**-teh
men / women	*Herren / Damen*	**hehr**-ehn / **dah**-mehn

You'll find some German words are similar to English if you're looking for a *Bank, Hotel, Restaurant,* or *Supermarkt.*

How Much?

How much is it?	*Wie viel kostet das?*	vee feel **kohs**-teht dahs
Write it down?	*Aufschreiben?*	**owf**-shrī-behn
Is it free?	*Ist es umsonst?*	ist ehs oom-**zohnst**
Included?	*Inklusive?*	in-kloo-**zee**-veh
Do you have...?	*Haben Sie...?*	**hah**-behn zee
Where can I buy...?	*Wo kann ich... kaufen?*	voh kahn ikh... **kow**-fehn
I'd like...	*Ich hätte gern...*	ikh **heh**-teh gehrn
We'd like...	*Wir hätten gern...*	veer **heh**-tehn gehrn
...this.	*...dies.*	deez
...just a little.	*...nur ein bißchen.*	noor īn **bis**-yehn
...more.	*...mehr.*	mehr
...a ticket.	*...eine Karte.*	**ī**-neh **kar**-teh
...a room.	*...ein Zimmer.*	īn **tsim**-mer
...the bill.	*...die Rechnung.*	dee **rehkh**-noong

How Many?

one	*eins*	īns
two	*zwei*	tsvī
three	*drei*	drī
four	*vier*	feer

five	*fünf*	fewnf
six	*sechs*	zehkhs
seven	*sieben*	**zee**-behn
eight	*acht*	ahkht
nine	*neun*	noyn
ten	*zehn*	tsayn

You'll find more to count on in the "Numbers" section (page 14).

When?

At what time?	*Um wie viel Uhr?*	oom vee feel oor
open	*geöffnet*	geh-**urf**-neht
closed	*geschlossen*	geh-**shloh**-sehn
Just a moment.	*Moment.*	moh-**mehnt**
Now.	*Jetzt.*	yehtst
Soon.	*Bald.*	bahlt
Later.	*Später.*	**shpay**-ter
Today.	*Heute.*	**hoy**-teh
Tomorrow.	*Morgen.*	**mor**-gehn

Be creative! You can combine these phrases to say: "Two, please," or "No, thank you," or "Open tomorrow?" or "Please, where can I buy a ticket?" Please is a magic word in any language. If you want something and you don't know the word for it, just point and say, "*Bitte*" (Please). If you know the word for what you want, such as the bill, simply say, "*Rechnung, bitte*" (Bill, please).

Struggling with German

Do you speak English?	*Sprechen Sie Englisch?*	**shprehkh**-ehn zee **ehng**-lish
A teeny weeny bit?	*Ein ganz klein bißchen?*	īn gahnts klīn **bis**-yehn
Please speak English.	*Bitte sprechen Sie Englisch.*	**bit**-teh **shprehkh**-ehn zee **ehng**-lish
You speak English well.	*Ihr Englisch ist sehr gut.*	eer **ehng**-lish ist zehr goot

I don't speak German.	*Ich spreche nicht Deutsch.*	ikh **shprehkh**-eh nikht doych
We don't speak German.	*Wir sprechen nicht Deutsch.*	veer **shprehkh**-ehn nikht doych
I speak a little German.	*Ich spreche ein bißchen Deutsch.*	ikh **shprehkh**-eh īn **bis**-yehn doych
Sorry, I speak only English.	*Es tut mir leid, ich spreche nur Englisch.*	ehs toot meer līt ikh **shprehkh**-eh noor **ehng**-lish
Sorry, we speak only English.	*Es tut mir leid, wir sprechen nur Englisch.*	ehs toot meer līt veer **shprehkh**-ehn noor **ehng**-lish
Does somebody nearby speak English?	*Spricht jemand in der Nähe Englisch?*	shprikht **yay**-mahnt in dehr **nay**-heh **ehng**-lish
Who speaks English?	*Wer kann Englisch?*	vehr kahn **ehng**-lish
What does this mean?	*Was bedeutet das?*	vas beh-**doy**-teht dahs
What is this in German / English?	*Wie heißt das auf Deutsch / Englisch?*	vee hīst dahs owf doych / **eng**-lish
Repeat?	*Noch einmal?*	nohkh **īn**-mahl
Please speak slowly.	*Bitte sprechen Sie langsam.*	**bit**-teh **shprehkh**-ehn zee **lahng**-zahm
Slower.	*Langsamer.*	**lahng**-zah-mer
I understand.	*Ich verstehe.*	ikh fehr-**shtay**-heh
I don't understand.	*Ich verstehe nicht.*	ikh fehr-**shtay**-heh nikht
Do you understand?	*Verstehen Sie?*	fehr-**shtay**-hehn zee
Write it down?	*Aufschreiben?*	**owf**-shrī-behn

Handy Questions

How much?	*Wie viel?*	vee feel
How many?	*Wie viele?*	vee **fee**-leh
How long is the trip?	*Wie lange dauert die Reise?*	vee lahng-eh **dow**-ert dee **rī**-zeh

How many minutes / hours?	Wie viele Minuten / Stunden?	vee **fee**-leh mee-**noo**-tehn / **shtoon**-dehn
How far?	Wie weit?	vee vīt
How?	Wie?	vee
Can you help me?	Können Sie mir helfen?	**kurn**-nehn zee meer **hehlf**-ehn
Can you help us?	Können Sie uns helfen?	**kurn**-nehn zee oons **hehlf**-ehn
Can I...?	Kann ich...?	kahn ik
Can we...?	Können wir...?	**kurn**-nehn veer
...have one	...eins haben	īns **hah**-behn
...go in for free	...umsonst rein	oom-**zohnst** rīn
...borrow that for a moment	...das für ein Moment leihen	dahs fewr īn moh-**mehnt lī**-hehn
...borrow that for an hour	...das für eine Stunde leihen	dahs fewr ī-neh **shtoon**-deh **lī**-hehn
...use the toilet	...die Toilette benützen	dee toh-**leh**-teh beh-**newts**-ehn
What? (didn't hear)	Wie bitte?	vee **bit**-teh
What is this / that?	Was ist dies / das?	vahs ist deez / dahs
What is better?	Was ist besser?	vahs ist **behs**-ser
What's going on?	Was ist los?	vahs ist lohs
When?	Wann?	vahn
What time is it?	Wie spät ist es?	vee shpayt ist ehs
At what time?	Um wie viel Uhr?	oom vee feel oor
On time? / Late?	Pünktlich? / Spät?	**pewnkt**-likh / shpayt
How long will it take?	Wie lange dauert es?	vee **lahng**-eh **dow**-ert ehs
When does this open / close?	Wann ist hier geöffnet / geschlossen	vahn ist heer geh-**urf**-neht / geh-**shloh**-sehn
Is this open daily?	Ist es täglich offen?	ist ehs **tayg**-likh **oh**-fehn
What day is this closed?	An welchem Tag ist es geschlossen?	ahn **vehlkh**-ehm tahg ist ehs geh-**shloh**-sehn
Do you have...?	Haben Sie...?	**hah**-behn zee

Where is...?	Wo ist...?	voh ist
Where are...?	Wo sind...?	voh zint
Where can I find / buy...?	Wo kann ich... finden / kaufen?	voh kahn ikh... **fin**-dehn / **kow**-fehn
Where can we find / buy...?	Wo können wir... finden / kaufen?	vo **kurn**-ehn veer... **fin**-dehn / **kow**-fehn
Is it necessary?	Ist das nötig?	ist dahs **nur**-tig
Is it possible...?	Ist es möglich...?	ist ehs **mur**-glikh
...to enter	...hinein zu gehen	hin-**īn** tsoo **gay**-hehn
...to picnic here	...hier zu picknicken	heer tsoo **pik**-nik-ehn
...to sit here	...hier zu sitzen	heer tsoo **zit**-sehn
...to look	...anzusehen	**ahn**-tsoo-zay-hehn
...to take a photo	...ein Foto zu machen	īn **foh**-toh tsoo **mahkh**-ehn
...to see a room	...ein Zimmer zu sehen	īn **tsim**-mer tsoo **zay**-hehn
Who?	Wer?	vehr
Why?	Warum?	vah-**room**
Why not?	Warum nicht?	vah-**room** nikht
Yes or no?	Ja oder nein?	yah **oh**-der nīn

To prompt a simple answer, ask, "*Ja oder nein?*" (Yes or no?). To turn a word or sentence into a question, ask it in a questioning tone. An easy way to ask, "Where is the toilet?" is to say, "*Toilette?*"

Das Yin und Yang

good / bad	gut / schlecht	goot / shlehkht
best / worst	beste / schlechteste	**bes**-teh / **shlehkh**-tehs-teh
a little / lots	wenig / viel	**vay**-nig / feel
more / less	mehr / weniger	mehr / **vay**-nig-er
cheap / expensive	billig / teuer	**bil**-lig / **toy**-er
big / small	groß / klein	grohs / klīn
hot / cold	heiß / kalt	hīs / kahlt
warm / cool	warm / kühl	varm / kewl
open / closed	geöffnet / geschlossen	geh-**urf**-neht / geh-**shloh**-sehn

entrance / exit	Eingang / Ausgang	**īn**-gahng / **ows**-gahng
push / pull	drücken / ziehen	**drewk**-ehn / **tsee**-hehn
arrive / depart	ankommen / abfahren	**ahn**-koh-mehn / **ahp**-fah-rehn
early / late	früh / spät	frew / shpayt
soon / later	bald / später	bahlt / **shpay**-ter
fast / slow	schnell / langsam	shnehl / **lahng**-zahm
here / there	hier / dort	heer / dort
near / far	nah / fern	nah / fayrn
indoors / outdoors	drinnen / draussen	**drin**-nehn / **drow**-sehn
mine / yours	mein / Ihr	mīn / eer
this / that	dies / das	deez / dahs
everybody / nobody	jeder / keiner	**yay**-der / **kī**-ner
easy / difficult	leicht / schwierig	līkht / **shvee**-rig
left / right	links / rechts	links / rehkhts
up / down	hoch / unter	hohkh / **oon**-ter
beautiful / ugly	schön / häßlich	shurn / **hehs**-likh
nice / mean	nett / gemein	neht / geh-**mīn**
smart / stupid	klug / dumm	kloog / doom
vacant / occupied	frei / besetzt	frī / beh-**zehtst**
with / without	mit / ohne	mit / **oh**-neh

Big Little Words

I	ich	ikh
you (formal)	Sie	zee
you (informal)	du	doo
we	wir	veer
he	er	ehr
she	sie	zee
they	sie	zee
and	und	oont
at	bei	bī
because	weil	vīl
but	aber	**ah**-ber
by (train, car, etc.)	mit	mit

for	*für*	fewr
from	*von*	fohn
here	*hier*	heer
if	*ob*	ohp
in	*in*	in
it	*es*	ehs
not	*nicht*	nikht
now	*jetzt*	yehtst
only	*nur*	noor
or	*oder*	**oh**-der
this / that	*dies / das*	deez / dahs
to	*nach*	nahkh
very	*sehr*	zehr

Very German Expressions

Ach so.	ahkh zoh	I see.
Achtung.	**ahkh**-toong	Attention. / Watch out.
Alles klar.	**ah**-lehs klar	Everything is clear. / I get it.
Ausgezeichnet.	ows-geht-**sīkh**-neht	Excellent.
Bitte.	**bit**-teh	Please. / You're welcome.
Kann ich Ihnen helfen?	kahn ikh **een**-ehn **helf**-ehn	Can I help you?
Es geht.	ehs gayt	So-so.
Gemütlich.	geh-**mewt**-likh	Cozy.
Gemütlichkeit.	geh-**mewt**-likh-kīt	Coziness.
Genau.	geh-**now**	Exactly.
Halt.	hahlt	Stop.
Hoppla!	**hohp**-lah	Oops!
Kein Wunder.	kīn **voon**-der	No wonder.
Mach schnell!	mahkh shnehl	Hurry up!
Macht's nichts.	mahkhts nikhts	It doesn't matter.
Natürlich.	nah-**tewr**-likh	Naturally.
Sonst noch etwas?	zohnst nohkh **eht**-vahs	Anything else?
Stimmt.	shtimt	Correct.
Super.	**zoo**-pehr	Great.

Warum nicht?	vah-**room** nikht	Why not?
Was ist los?	vahs ist lohs	What's going on?
Wie geht's?	vee gayts	How's it going?

Gemütlich (the adjective) and *Gemütlichkeit* (the noun) refer to a special local coziness. A candlelit dinner, a friendly pub, a strolling violinist under a grape arbor on a balmy evening...this is *gemütlich*.

COUNTING

NUMBERS

0	*null*	nool
1	*eins*	īns
2	*zwei*	tsvī
3	*drei*	drī
4	*vier*	feer
5	*fünf*	fewnf
6	*sechs*	zehkhs
7	*sieben*	**zee**-behn
8	*acht*	ahkht
9	*neun*	noyn
10	*zehn*	tsayn
11	*elf*	ehlf
12	*zwölf*	tsvurlf
13	*dreizehn*	**drī**-tsayn
14	*vierzehn*	**feer**-tsayn
15	*fünfzehn*	**fewnf**-tsayn
16	*sechzehn*	**zehkh**-tsayn
17	*siebzehn*	**zeeb**-tsayn
18	*achtzehn*	**ahkht**-tsayn
19	*neunzehn*	**noyn**-tsayn
20	*zwanzig*	**tsvahn**-tsig
21	*einundzwanzig*	**īn**-oont-tsvahn-tsig
22	*zweiundzwanzig*	**tsvī**-oont-tsvahn-tsig

23	*dreiundzwanzig*	**drī**-oont-tsvahn-tsig
30	*dreißig*	**drī**-sig
31	*einunddreißig*	**īn**-oont-drī-sig
40	*vierzig*	**feer**-tsig
41	*einundvierzig*	**īn**-oont-feer-tsig
50	*fünfzig*	**fewnf**-tsig
60	*sechzig*	**zehkh**-tsig
70	*siebzig*	**zeeb**-tsig
80	*achtzig*	**ahkht**-tsig
90	*neunzig*	**noyn**-tsig
100	*hundert*	**hoon**-dert
101	*hunderteins*	hoon-dert-**īns**
102	*hundertzwei*	hoon-dert-**tsvī**
200	*zweihundert*	**tsvī**-hoon-dert
1000	*tausend*	**tow**-zehnd
2000	*zweitausend*	**tsvī**-tow-zehnd
2001	*zweitausendeins*	**tsvī**-tow-zehnd-**īns**
2002	*zweitausendzwei*	**tsvī**-tow-zehnd-**tsvī**
2003	*zweitausenddrei*	**tsvī**-tow-zehnd-**drī**
2004	*zweitausendvier*	**tsvī**-tow-zehnd-**feer**
2005	*zweitausendfünf*	**tsvī**-tow-zehnd-**fewnf**
2006	*zweitausendsechs*	**tsvī**-tow-zehnd-**zehkhs**
2007	*zweitausendsieben*	**tsvī**-tow-zehnd-**zee**-behn
2008	*zweitausendacht*	**tsvī**-tow-zehnd-**ahkht**
2009	*zweitausendneun*	**tsvī**-tow-zehnd-**noyn**
2010	*zweitausendzehn*	**tsvī**-tow-zehnd-**tsayn**
million	*eine Million*	**ī**-neh mil-**yohn**
billion	*eine Milliarde*	**ī**-neh mil-**yar**-deh
number one	*Nummer eins*	**noo**-mer **īns**
first	*erste*	**ehr**-steh
second	*zweite*	**tsvī**-teh
third	*dritte*	**drit**-teh
once / twice	*ein Mal / zwei Mal*	īn mahl / tsvī mahl
a quarter	*ein Viertel*	īn **feer**-tehl
a third	*ein Drittel*	īn **drit**-tehl
half	*Halb*	hahlp
this much	*so viel*	zoh feel
a dozen	*ein Dutzend*	īn **doot**-tsehnd
some	*einige*	**ī**-ni-geh

enough	genug	geh-**noog**
a handful	eine Hand voll	**ī**-neh hahnt fohl
50%	fünfzig Prozent	**fewnf**-tsig proh-**tsehnt**
100%	hundert Prozent	**hoon**-dert proh-**tsehnt**

The number *zwei* (two) is sometimes pronounced "tsvoh" to help distinguish it from the similar sound of *eins* (one).

Remember the nursery rhyme about the four-and-twenty blackbirds? That's how Germans say the numbers from 21 to 99 (e.g., 59 = *neunundfünfzig* = nine-and-fifty).

COUNTING

MONEY

Where is a cash machine?	Wo ist ein Geldautomat?	voh ist īn **gelt**-ow-toh-maht
My ATM card has been...	Meine Kontokarte wurde...	**mī**-neh **kohn**-toh-kar-teh **voor**-deh
...demagnetized.	...entmagnetisiert.	ehnt-mahg-neh-teh-**zeert**
...stolen.	...gestohlen.	geh-**shtoh**-lehn
...eaten by the machine.	...von der Maschine geschluckt.	fohn dehr mahs-**shee**-neh geh-**shlookt**

Key Phrases: Money

euro (€)	Euro	**oy**-roh
money	Geld	gehlt
cash	Bargeld	**bar**-gehlt
credit card	Kreditkarte	kreh-**deet**-kar-teh
bank	Bank	bahnk
cash machine	Geldautomat, Bankomat	**gelt**-ow-toh-maht, **bahnk**-oh-maht
Where is a cash machine?	Wo ist ein Bankomat?	voh ist īn **bahnk**-oh-maht
Do you accept credit cards?	Akzeptieren Sie Kreditkarten?	ahk-tsehp-**teer**-ehn zee kreh-**deet**-kar-tehn

Do you accept credit cards?	Akzeptieren Sie Kreditkarten?	ahk-tsehp-**teer**-ehn zee kreh-**deet**-kar-tehn
Can you change dollars?	Können Sie Dollar wechseln?	**kurn**-nehn zee **dohl**-lar **vehkh**-sehln
What is your exchange rate for dollars...?	Was ist ihr Wechselkurs für Dollars...?	vahs ist eer **vehkh**-sehl-koors fewr **dohl**-lars
...in traveler's checks	...in Reisechecks	in **rī**-zeh-shehks
What is the commission?	Wie viel ist die Kommission?	vee feel ist dee koh-mis-see-**ohn**
Any extra fee?	Extra Gebühren?	**ehx**-trah geh-**bew**-rehn
Can you break this? (big bills into smaller bills)	Können Sie dies wechseln?	**kurn**-nehn zee deez **vehkh**-sehln
I would like...	Ich hätte gern...	ikh **heht**-teh gehrn
...small bills.	...kleine Banknoten.	**klī**-neh **bahnk**-noh-tehn
...large bills.	...große Banknoten.	**groh**-seh **bahnk**-noh-tehn
...coins.	...Münzen.	**mewn**-tsehn
€50	fünfzig Euro	**fewnf**-tsig **oy**-roh
Is this a mistake?	Ist das ein Fehler?	ist dahs īn **fay**-ler
This is incorrect.	Das stimmt nicht.	dahs shtimt nikht
Did you print these today?	Haben Sie die heute gedruckt?	**hah**-ben zee dee **hoy**-teh geh-**drookt**
I'm broke / poor / rich.	Ich bin pleite / arm / reich.	ikh bin **plī**-teh / arm / **rīkh**
I'm Bill Gates.	Ich bin Bill Gates.	ikh bin "Bill Gates"
Where is the nearest casino?	Wo ist das nächste Kasino?	voh ist dahs **nehkh**-steh kah-**see**-noh

COUNTING

Germany and Austria use the euro currency. Euros (€) are divided into 100 cents. Switzerland has held fast to its francs (Fr), which are divided into 100 centimes (c) or rappen (Rp). Use your common cents—cents and centimes are like pennies, and the euro and franc currency each have coins like nickels, dimes, and half-dollars.

Money Words

euro (€)	Euro	**oy**-roh
cents	Cent	sehnt
money	Geld	gehlt
cash	Bargeld	**bar**-gehlt
cash machine	Geldautomat, Bankomat	**gelt**-ow-toh-maht, **bahnk**-oh-maht
bank	Bank	bahnk
credit card	Kreditkarte	kreh-**deet**-kar-teh
change money	Geld wechseln	gehlt **vehkh**-sehln
exchange	Wechsel	**vehkh**-sehl
buy / sell	kaufen / verkaufen	**kow**-fehn / fehr-**kow**-fehn
commission	Kommission	koh-mis-see-**ohn**
cash advance	Vorschuß in Bargeld	**for**-shoos in **bar**-gehlt
cashier	Kassierer	kahs-**seer**-er
bills	Banknoten	**bahnk**-noh-tehn
coins	Münzen	**mewn**-tsehn
receipt	Beleg	beh-**lehg**

Every cash mashine (**Geldautomat** in Germany, **Bankomat** in Austria and Switzerland) is multilingual, but if you want to be adventuresome, **Bestätigung** means confirm, **Korrektur** means change or correct, and **Abbruch** is cancel. Your PIN code is a **Geheimnummer**.

TIME

What time is it?	Wie spät ist es?	vee shpayt ist ehs
It's...	Es ist...	ehs ist
...8:00 in the morning.	...acht Uhr morgens.	ahkht oor **mor**-gehns
...16:00.	...sechzehn Uhr.	**zehkh**-tsayn oor
...4:00 in the afternoon.	...vier Uhr nachmittags.	feer oor **nahkh**-mit-tahgs
...10:30 in the evening.	...halb elf Uhr abends. ("half-eleven")	hahlp ehlf oor **ah**-behnts

Key Phrases: Time

minute	*Minute*	mee-**noo**-teh
hour	*Stunde*	**shtoon**-deh
day	*Tag*	tahg
week	*Woche*	**vohkh**-eh
What time is it?	*Wie spät ist es?*	vee shpayt ist ehs
It's...	*Es ist...*	ehs ist
...8:00.	*...acht Uhr.*	ahkht oor
...16:00.	*...sechzehn Uhr.*	**zehkh**-tsayn oor
When does this open / close?	*Wann ist hier geöffnet / geschossen?*	vahn ist heer geh-**urf**-neht / geh-**shloh**-sehn

...a quarter past nine.	*...Viertel nach neun.*	**feer**-tehl nahkh noyn
...a quarter to eleven.	*...Viertel vor elf.*	**feer**-tehl for ehlf
...noon.	*...Mittag.*	**mit**-tahg
...midnight.	*...Mitternacht*	**mit**-ter-nahkht
...early / late.	*...früh / spät.*	frew / shpayt
...on time.	*...pünktlich.*	**pewnkt**-likh
...sunrise.	*...Sonnenaufgang.*	zoh-nehn-**owf**-gahng
...sunset.	*...Sonnenuntergang.*	zoh-nehn-**oon**-ter-gahng
It's my bedtime.	*Es ist meine Zeit fürs Bett.*	ehs ist **mī**-neh tsīt fewrs beht

Timely Expressions

I will / We will....	*Ich bin / Wir sind...*	ikh bin / veer zint
...be back at 11:20.	*...um elf Uhr zwanzig zurück.*	oom ehlf oor **tsvahn**-tsig tsoo-**rewk**
I will / We will...	*Ich bin / Wir sind...*	ikh bin / veer zint
...be there by 18:00.	*...um achtzehn Uhr dort.*	oom **ahkht**-tsayn oor dort
When is check-out time?	*Wann muß ich das Zimmer verlassen?*	vahn mus ikh dahs **tsim**-mer fehr-**lah**-sehn

When does this open / close?	Wann ist hier geöffnet / geschossen	vahn ist heer geh-**urf**-neht / geh-**shloh**-sehn
When...?	Wann...?	vahn
...does this train / bus leave for ___	...geht der Zug / Bus nach ___	gayt dehr tsoog / boos nahkh
...does the next train / bus leave for ___	...geht der nächste Zug / Bus nach ___	gayt dehr **nehkh**-steh tsoog / boos nahkh
...does the train / bus arrive in ___	...kommt der Zug / Bus in ___ an	kohmt dehr tsoog / boos in ___ ahn
I want / We want...	Ich möchte / Wir möchten...	ikh **merkh**-teh / veer **merkh**-tehn
...to take the 16:30 train.	...den Zug um sechzehn Uhr dreißig nehmen.	dehn tsoog oom **zehkh**-tsayn oor **drī**-sig **nay**-mehn
Is the train / bus...?	Ist der Zug / Bus...?	ist dehr tsoog / boos
...early / late	...früh / spät	frew / shpayt
...on time	...pünktlich	**pewnkt**-likh

In Germany, Austria, and Switzerland, the 24-hour clock (or military time) is used by hotels, for the opening and closing hours of museums, and for train, bus, and boat schedules. Informally, Europeans usually use the same 12-hour clock we use.

About Time

minute	Minute	mee-**noo**-teh
hour	Stunde	**shtoon**-deh
in the morning	am Morgen	ahm **mor**-gehn
in the afternoon	am Nachmittag	ahm **nahkh**-mit-tahg
in the evening	am Abend	ahm **ah**-behnt
at night	in der Nacht	in dehr nahkht
at 6:00 sharp	Punkt sechs Uhr	poonkt zehkhs oor
from 8:00 to 10:00	von acht bis zehn	fohn ahkht bis tsayn
in half an hour	in einer halben Stunde	in **ī**-ner **hahl**-behn **shtoon**-deh

in one hour	in einer Stunde	in **ī**-ner **shtoon**-deh
in three hours	in drei Stunden	in drī **shtoon**-dehn
anytime	jederzeit	yay-der-**tsīt**
immediately	jetzt	yehtst
every hour	jede Stunde	**yay**-deh **shtoon**-deh
every day	jeden Tag	**yay**-dehn tahg
daily	täglich	**tay**-glikh
last	letzte	**lehts**-teh
this	diese	**dee**-zeh
next	nächste	**nehkh**-steh
May 15	fünfzehnten Mai	**fewnf**-tsayn-tehn mī
high season	Hochsaison	**hohkh**-zay-zohn
low season	Nebensaison	**neh**-behn-zay-zohn
in the future	in Zukunft	in **tsoo**-koonft
in the past	in der Vergangenheit	in dehr fehr-**gahng**-ehn-hīt

COUNTING

The Day

day	Tag	tahg
today	heute	**hoy**-teh
yesterday	gestern	**geh**-stern
tomorrow	morgen	**mor**-gehn
tomorrow morning	morgen früh	**mor**-gehn frew
day after tomorrow	übermorgen	**ew**-ber-mor-gehn

The Week

week	Woche	**vohkh**-eh
last / this / next week	letzte / diese / nächste Woche	**lehts**-teh / **dee**-zeh / **nehkh**-steh **vohkh**-eh
Monday	Montag	**mohn**-tahg
Tuesday	Dienstag	**deen**-stahg
Wednesday	Mittwoch	**mit**-vohkh
Thursday	Donnerstag	**dohn**-ner-stahg
Friday	Freitag	**frī**-tahg
Saturday	Samstag, Sonnabend	**zahm**-stahg, **zohn**-ah-behnt
Sunday	Sonntag	**zohn**-tahg

The Month

month	*Monat*	**moh**-naht
January	*Januar*	**yah**-noo-ar
February	*Februar*	**fay**-broo-ar
March	*März*	mehrts
April	*April*	ah-**pril**
May	*Mai*	mī
June	*Juni*	**yoo**-nee
July	*Juli*	**yoo**-lee
August	*August*	ow-**goost**
September	*September*	zehp-**tehm**-ber
October	*Oktober*	ohk-**toh**-ber
November	*November*	noh-**vehm**-ber
December	*Dezember*	day-**tsehm**-ber

For dates, take any number, add the sound "-ten" to the end, then say the month. June 19 is *neunzehnten Juni.*

The Year

year	*Jahr*	yar
spring	*Frühling*	**frew**-ling
summer	*Sommer*	**zohm**-mer
fall	*Herbst*	hehrpst
winter	*Winter*	**vin**-ter

Holidays and Happy Days

holiday	*Feiertag*	**fī**-er-tahg
national holiday	*staatlicher Feiertag*	**shtaht**-likh-er **fī**-er-tahg
school holiday	*Schulferien*	**shool**-fehr-ee-ehn
religious holiday	*religiöser Feiertag*	reh-lig-ee-**ur**-zer **fī**-er-tahg
Is today / tomorrow a holiday?	*Ist heute / morgen ein Feiertag?*	ist **hoy**-teh / **mor**-gehn īn **fī**-er-tahg
Is a holiday coming up soon?	*Ist bald ein Feiertag?*	ist bahlt īn **fī**-er-tahg

When?	*Wann?*	vahn
What is the holiday?	*Welcher Feiertag ist das?*	**vehlkh**-er **fī**-er-tahg ist dahs
Merry Christmas!	*Fröhliche Weihnachten!*	**frur**-likh-eh **vī**-nahkh-tehn
Happy New Year!	*Glückliches Neues Jahr!*	**glewk**-likh-ehs **noy**-ehs yar
Easter	*Ostern*	**ohs**-tern
Happy anniversary!	*Herzlichen Glückwunsch!*	**hehrts**-likh-ehn **glewk**-voonsh
Happy birthday!	*Herzlichen Glückwunsch zum Geburtstag!*	**hehrts**-likh-ehn **glewk**-voonsh tsoom geh-**boorts**-tahg

German-speakers sing "Happy Birthday" to the tune we use, sometimes even in English. The German version means "On your birthday, best wishes": *Zum Geburtstag, viel Glück, Zum Geburtstag, viel Glück, Zum Geburtstag, liebe ___, Zum Geburtstag, viel Glück.*

Traditional Germanic celebrations include *Karneval* (a.k.a *Fascnacht, Fasnet,* or *Fasching*), a week-long festival of parades and partying that happens before Lent in February. The centers of revelry are Köln (Germany), Mainz (Germany), and Basel (Switzerland), though celebrations happen in cities and towns throughout southern Germany, western Austria, and northern Switzerland. *Christi Himmelfahrt,* or the Ascension of Christ, comes in May, and doubles for Father's Day. You'll see men in groups on pilgrimages through the countryside, usually carrying beer or heading toward it.

Germany's national holiday is October 3, Austria's is October 26, and Switzerland's is August 1.

TRAVELING

The German word for journey or trip is *Fahrt*. Many tourists enjoy collecting *Fahrts*. In German-speaking areas, you'll see signs for *Einfahrt* (entrance), *Rundfahrt* (round trip), *Rückfahrt* (return trip), *Panoramafahrt* (scenic journey), *Zugfahrt* (train trip), *Ausfahrt* (trip out), and throughout your trip, people will smile and wish you a *"Gute Fahrt."*

FLIGHTS

All airports have bilingual signage with German and English. Also, nearly all airport service personnel and travel agents speak English these days. Still, these words and phrases could conceivably come in handy.

Making a Reservation

I'd like to... my reservation / ticket.	*Ich möchte meine Reservierung / Flugschein...*	ikh **murkh**-teh **mī**-neh reh-zer-**feer**-oong / **floog**-shīn
We'd like to... our reservation / ticket.	*Wir möchten unsere Reservierung / Flugschein...*	veer **murkh**-tehn **oon**-zer-eh reh-zer-**feer**-oong / **floog**-shīn
...confirm	*...bestätigen.*	beh-**shtay**-teh-gehn
...reconfirm	*...nochmals bestätigen.*	**nohkh**-mahls beh-**shtay**-teh-gehn

24

...change	...ändern.	**ehn**-dern
...cancel	...annulieren.	ah-nool-**eer**-ehn
aisle seat /	Sitz am Gang /	zits ahm gahng /
window seat	Sitz am Fenster	zits ahm **fehn**-ster

At the Airport

Which terminal?	Welches Terminal?	**vehlkh**-ehs ter-mee-**nahl**
international flights	internationale	in-ter-naht-see-oh-**nah**-leh
	Flüge	**flew**-geh
domestic flights	inländische Flüge	**in**-lehnd-ish-eh **flew**-geh
arrival	Ankunft	**ahn**-koonft
departure	Abflug	**ahp**-floog
baggage check	Gepäckaufgabe	geh-**pehk**-owf-gah-beh
baggage claim	Gepäckausgabe	geh-**pehk**-ows-gah-beh
Nothing to declare	Nichts zu	nihkts tsoo
	deklarieren	dehk-lah-**reer**-ehn
I have only	Ich habe nur	ikh **hah**-beh noor
carry-on luggage.	Handgepäck.	**hahnd**-geh-pehk
flight number	Flugnummer	**floog**-noo-mer
departure gate	Abflugtor	**ahp**-floog-tor
duty free	zollfrei	**tsohl**-frī
luggage cart	Gepäckwagen	geh-**pehk**-vah-gehn
jet lag	Jetlag	"jet lag"

Getting to/from the Airport

Approximately how	Wie viel ungefähr ist	vee feel **oon**-geh-fehr ist
much is a	die Taxifahrt...?	dee **tahk**-see-fart
taxi ride...?		
...to downtown	...zur Stadtmitte	tsoor **shtaht**-mit-teh
...to the train	...zum Bahnhof	tsoom **bahn**-hohf
station		
...to the airport	...zum Flughafen	tsoom **floog**-hah-fehn
Does a bus	Fährt ein Bus	fayrt īn boos
(or train) run...?	(oder Zug)...?	(**oh**-der tsoog)
...from the airport	...vom Flughafen	fohm **floog**-hah-fehn
to downtown	zur Stadtmitte	tsoor **shtaht**-mit-teh

...to the airport from downtown	...zum Flughafen von der Stadtmitte	tsoom **floog**-hah-fehn fohn dehr **shtaht**-mit-teh
How much is it?	Wie viel kostet das?	vee feel **kohs**-teht dahs
Where does it leave from...?	Von wo fährt er ab...?	fohn voh fayrt ehr ahp
Where does it arrive at...?	Wo kommt er an...?	voh kohmt ehr ahn
...at the airport	...am Flughafen	ahm **floog**-hah-fehn
...downtown	...in der Stadtmitte	in dehr **shtaht**-mit-teh
How often does it run?	Wie oft fährt er?	vee ohft fayrt ehr

TRAINS

The Train Station

Where is the...?	Wo ist der...?	voh ist dehr
...(central) train station	...(Haupt-)Bahnhof	(**howpt**-)**bahn**-hohf
German Railways	Deutsche Bahn (DB)	**doy**-cheh bahn (day bay)
Swiss Railways	Schweizer Bundesbahn (SBB)	**shvīt**-ser **boon**-dehs-bahn (ehs bay bay)
Austrian Railways	Österreichische Bundesbahn (ÖBB)	**urs**-ter-**rīkh**-is-sheh **boon**-dehs-bahn (ur bay bay)
train information	Zugauskunft	tsoog-**ows**-koonft
train	Zug	tsoog
high-speed train	Intercity, Schnellzug	"inter-city," **shnehl**-tsoog
highest-speed train	ICE	ee tsay ay
fast / faster	schnell / schneller	shnehl / **shnehl**-ler
arrival	Ankunft	**ahn**-koonft
departure	Abfahrt	**ahp**-fart
delay	Verspätung	fehr-**shpay**-toong
toilet	Toilette, WC	toh-**leh**-teh, vay-**tsay**
waiting room	Wartesaal	**var**-teh-zahl
lockers	Schließfächer	**shlees**-fehkh-er

baggage check room	Gepäckaufgabe	geh-**pehk**-owf-gah-beh
lost and found office	Fundbüro	**foond**-bew-roh
tourist information	Touristen-information	too-**ris**-tehn-in-for-maht-see-**ohn**
platform	Bahnsteig	**bahn**-shtīg
to the trains	zu den Zugen	tsoo dayn **tsoo**-gehn
track	Gleis	glīs
train car	Wagen	**vah**-gehn
dining car	Speisewagen	**shpī**-zeh-vah-gehn
sleeper car	Liegewagen	**lee**-geh-vah-gehn
conductor	Schaffner	**shahf**-ner

You'll encounter several types of trains in Germany. Along with the various local and milk-run trains, there are the:

- slow *RB* (*RegionalBahn*) and *RE* (*RegionalExpress*) trains,
- the medium-speed *IR* (*InterRegio*) and *IRE* (*InterRegioExpress*) trains,
- the fast *IC* (*InterCity*, domestic routes) and *EC* (*EuroCity*, international routes) trains, and
- the super-fast *ICE* trains (*InterCityExpress*).

Railpasses cover travel on all of these trains, except for the rare *Metropolitan* train between Köln and Hamburg. Seat reservations are not required on most daytime trains.

TRAVELING

Getting a Ticket

Where can I buy a ticket?	Wo kann ich eine Fahrkarte kaufen?	voh kahn ikh **ī**-neh **far**-kar-teh **kow**-fehn
A ticket to ___.	Eine Fahrkarte nach ___.	**ī**-neh **far**-kar-teh nahkh
Where can we buy tickets?	Wo können wir Fahrkarten kaufen?	voh **kurn**-nehn veer **far**-kar-tehn **kow**-fehn
Two tickets to ___.	Zwei Fahrkarten nach ___.	tsvī **far**-kar-tehn nahkh
Is this the line for...?	Ist das die Schlange für...?	ist dahs dee **shlahng**-eh fewr
...tickets	...Fahrkarten	**far**-kar-tehn

TRAVELING

...reservations	...Reservierungen	reh-zer-**feer**-oong-ehn
How much is a ticket to ___?	Wie viel kostet eine Fahrkarte nach ___?	vee feel **kohs**-teht **ī**-neh **far**-kar-teh nahkh
Is this ticket valid for ___?	Ist diese Fahrkarte gültig für ___?	ist **dee**-zeh **far**-kar-teh **gewl**-tig fewr
How long is this ticket valid?	Wie lange ist diese Fahrkarte gültig?	vee **lahng**-eh ist **dee**-zeh **far**-kar-teh **gewl**-tig
When is the next train?	Wann ist der nächste Zug?	vahn ist dehr **nehkh**-steh tsoog
Do you have a schedule for all trains departing today / tomorrow for ___?	Haben Sie einen Fahrplan für alle Züge heute / morgen nach ___?	**hah**-behn zee **ī**-nehn **far**-plahn fewr **ahl**-leh **tsew**-geh **hoy**-teh / **mor**-gehn nahkh
I'd like to leave...	Ich möchte... abfahren.	ikh **murkh**-teh... **ahp**-fah-rehn
We'd like to leave...	Wir möchten... abfahren.	veer **murkh**-tehn... **ahp**-fah-rehn
I'd like to arrive...	Ich möchte... ankommen.	ikh **murkh**-teh... **ahn**-koh-mehn
We'd like to arrive...	Wir möchten... ankommen.	veer **murkh**-tehn... **ahn**-koh-mehn
...by ___	... vor ___	for
...in the morning.	...am Morgen	ahm **mor**-gehn
...in the afternoon.	...am Nachmittag	ahm **nahkh**-mit-tahg
...in the evening.	...am Abend	ahm **ah**-behnt
Is there a...?	Gibt es einen...?	gipt ehs **ī**-nehn
...later train	...späterer Zug	**shpay**-ter-er tsoog
...earlier train	...früherer Zug	**frew**-her-er tsoog
...overnight train	...Nachtzug	**nahkht**-tsoog
...cheaper train	...billigere Zug	**bil**-lig-er-eh tsoog
...cheaper option	...billigere Möglichkeit	**bil**-lig-er-eh **murg**-likh-kīt
...local train	...Regionalzug	reh-gee-oh-**nahl**-tsoog
...express train	...Schnellzug	**shnehl**-tsoog
What track does the train leave from?	Von welches Gleis fährt er ab?	fohn **vehlkh**-ehs glīs fayrt ehr ahp

Key Phrases: Trains

(central) train station	*(Haupt-) Bahnhof*	(**howpt**-) **bahn**-hohf
train	*Zug*	tsoog
ticket	*Fahrkarte*	**far**-kar-teh
transfer (verb)	*umsteigen*	**oom**-shtī-gehn
supplement	*Zuschlag*	**tsoo**-shlahg
arrival	*Ankunft*	**ahn**-koonft
departure	*Abfahrt*	**ahp**-fart
platform	*Bahnsteig*	**bahn**-shtīg
track	*Gleis*	glīs
train car	*Wagen*	**vah**-gehn
A ticket to ___.	*Eine Fahrkarte nach ___.*	**ī**-neh **far**-kar-teh nahkh
Two tickets to ___.	*Zwei Fahrkarten nach ___.*	tsvī **far**-kar-tehn nahkh
When is the next train?	*Wann ist der nächste Zug?*	vahn ist dehr **nehk**-steh tsoog
Where does the train leave from?	*Von wo fährt der Zug ab?*	fohn voh fayrt dehr tsoog ahp
Which train to ___?	*Welcher Zug nach ___?*	**vehlkh**-er tsoog nahkh

TRAVELING

On time?	*Pünktlich?*	**pewnkt**-likh
Late?	*Spät?*	shpayt

Reservations, Supplements, and Discounts

Is a reservation required?	*Brauche ich eine Platzkarte?*	**browkh**-eh ikh **ī**-neh **plahts**-kar-teh
I'd like to reserve...	*Ich möchte... reservieren.*	ikh **murkh**-teh... reh-zer-**vee**-rehn
...a seat.	*...einen Sitzplatz*	**ī**-nehn **zits**-plahts
...a berth.	*...einen Liegewagenplatz*	**ī**-nehn **lee**-geh-vah-gehn-plahts

...a sleeper.	...einen Schlafwagenplatz	**ī**-nehn **shlahf**-vah-gehn-plahts
...the entire train.	...den ganzen Zug	dayn **gahn**-tsehn tsoog
We'd like to reserve...	Wir möchten... reservieren.	veer **murkh**-tehn... reh-zer-**vee**-rehn
...two seats.	...zwei Sitzplätze	tsvī **zits**-pleht-seh
...two couchettes.	...zwei Liegewagen- plätze	tsvī **lee**-geh-vah-gehn- pleht-seh
...two sleepers.	...zwei Schlafwagen- plätze	tsvī **shlahf**-vah-gehn- pleht-seh
Is there a supplement?	Kostet das einen Zuschlag?	**kohs**-teht dahs **ī**-nehn **tsoo**-shlahg
Does my railpass cover the supplement?	Ist der Zuschlag in meinem Railpass enthalten?	ist dehr **tsoo**-shlahg in **mī**-nehm **rayl**-pahs ehnt-**hahl**-tehn
Is there a discount for...?	Gibt es eine Ermäßigung für...?	gipt ehs **ī**-neh ehr-**may**-see-goong fewr
...youths	...Jugendliche	**yoo**-gehnd-likh-eh
...seniors	...Senioren	zehn-**yor**-ehn
...families	...Familien	fah-**mee**-lee-ehn

Ticket Talk

ticket window	Fahrscheine	far-**shī**-neh
reservations window	Reservierungen	reh-zer-**feer**-oong-ehn
national / international	Inland / Ausland	**in**-lahnt / **ows**-lahnt
ticket	Fahrkarte	**far**-kar-teh
one-way ticket	Hinfahrkarte	**hin**-far-kar-teh
roundtrip ticket	Rückfahrkarte	**rewk**-far-kar-teh
first class	erste Klasse	**ehr**-steh **klah**-seh
second class	zweite Klasse	**tsvī**-teh **klah**-seh
non-smoking	Nichtraucher	**nikht**-rowkh-er
validate	abstempeln	**ahp**-shtehm-pehln
schedule	Fahrplan	**far**-plahn
departure	Abfahrtszeit	**ahp**-farts-tsīt

direct	*Direkt*	dee-**rehkt**
transfer (verb)	*umsteigen*	**oom**-shtī-gehn
connection	*Anschluß*	**ahn**-shloos
with supplement	*mit Zuschlag*	mit **tsoo**-shlahg
reservation	*Platzkarte*	**plahts**-kar-teh
seat	*Platz*	plahts
window seat	*Fensterplatz*	**fehn**-ster-plahts
aisle seat	*Platz am Gang*	plahts ahm gahng
berth...	*Liege...*	**lee**-geh
...upper	*...obere*	**oh**-ber-eh
...middle	*...mittlere*	**mit**-leh-reh
...lower	*...untere*	**oon**-ter-eh
refund	*Rückvergütung*	**rewk**-fehr-gew-toong
reduced fare	*verbilligte Karte*	fehr-**bil**-lig-teh **kar**-teh

Changing Trains

Is it direct?	*Direktverbindung?*	dee-**rehkt**-fehr-bin-doong
Must I transfer?	*Muß ich umsteigen?*	mus ikh **oom**-shtī-gehn
Must we transfer?	*Müssen wir umsteigen?*	**mew**-sehn veer **oom**-shtī-gehn
When? / Where?	*Wann? / Wo?*	vahn / voh
Do I / Do we change here for ___?	*Muß ich / Müssen wir hier umsteigen nach ___?*	mus ikh / **mew**-sehn veer heer **oom**-shtī-gehn nahkh
Where do I / do we change for ___?	*Wo muß ich / müssen wir umsteigen für ___?*	voh mus ikh / **mew**-sehn veer **oom**-shtī-gehn fewr
At what time?	*Um wie viel Uhr?*	oom vee feel oor
From what track does my / our connecting train leave?	*Auf welchem Gleis fährt mein / unser Verbindungszug?*	owf **wehlkh**-ehm glīs fayrt mīn / **oon**-ser fehr-**bin**-doongs-tsoog
How many minutes in ___ to change trains?	*Wie viele Minuten zum Umsteigen in ___?*	vee **fee**-leh mee-**noo**-tehn tsoom **oom**-shtī-gehn in

On the Platform

Where is...?	*Wo ist...?*	voh ist
Is this...?	*Ist das...?*	ist dahs
...the train to ___	*...der Zug nach ___*	dehr tsoog nahkh
Which train to ___?	*Welcher Zug nach ___?*	**vehlkh**-er tsoog nahkh
Which train car to ___?	*Welcher Wagen nach ___?*	**vehlkh**-er **vah**-gehn nahkh
Where is first class?	*Wo ist die erste Klasse?*	voh ist dee **ehr**-steh **klah**-seh
...front / middle / back	*...vorne / mitte / hinten*	**for**-neh / **mit**-teh / **hin**-tehn
Where can I validate my ticket?	*Wo kann ich meine Fahrkarte abstempeln?*	voh kahn ikh **mī**-neh **far**-kar-teh **ahp**-shtehm-pehln

At the platform, you'll often see a sign that says *Etwa 10 Min. später.* This means that the train is running about (*etwa*) 10 minutes later (*später*) than expected.

On the Train

Is this seat free?	*Ist dieser Platz frei?*	ist **dee**-zer plahts frī
May I / May we...?	*Darf ich / Dürfen wir...?*	darf ikh / **dewr**-fehn veer
...sit here	*...hier sitzen*	heer **zit**-sehn
...open the window	*...das Fenster öffnen*	dahs **fehn**-ster **urf**-nehn
...eat your meal	*...Ihre Mahlzeit essen*	**eer**-eh **mahl**-tsīt **ehs**-sehn
Save my place?	*Halten Sie meinen Platz frei?*	**hahl**-tehn zee **mī**-nehn plahts frī
Save our places?	*Halten Sie unsere Plätze frei?*	**hahl**-tehn zee **oon**-zer-eh **pleht**-seh frī
That's my seat.	*Das ist mein Platz.*	dahs ist mīn plahts
These are our seats.	*Das sind unsere Plätze.*	dahs zint **oon**-zer-eh **pleht**-seh
Where are you going?	*Wohin fahren Sie?*	voh-hin **far**-ehn zee

I'm going to __.	*Ich fahre nach __.*	ikh **far**-eh nahkh
We're going to __.	*Wir fahren nach __.*	veer **far**-ehn nahkh
Can you tell me / us when to get off?	*Können Sie mir / uns Bescheid sagen?*	**kurn**-nehn zee meer / oons beh-**shīt** zah-gehn
Where is a (good looking) conductor?	*Wo ist ein (hübscher) Schaffner?*	voh ist īn (**hewb**-sher) **shahf**-ner
Does this train stop in __?	*Hält dieser Zug in __?*	hehlt **dee**-zer tsoog in
When will it arrive in __?	*Wann kommt er in __ an?*	vahn kohmt ehr in __ ahn
When will it arrive?	*Wann kommt er an?*	vahn kohmt ehr ahn

As you approach a station on the train, you will hear an announcement such as: *In wenigen Minuten erreichen wir in München* (In a few minutes, we will arrive in Munich).

Reading Train and Bus Schedules

European schedules use the 24-hour clock. It's like American time until noon. After that, subtract twelve and add P.M. So 13:00 is 1 P.M., 19:00 is 7 P.M., and midnight is 24:00. If your train is scheduled to depart at 00:01, it'll leave one minute after midnight.

Abfahrt	departure
Ankunft	arrival
auch	also
außer	except
bis	until
Feiertag	holiday
Gleis	track
jeden	every
nach	to
nicht	not
nur	only
Richtung	direction
Samstag	Saturday

Sonntag	Sunday
täglich (tgl.)	daily
tagsüber	days
über	via
verspätet	late
von	from
Werktags	Monday–Saturday (workdays)
Wochentags	weekdays
Zeit	time
Ziel	destination
1-5, 6, 7	Monday–Friday, Saturday, Sunday

Major Transportation Lines in Germany, Austria, and Switzerland

Going Places

Germany	*Deutschland*	**doych**-lahnd
Munich	*München*	**mewnkh**-ehn
Bavaria	*Bayern*	**bī**-ehrn
Black Forest	*Schwarzwald*	**shvahrts**-vahlt
Danube	*Donau*	**doh**-now
Austria	*Österreich*	**urs**-ter-rīkh
Vienna	*Wien*	veen
Switzerland	*Schweiz*	shvīts
Belgium	*Belgien*	**behl**-gee-ehn
Czech Republic	*Tschechien*	**shehkh**-ee-ehn
Prague	*Prag*	prahk
Denmark	*Dänemark*	**deh**-neh-mark
France	*Frankreich*	**frahnk**-rīkh
Great Britain	*Großbritannien*	grohs-brit-**ahn**-ee-ehn
Greece	*Griechenland* ·	**greekh**-ehn-lahnd
Ireland	*Irland*	**ihr**-lahnd
Italy	*Italien*	i-**tah**-lee-ehn
Venice	*Venedig*	veh-**neh**-dig
Netherlands	*Niederlande*	**nee**-der-lahn-deh
Norway	*Norwegan*	**nor**-vay-gehn
Portugal	*Portugal*	**pohr**-too-gahl
Scandinavia	*Skandinavien*	shkahn-dee-**nah**-vee-ehn
Spain	*Spanien*	**shpahn**-ee-ehn
Sweden	*Schweden*	**shvay**-dehn
Turkey	*Türkei*	tewr-**kī**
Europe	*Europa*	oy-**roh**-pah
EU (European Union)	*EU*	ay oo
Russia	*Rußland*	**roos**-lahnd
Africa	*Afrika*	**ah**-free-kah
United States	*USA* (Vereinigten Staaten)	oo ehs ah (fehr-**ī**-nig-tehn **shtah**-tehn)
Canada	*Kanada*	**kah**-nah-dah
world	*Welt*	vehlt

If you're using the *Rick Steves'* guidebooks on Germany, Switzerland, and Austrian cities, you're also likely to see these place names:

Bacharach (Ger.)	**bahkh**-ah-rahkh
Jungfrau (Switz.)	**yoong**-frow
Kleine Scheidegg (Switz.)	**klī**-neh **shī**-dehg
Köln (Ger.)	kurln
Mosel (Ger.)	**moh**-zehl
Neuschwanstein (Ger.)	noysh-**vahn**-shtīn
Reutte (Aus.)	**roy**-teh
Rothenburg (Ger.)	**roh**-tehn-boorg

BUSES AND SUBWAYS

At the Bus Station or Metro Stop

ticket	Fahrkarte	**far**-kar-teh
day ticket	Tageskarte	**tahg**-ehs-kar-teh
short-ride ticket	Kurzstrecke	**koorts**-streh-keh
city bus	Linienbus	**lee**-nee-ehn-boos
regional / long-distance bus	Regionalbus / Fernbus	reh-gee-ohn-**ahl**-boos / **fayrn**-boos
bus stop	Bushaltestelle	**boos**-hahl-teh-shtehl-leh
bus station	Busbahnhof	**boos**-bahn-hohf
subway	U-Bahn	**oo**-bahn
subway station	U-Bahn-Station	**oo**-bahn-stah-tsee-ohn
subway map	U-Bahn-Streckenplan	**oo**-bahn-**shtrehk**-ehn-plahn
subway entrance	U-Bahn-Eingang	**oo**-bahn-**īn**-gahng
subway stop	U-Bahn-Haltestelle	**oo**-bahn-**hahl**-teh-shtehl-leh
subway exit	U-Bahn-Ausgang	**oo**-bahn-**ows**-gahng
direct	Direkt	dee-**rehkt**
direction	Richtung	**rikh**-toong
connection	Anschluß	**ahn**-shlus
pickpocket	Taschendieb	**tahsh**-ehn-deep

Most big cities offer deals on transportation, such as one-day tickets, cheaper fares for youths and seniors, or a discount for buying a batch of tickets (which you can share with friends). If you're taking a short trip (usually four stops or fewer), buy a discounted *Kurzstrecke* ("short stretch" ticket). Major cities in Germany, such as Munich and Berlin, have an *U-Bahn* (subway) and an *S-Bahn* (urban rail system). If your Eurailpass is active on the day you're traveling, it covers the *S-Bahn* for free. On a map, *Standort* means "You are here."

Taking Buses and Subways

How do I get to __?	*Wie komme ich zu __?*	vee **koh**-meh ikh tsoo
How do we get to __?	*Wie kommen wir zu __?*	vee **koh**-mehn veer tsoo
How much is a ticket?	*Wie viel kostet eine Fahrkarte?*	vee feel **kohs**-teht **ī**-neh far-kar-teh
Where can I buy a ticket?	*Wo kaufe ich eine Fahrkarte?*	voh **kow**-feh ikh **ī**-neh **far**-kar-teh

Key Phrases: Buses and Subways

bus	*Bus*	boos
subway	*U-Bahn*	**oo**-bahn
ticket	*Fahrkarte*	**far**-kar-teh
How do I get to __?	*Wie komme ich zu __?*	vee **koh**-meh ikh tsoo
How do we get to __?	*Wie kommen wir zu __?*	vee **koh**-mehn veer tsoo
Which stop for __?	*Welche Haltestelle für __?*	**vehlkh**-eh **hahl**-teh-shtehl-leh fewr
Can you tell me / us when to get off?	*Können Sie mir / uns Bescheid sagen?*	**kurn**-nehn zee meer / oons beh-**shīt** zah-gehn

Where can we buy tickets?	Wo kaufen wir Fahrkarten?	voh **kow**-fehn veer **far**-kar-tehn
One ticket, please.	Eine Fahrkarte, bitte.	**ī**-neh **far**-kar-teh, **bit**-teh
Two tickets.	Zwei Fahrkarten.	tsv**i** **far**-kar-tehn
Is this ticket valid (for ___)?	Ist diese Fahrkarte gültig (für ___)?	ist **dee**-zeh **far**-kar-teh **gewl**-tig (fewr ___)
Is there a...?	Gibt es eine...?	gipt ehs **ī**-neh
...one-day pass	...Tageskarte	**tahg**-ehs-kar-teh
...discount if I buy more tickets	...Preisnachlaß, wenn ich mehrere Fahrkarten kaufe	prīs-**nahkh**-lahs vehn ikh **meh**-reh-reh **far**-kar-tehn **kow**-feh
Which bus to ___?	Welcher Bus nach ___?	**vehlkh**-er boos nahkh
Does it stop at ___?	Hält er in ___?	hehlt ehr in
Which bus stop for ___?	Welche Haltestelle für ___?	**vehlkh**-eh **hahl**-teh-shtehl-leh fewr
Which metro stop for ___?	Welcher Halt für ___?	**vehlkh**-er hahlt fewr
Which direction for ___?	Welche Richtung nach ___?	**vehlkh**-eh **rikh**-toong nahkh
Must I transfer?	Muß ich umsteigen?	mus ikh **oom**-shtī-gehn
Must we transfer?	Müssen wir umsteigen?	**mew**-sehn veer **oom**-shtī-gehn
When is the...?	Wann fährt der... ab?	vahn fayrt dehr... ahp
...first / next / last	...erste / nächste / letzte	**ehr**-steh / **nehkh**-steh / **lehts**-teh
...bus / subway	...Bus / U-Bahn	boos / **oo**-bahn
What's the frequency per hour / day?	Wie oft pro Stunde / Tag?	vee ohft pro **shtoon**-deh / tahg
Where does it leave from?	Von wo fährt er ab?	fohn voh fayrt ehr ahp
What time does it leave?	Um wie viel Uhr fährt er ab?	oom vee feel oor fayrt ehr ahp
I'm going to ___.	Ich fahre nach ___.	ikh **far**-eh nahkh
We're going to ___.	Wir fahren nach ___.	veer **far**-ehn nahkh

| Can you tell me / us when to get off? | *Können Sie mir / uns Bescheid sagen?* | **kurn**-nehn zee meer / oons beh-**shīt** zah-gehn |

TAXIS

Getting a Taxi

Taxi!	*Taxi!*	**tahk**-see
Can you call a taxi?	*Können Sie mir ein Taxi rufen?*	**kurn**-nehn zee meer īn **tahk**-see **roo**-fehn
Where can I get a taxi?	*Wo finde ich ein Taxi?*	voh fin-deh ikh īn **tahk**-see
Where can we get a taxi?	*Wo finden wir ein Taxi?*	voh fin-dehn veer īn **tahk**-see
Where is a taxi stand?	*Wo ist ein Taxistand?*	voh ist īn **tahk**-see-shtahnt
Are you free?	*Sind Sie frei?*	zint zee frī
Occupied.	*Besetzt.*	beh-**zehtst**
To ___, please.	*Zu ___, bitte.*	tsoo ___ **bit**-teh
To this address.	*Zu dieser Adresse.*	tsoo **dee**-zer ah-**dreh**-seh
Take me / us to ___.	*Bringen Sie mich / uns zu ___.*	**bring**-ehn zee mikh / oons tsoo ___
Approximately how much will it cost for a trip...?	*Wie viel ungefähr kostet die Fahrt...?*	vee feel **oon**-geh-fehr **kohs**-teht dee fart
...to ___	*...zu ___*	tsoo
...to the airport	*...zum Flughafen*	tsoom **floog**-hah-fehn
...to the train station	*...zum Bahnhof*	tsoom **bahn**-hohf
...to this address	*...zu dieser Adresse*	tsoo **dee**-zer ah-**dreh**-seh
No extra supplements?	*Keine Zuschläge?*	**kī**-neh **tsoo**-shleh-geh
Too much.	*Zu viel.*	tsoo feel
Can you take ___ people?	*Können Sie ___ Personen mitnehmen?*	**kurn**-nehn zee ___ pehr-**zoh**-nehn **mit**-nay-mehn

Any extra fee?	*Extra Gebühren?*	**ex**-trah geh-**bew**-rehn
Do you have an hourly rate?	*Haben Sie einen Stundenansatz?*	**hah**-behn zee **ī**-nehn **shtoon**-dehn-ahn-zahts
How much for a one-hour city tour?	*Wie viel für eine Stunde Stadtbesichtigung?*	vee feel fewr **ī**-neh **shtoon**-deh **shtaht**-beh-**sikh**-ti-goong

Ride in style in a German taxi—usually a BMW or Mercedes. If you're having a tough time hailing a taxi, ask for the nearest taxi stand (**Taxistand**). The simplest way to tell a cabbie where you want to go is by stating your destination followed by "please" (**"Hofbräuhaus, bitte"**). Tipping isn't expected, but it's polite to round up. So if the fare is €19, round up to €20.

In the Taxi

The meter, please.	*Den Zähler, bitte.*	dayn **tsay**-ler **bit**-teh
Where is the meter?	*Wo ist der Zähler?*	voh ist dehr **tsay**-ler
I'm in a hurry.	*Ich bin in Eile.*	ikh bin in **ī**-leh
We're in a hurry.	*Wir sind in Eile.*	veer zint in **ī**-leh
Slow down.	*Fahren Sie langsamer.*	**fahr**-ehn zee **lahng**-zah-mer
If you don't slow down, I'll throw up.	*Wenn Sie nicht langsamer fahren, muß ich kotzen.*	vehn zee nikht **lahng**-zah-mer **far**-ehn mus ikh **koht**-sehn
Left / Right / Straight.	*Links / Rechts / Geradeaus.*	links / rehkhts / geh-rah-deh-**ows**
I'd like / We'd like to stop here briefly.	*Ich möchte / Wir möchten hier kurz anhalten.*	ikh **murkh**-teh / veer **murkh**-tehn heer koorts **ahn**-hahl-tehn
Please stop here for ___ minutes.	*Bitte halten Sie hier für ___ Minuten.*	**bit**-teh **hahl**-tehn zee heer fewr ___ mee-**noo**-tehn
Can you wait?	*Können Sie warten?*	**kurn**-nehn zee **var**-tehn
Crazy traffic, isn't it?	*Verrückter Verkehr, nicht wahr?*	fehr-**rewk**-ter fehr-**kehr**, nikht var

---

Key Phrases: Taxis

Taxi!	*Taxi!*	**tahk**-see
Are you free?	*Sind Sie frei?*	zint zee frī
To ___, please.	*Zu ___, bitte.*	tsoo ___ **bit**-teh
meter	*Zähler*	**tsay**-ler
Stop here.	*Halten Sie hier.*	**hahl**-tehn zee heer
Keep the change.	*Stimmt so.*	shtimt zoh

You drive like...	*Sie fahren wie...*	zee **far**-ehn vee
...a madman!	*...ein Verrückter!*	īn fehr-**rewk**-ter
...Michael Schumacher.	*...Michael Schumacher.*	**mee**-kay-ehl "Schumacher"
You drive very well.	*Sie fahren sehr gut.*	zee **far**-ehn zehr goot
Where did you learn to drive?	*Wo haben Sie Auto fahren gelernt?*	voh **hah**-behn zee **ow**-toh **far**-ehn geh-**lehrnt**
Stop here.	*Halten Sie hier.*	**hahl**-tehn zee heer
Here is fine.	*Hier ist gut.*	heer ist goot
At this corner.	*An dieser Ecke.*	ahn **dee**-zer **ehk**-eh
The next corner.	*An der nächsten Ecke.*	ahn dehr **nehkh**-stehn **ehk**-eh
My change, please.	*Mein Wechselgeld, bitte.*	mīn **vehkh**-sehl-gehlt **bit**-teh
Keep the change.	*Stimmt so.*	shtimt zoh
This ride is / was more fun than Disneyland.	*Diese Fahrt ist / war lustiger als Disneyland.*	**dee**-zer fart ist / var **loos**-ti-ger ahls "Disneyland"

TRAVELING

DRIVING

Rental Wheels

car rental agency	*Autovermietung*	**ow**-toh-fehr-**mee**-toong
I'd like to rent a...	*Ich möchte ein... mieten.*	ikh **murkh**-teh īn... **mee**-tehn

We'd like to rent a...	Wir möchten ein... mieten.	veer **murkh**-tehn īn... **mee**-tehn
...car.	...Auto	**ow**-toh
...station wagon.	...Kombi	**kohm**-bee
...van.	...Kleinbus	**klīn**-boos
...motorcycle.	...Motorrad	**moh**-tor-raht
...motor scooter.	...Motorroller	**moh**-tor-roh-ler
...tank.	...Panzer	**pahn**-tser
How much per...?	Wie viel pro...?	vee feel proh
...hour	...Stunde	**shtoon**-deh
...half day	...halben Tag	**hahl**-behn tahg
...day	...Tag	tahg
...week	...Woche	**vohkh**-eh
Unlimited mileage?	Unbegrenzte Kilometer?	oon-beh-**grents**-teh kee-loh-**may**-ter
When must I bring it back?	Wann muß ich es zurückbringen?	vahn mus ikh ehs tsoo-**rewk**-bring-ehn
Is there a...?	Gibt es eine...?	gipt ehs **ī**-neh
...helmet	...Helm	hehlm
...discount	...Ermäßigung	ehr-**may**-see-goong
...deposit	...Kaution	kowt-see-**ohn**
...insurance	...Versicherung	fehr-**zikh**-er-oong

At the Gas Station

gas station	Tankstelle	**tahnk**-shtehl-leh
The nearest gas station?	Die nächste Tankstelle?	dee **nehkh**-steh **tahnk**-shtehl-leh
Self-service?	Selbstbedienung?	**zehlpst**-beh-dee-noong
Fill the tank.	Volltanken.	**fohl**-tahnk-ehn
Wash the windows.	Scheiben putzen.	**shī**-behn **poots**-ehn
I need...	Ich brauche...	ikh **browkh**-eh
We need...	Wir brauchen...	veer **browkh**-ehn
...gas.	...Benzin.	behn-**tseen**
...unleaded.	...Bleifrei.	**blī**-frī
...regular.	...Normal.	nor-**mahl**
...super.	...Super.	**zoo**-per

Key Phrases: Driving

car	*Auto*	**ow**-toh
gas station	*Tankstelle*	**tahnk**-shtehl-leh
parking lot	*Parkplatz*	**park**-plahts
accident	*Unfall*	**oon**-fahl
left / right	*links / rechts*	links / **rehkhts**
straight ahead	*geradeaus*	geh-rah-deh-**ows**
downtown	*Zentrum*	**tsehn**-troom
How do I get to __?	*Wie komme ich nach __?*	vee **koh**-meh ikh nahkh
Where can I park?	*Wo kann ich parken?*	voh kahn ikh **par**-ken

---

...diesel.	*...Diesel.*	**dee**-zehl
Check...	*Sehen Sie nach...*	**zay**-ehn zee nahkh
... the oil.	*...dem Öl.*	daym url
...the air in the tires.	*...dem Luftdruck in Reifen.*	daym **looft**-drook in ** rī**-fehn
...the radiator.	*...dem Kühler.*	daym **kew**-ler
...the battery.	*...der Batterie.*	dehr bah-teh-**ree**
...the sparkplugs.	*...den Zündkerzen.*	dayn **tsewnt**-ker-tsehn
...the headlights.	*...den Scheinwerfern.*	dayn **shīn**-vehr-fern
...the tail lights.	*...den Rücklichtern.*	dayn **rewk**-likht-ern
...the directional signal.	*...dem Blinker.*	daym **blink**-er
...the brakes.	*...den Bremsen.*	dayn **brehm**-zehn
...the transmission fluid.	*...dem Getriebeöl.*	daym geh-**treeb**-eh-url
...the windshield wipers.	*...den Scheibenwischern.*	dayn **shī**-behn-vish-ern
...the fuses.	*...den Sicherungen.*	dayn **zikh**-eh-roong-ehn
...the fanbelt.	*...dem Keilriemen.*	daym **kīl**-ree-mehn
...my pulse.	*...meinem Puls.*	**mī**-nehm pools
...my husband / my wife.	*...meinem Mann / meiner Frau.*	**mī**-nehm mahn / **mī**-ner frow

Getting gas is a piece of *Strudel.* Regular is *normal* and super is *super.* Prices are listed per liter; there are about four liters in a gallon.

Car Trouble

accident	*Unfall*	**oon**-fahl
breakdown	*Panne*	**pah**-neh
dead battery	*leere Batterie*	**lehr**-eh baht-teh-**ree**
funny noise	*komisches Geräusch*	**koh**-mish-ehs geh-**roysh**
electrical problem	*elektrische Schwierigkeiten*	eh-**lehk**-trish-eh **shvee**-rig-kī-tehn
flat tire	*Reifenpanne*	**rī**-fehn-pah-neh
repair shop	*Garage*	gah-**rah**-zheh
My car won't start.	*Mein Auto springt nicht an.*	mīn **ow**-toh shpringt nikht ahn
My car is broken.	*Mein Auto ist kaputt.*	mīn **ow**-toh ist kah-**poot**
This doesn't work.	*Das geht nicht.*	dahs gayt nikht
It's overheating.	*Es überhitzt.*	ehs **ew**-ber-hitst
It's a lemon (useless box).	*Es ist eine Schrottkiste.*	ehs ist ī-neh **shroht**-kis-teh
I need a...	*Ich brauche einen...*	ikh **browkh**-eh ī-nehn
We need a...	*Wir brauchen einen...*	veer **browkh**-ehn ī-nehn
...tow truck.	*...Abschleppwagen.*	**ahp**-shlehp-vah-gehn
...mechanic.	*...Mechaniker.*	mehkh-**ahn**-i-ker
...stiff drink.	*...Schnaps.*	shnahps

For help with repair, see "Repair" on page 162 of the Services chapter.

Parking

parking lot	*Parkplatz*	**park**-plahts
parking garage	*Garage*	gah-**rah**-zheh
parking meter	*Parkuhr*	**park**-oor
parking clock (to put on dashboard)	*Parkscheibe*	**park**-shī-beh
Where can I park?	*Wo kann ich parken?*	voh kahn ikh **par**-kehn

Is parking nearby?	Gibt es Parkplätze in der Nähe?	gipt ehs **park**-pleht-seh in dehr **nay**-heh
Can I park here?	Darf ich hier parken?	darf ikh heer **par**-kehn
Is this a safe place to park?	Ist dies ein sicherer Parkplatz?	ist deez īn **zikh**-her-er **park**-plahts
How long can I park here?	Wie lange darf ich hier parken?	vee **lahng**-eh darf ikh heer **par**-kehn
Must I pay to park here?	Kostet Parken hier etwas?	**kohs**-teht **par**-kehn heer **eht**-vahs
How much per hour / day?	Wie viel pro Stunde / Tag?	vee feel proh **shtoon**-deh / tahg

Free but time-limited parking spaces use the "cardboard clock" (*Parkscheibe;* you'll usually find one in your rental car). Put the clock on your dashboard with your arrival time so parking attendants can see you've been there less than the posted maximum stay. At pay parking spaces, you'll pre-pay for the length of your stay. Find the parking meter (usually about one or two per block), pay for the amount of time you need, then put the ticket (*Parkschein*) on your dashboard. If you're not sure what to do, check the dashboards of the cars around you.

TRAVELING

FINDING YOUR WAY

I'm going on foot to ___.	Ich gehe nach ___.	ikh **gay**-heh nahkh
We're going on foot to ___.	Wir gehen nach ___.	veer **gay**-hehn nahkh
I'm going to ___. (using wheels)	Ich fahre nach ___.	ikh **fah**-reh nahkh
We're going to ___. (using wheels)	Wir fahren nach ___.	veer **fah**-rehn nahkh
How do I get to ___?	Wie komme ich nach ___?	vee **koh**-meh ikh nahkh ___
How do we get to ___?	Wie kommen wir nach ___?	vee **koh**-mehn veer nahkh ___
Do you have a...?	Haben Sie eine...?	**hah**-behn zee ī-neh

TRAVELING

English	German	Pronunciation
...city map	...Stadtplan	**shtaht**-plahn
...road map	...Straßenkarte	**shtrah**-sehn-kar-teh
How many minutes / hours...?	Wie viele Minuten / Stunden...?	vee **fee**-leh mee-**noo**-tehn / **shtoon**-dehn
...on foot	...zu Fuß	tsoo foos
...by bicycle	...mit dem Rad	mit daym raht
...by car	...mit dem Auto	mit daym **ow**-toh
How many kilometers to ___?	Wie viele Kilometer sind es nach ___?	vee **fee**-leh kee-loh-**may**-ter zint ehs nahkh
What's the... route to Berlin?	Was ist der... Weg nach Berlin?	vahs ist dehr... vehg nahkh behr-**leen**
...most scenic	...schönste	**shurn**-steh
...fastest	...schnellste	**shnehl**-steh
...most interesting	...interessanteste	in-ter-ehs-**sahn**-tehs-teh
Point it out?	Zeigen Sie es mir?	**tsi**-gehn zee ehs meer
I'm lost. (if you're on foot)	Ich habe mich verlaufen.	ikh **hah**-beh mikh fehr-**lowf**-ehn
We're lost. (on foot)	Wir haben uns verlaufen.	veer **hah**-behn oons fehr-**lowf**-ehn
I'm lost. (if you're in a car)	Ich habe mich verfahren.	ikh **hah**-beh mikh fehr-**far**-ehn
We're lost. (by car)	Wir haben uns verfahren.	veer **hah**-behn oons fehr-**far**-ehn
Where am I?	Wo bin ich?	voh bin ikh
Where is...?	Wo ist...?	voh ist
The nearest...?	Der nächste...?	dehr **nehkh**-steh
Where is this address?	Wo ist diese Adresse?	voh ist **dee**-zeh ah-**drehs**-seh

Route-Finding Words

English	German	Pronunciation
city map	Stadtplan	**shtaht**-plahn
road map	Straßenkarte	**shtrah**-sehn-kar-teh

downtown	*Zentrum, Stadtzentrum*	**tsehn**-troom, **shtaht**-tsehn-troom
straight ahead	*geradeaus*	geh-rah-deh-**ows**
left	*links*	links
right	*rechts*	rehkhts
first	*erste*	**ehr**-steh
next	*nächste*	**nehkh**-steh
intersection	*Kreuzung*	**kroy**-tsoong
corner	*Ecke*	**ehk**-eh
block	*Häuserblock*	**hoy**-zer-blohk
roundabout	*Kreisel*	**krī**-zehl
ring road	*Ringstraße*	**ring**-shtrah-seh
stoplight	*Ampel*	**ahm**-pehl
(main) square	*(Markt-)platz*	**(markt-)**plahts
street	*Straße*	**shtrah**-seh
bridge	*Brücke*	**brew**-keh
tunnel	*Tunnel*	**too**-nehl
highway	*Landstraße*	**lahnd**-shtrah-seh
national highway	*Fernstraße*	**fayrn**-shtrah-seh
freeway	*Autobahn*	**ow**-toh-bahn
north	*Nord*	nord
south	*Süd*	zewd
east	*Ost*	ohst
west	*West*	vehst

TRAVELING

The shortest distance between any two points in Germany is the *Autobahn.* The right to no speed limit is as close to the average German driver's heart as the right to bear arms is to many American hearts. To survive, never cruise in the passing lane. While all roads seem to lead to the little town of *Ausfahrt,* that is the German word for exit. The *Autobahn* information magazine, available at any *Autobahn Tankstelle* (gas station), lists all road signs, interchanges, and the hours and facilities available at various rest stops. Missing a turnoff can cost you lots of time and miles— be alert for *Autobahn Kreuz* (interchange) signs.

The Police

As in any country, the flashing lights of a patrol car are a sure sign that someone's in trouble. If it's you, try this handy phrase: *"Entschuldigung, ich bin Tourist"* (Sorry, I'm a tourist). Or, for the adventurous: *"Wenn es Ihnen nicht gefällt, wie ich Auto fahre, gehen Sie doch vom Gehweg runter."* (If you don't like how I drive, stay off the sidewalk.)

I'm late for my tour.	*Ich bin zu spät für meine Gruppenreise.*	ikh bin tsoo shpayt fewr **mī**-neh **groop**-ehn-**rī**-zeh
Can I buy your hat?	*Kann ich Ihren Hut kaufen?*	kahn ikh **eer**-ehn hoot **kowf**-ehn
What seems to be the problem?	*Was ist los?*	vas ist lohs
Sorry, I'm a tourist.	*Entschuldigung, ich bin Tourist.*	ehnt-**shool**-dig-oong ikh bin **too**-rist

TRAVELING

Reading Road Signs

Alle Richtungen	Out of town (all destinations)
Ausfahrt	Exit
Autobahn Kreuz	Freeway interchange
Baustelle	Construction
Dreieck ("three-corner")	fork
Einbahnstraße	One-way street
Einfahrt	Entrance
Fußgänger	Pedestrians
Gebühr	Toll
Langsam	Slow down
Nächste Ausfart	Next exit
Parken verboten	No parking
Stadtmitte	To the center of town
Stopp	Stop
Straßenarbeiten	Road workers ahead
Umleitung	Detour
Vorfahrt beachten	Yield
Zentrum	To the center of town

Standard Road Signs

 AND LEARN THESE ROAD SIGNS

Speed Limit
(km/hr)

Yield

No Passing

End of
No Passing
Zone

One Way

Intersection

Main
Road

Freeway

Danger

No Entry

No Entry
for cars

All Vehicles
Prohibited

Parking

No Parking

Customs

Peace

Other Signs You May See

TRAVELING

Belegt	No vacancy
Besetzt	Occupied
Bissiger Hund	Mean dog
Damen	Ladies
Drücken / Ziehen	Push / Pull
Einfahrt freihalten	Keep entrance clear
Eintritt frei	Free admission
Fahrrad	Bicycle
Gefahr	Danger
Geöffnet von ___ bis ___	Open from ___ to ___
Geöffnet	Open
Geschlossen	Closed
Herren	Men
Kein Eingang, Keine Einfahrt	No entry
Kein Trinkwasser	Undrinkable water
Keine Werbung	No soliciting
Lebensgefährlich	Extremely dangerous
Nicht rauchen	No smoking
Notausgang	Emergency exit
Ruhetag ("quiet day")	Closed
Stammtisch	Reserved table for regulars
Toiletten	Toilets
Verboten	Forbidden
Vorsicht	Caution
WC	Toilet
Wegen Umbau geschlossen	Closed for restoration
Wegen Ferien geschlossen	Closed for vacation
Ziehen / Drücken	Pull / Push
Zimmer frei	Rooms available
Zu verkaufen	For sale
Zu vermieten	For rent or for hire
Zugang verboten	Keep out

SLEEPING

Places to Stay

hotel	*Hotel*	hoh-**tehl**
small hotel	*Pension*	pehn-see-**ohn**
country inn	*Gasthaus, Gasthof*	**gahst**-hows, **gahst**-hohf
family-run place	*Familienbetrieb*	fah-**mee**-lee-ehn-beh-treeb
room in a home,	*Gästezimmer,*	**gehs**-teh-tsim-mer,
bed & breakfast	*Fremdenzimmer*	**frehm**-dehn-tsim-mer
youth hostel	*Jugendherberge*	**yoo**-gehnd-hehr-behr-geh
vacancy	*Zimmer frei*	**tsim**-mer frī
no vacancy	*belegt*	beh-**lehgt**

The word *garni* in a hotel name means "without restaurant."

Reserving a Room

I like to reserve rooms a few days in advance as I travel. But if my itinerary is set, I reserve before I leave home. To reserve from home by email or fax, use the handy form in the appendix (online at www.ricksteves.com/reservation).

Hello.	*Guten Tag.*	**goo**-tehn tahg
Do you speak	*Sprechen Sie*	**shprehkh**-ehn zee
English?	*Englisch?*	**ehng**-lish
Do you have a	*Haben Sie ein*	**hah**-behn zee īn
room for...?	*Zimmer für...?*	**tsim**-mer fewr

51

SLEEPING

Key Phrases: Sleeping

I want to make / confirm a reservation.	Ich möchte eine Reservierung machen / bestätigen.	ikh **murkh**-teh **ī**-neh reh-zer-**feer**-oong **mahkh**-ehn / beh-**shtay**-teh-gehn
I'd like a room (for two people), please.	Ich möchte ein Zimmer (für zwei Personen), bitte.	ikh **murkh**-teh īn **tsim**-mer (fewr tsvī pehr-**zoh**-nehn) **bit**-teh
...with/without/and	...mit / ohne / und	mit / **oh**-neh / oont
...toilet	...Toilette	toh-**leh**-teh
...shower	...Dusche	**doo**-sheh
Can I see the room?	Kann ich das Zimmer sehen?	kahn ikh dahs **tsim**-mer **zay**-hehn
How much is it?	Wie viel kostet das?	vee feel **kohs**-teht dahs
Credit card O.K.?	Kreditkarte O.K.?	kreh-**deet**-kar-teh "O.K."

...one person	...eine Person	**ī**-neh pehr-**zohn**
...two people	...zwei Personen	tsvī pehr-**zoh**-nehn
...tonight	...heute Abend	**hoy**-teh **ah**-behnt
...two nights	...zwei Nächte	tsvī **naykh**-teh
...Friday	...Freitag	**frī**-tahg
...June 21	...einundzwanzigsten Juni	**īn**-oont-tsvahn-tsig-stehn **yoo**-nee
Yes or no?	Ja oder nein?	yah **oh**-der nīn
I'd like...	Ich möchte...	ikh **murkh**-teh
We'd like...	Wir möchten...	veer **murkh**-tehn
...a private bathroom	...eigenes Bad.	**ī**-geh-nehs baht
...your cheapest room.	...ihr billigstes Zimmer.	eer **bil**-lig-stehs **tsim**-mer
...___ bed(s) for ___ people in ___ room(s).	...___ Bett(en) für ___ Personen in ___ Zimmer(n).	beht-(tehn) fewr pehr-**zoh**-nehn in **tsim**-mer(n)
How much is it?	Wie viel kostet das?	vee feel **kohs**-teht dahs

Anything cheaper?	*Etwas Billigeres?*	**eht**-vahs **bil**-lig-er-ehs
I'll take it.	*Ich nehme es.*	ikh **nay**-meh ehs
My name is ___.	*Ich heiße ___.*	ikh **hī**-seh
I'll stay...	*Ich bleibe...*	ikh **blī**-beh
We'll stay...	*Wir bleiben...*	veer **blī**-behn
...for one night.	*...für eine Nacht.*	fewr **ī**-neh nahkht
...for ___ nights.	*...für ___ Nächte.*	fewr ___ **nehkh**-teh
I'll come...	*Ich komme...*	ikh **koh**-meh
We'll come...	*Wir kommen...*	veer **koh**-mehn
...in the morning.	*...am Morgen.*	ahm **mor**-gehn
...in the afternoon.	*...am Nachmittag.*	ahm **nahkh**-mit-tahg
...in the evening.	*...am Abend.*	ahm **ah**-behnt
...in one hour.	*...in einer Stunde.*	in **ī**-ner **shtoon**-deh
...before 4:00 in the afternoon.	*...vor vier Uhr abends.*	for feer oor **ah**-behnts
...Friday before 6 P.M.	*...Freitag vor sechs Uhr abends.*	**frī**-tahg for zehx oor **ah**-behnts
Thank you.	*Danke.*	**dahng**-keh

Using a Credit Card

If you need to secure your reservation with a credit card, here's the lingo.

Do you need a deposit?	*Brauchen Sie eine Anzahlung?*	**browkh**-ehn zee **ī**-neh **ahn**-tsahl-oong
Credit card O.K.?	*Kreditkarte O.K.?*	kreh-**deet**-kar-teh "O.K."
credit card	*Kreditkarte*	kreh-**deet**-kar-teh
debit card	*Kontokarte*	**kohn**-toh-kar-teh
The name on the card is ___.	*Der Name auf der Karte ist ___.*	der **nah**-meh owf dehr **kar**-teh ist
The credit card number is...	*Die Kreditkarten- nummer ist...*	dee kreh-**deet**-kar-tehn-**noo**-mer ist
0	*null*	nool
1	*eins*	īns
2	*zwei*	tsvī
3	*drei*	drī

4	*vier*	feer
5	*fünf*	fewnf
6	*sechs*	zehx
7	*sieben*	**zee**-behn
8	*acht*	ahkht
9	*neun*	noyn
Valid until ___.	*Gültig bis ___.*	**gool**-tig bis
January	*Januar*	**yah**-noo-ar
February	*Februar*	**fay**-broo-ar
March	*März*	mehrts
April	*April*	ah-**pril**
May	*Mai*	mī
June	*Juni*	**yoo**-nee
July	*Juli*	**yoo**-lee
August	*August*	ow-**goost**
September	*September*	zehp-**tehm**-ber
October	*Oktober*	ohk-**toh**-ber
November	*November*	noh-**vehm**-ber
December	*Dezember*	day-**tsehm**-ber
2009	*zweitausendneun*	**tsvī**-tow-zehnd-**noyn**
2010	*zweitausendzehn*	**tsvī**-tow-zehnd-**tsayn**
2011	*zweitausendelf*	**tsvī**-tow-zehnd-**ehlf**
2012	*zweitausendzwölf*	**tsvī**-tow-zehnd-**tsvurlf**
2013	*zweitausenddreizehn*	**tsvī**-tow-zehnd-**drī**-tsayn
2014	*zweitausendvierzehn*	**tsvī**-tow-zehnd-**feer**-tsayn
2015	*zweitausend-fünfzehn*	**tsvī**-tow-zehnd-**fewnf**-tsayn
2016	*zweitausend-sechzehn*	**tsvī**-tow-zehnd-**zehkh**-tsayn
Can I reserve with a credit card and pay in cash?	*Kann ich mit der Karte reservieren und bar zahlen?*	kahn ikh mit dehr **kar**-teh reh-ser-**veer**-ehn und bar **tsah**-lehn
I have another card.	*Ich habe eine andere Karte.*	ikh **hah**-beh ī-neh **ahn**-deh-reh **kar**-teh

If your *Kreditkarte* (credit card) is not approved, you can say "*Ich habe eine andere Karte*" (I have another card)—if you do.

Das Alphabet

If phoning, you can use the code alphabet below to spell out your name if necessary. Unless you're giving the hotelier your name as it appears on your credit card, consider using a shorter version of your name to make things easier.

a	ah	*Anna*	**ah**-nah
ä	ay	*Ärger (anger)*	**ehr**-ger
b	bay	*Bertha*	**behr**-tah
c	tsay	*Cäsar*	**tseh**-zar
d	day	*Daniel*	**dah**-nee-ehl
e	ay	*Emil*	**eh**-meel
f	"f"	*Friedrich*	**freed**-rikh
g	gay	*Gustav*	**goo**-stahf
h	hah	*Heinrich*	**hīn**-rikh
i	ee	*Ida*	**ee**-dah
j	yot	*Jakob*	**yah**-kohp
k	kah	*Kaiser (emperor)*	**kī**-zer
l	"l"	*Leopold*	**lay**-oh-pohld
m	"m"	*Martha*	**mar**-tah
n	"n"	*Niklaus*	**nik**-lows
o	"o"	*Otto*	**oh**-toh
ö	ur	*Ökonom*	urk-oh-**nohm**
p	pay	*Peter*	**pay**-ter
q	koo	*Quelle*	**kveh**-leh
r	ehr	*Rosa*	**roh**-zah
s	"s"	*Sophie*	zoh-**fee**
t	tay	*Theodor*	**tay**-oh-dor
u	oo	*Ulrich*	**ool**-rikh
ü	ew	*Übel (evil)*	**ew**-behl
v	fow	*Viktor*	**veek**-tor
w	vay	*Wilhelm*	**vil**-hehlm
x	eeks	*Xaver*	**ksah**-ver
y	**ewp**-sil-lohn	*Ypsilon*	**ewp**-sil-lohn
z	tseht	*Zeppelin*	**tseh**-peh-lin
β	**es**-tseht	*Ziss*	tsis

Just the Fax, Ma'am

If you're booking a room by fax...

I want to send a fax.	Ich möchte einen Fax senden.	ikh **murkh**-teh **ī**-nehn fahx **zehn**-dehn
What is your fax number?	Was ist Ihre Faxnummer?	vahs ist **eer**-eh **fahx**-noo-mer
Your fax number is not working.	Ihre Faxnummer funktioniert nicht.	**eer**-eh **fahx**-noo-mer foonk-tsee-ohn-**eert** nikht
Please turn on your fax machine.	Bitte stellen Sie Ihren Fax an.	**bit**-teh **shtehl**-lehn zee **eer**-ehn fahx ahn

Getting Specific

I'd like a room...	Ich möchte ein Zimmer...	ikh **murkh**-teh īn **tsim**-mer
We'd like a room...	Wir möchten ein Zimmer...	veer **murkh**-tehn īn **tsim**-mer
...with / without / and	...mit / ohne / und	mit / **oh**-neh / oont
...toilet	...Toilette	toh-**leh**-teh
...shower	...Dusche	**doo**-sheh
...shower down the hall	...Dusche im Gang	**doo**-sheh im gahng
...bathtub	...Badewanne	**bah**-deh-vah-neh
...double bed	...Doppelbett	**doh**-pehl-beht
...twin beds	...Einzelbetten	**īn**-tsehl-beht-tehn
...balcony	...Balkon	bahl-**kohn**
...view	...Ausblick	**ows**-blick
...with only a sink	...nur mit Waschbecken	noor mit **vahsh**-behk-ehn
...on the ground floor	...im Erdgeschoß	im **ehrd**-geh-shohs
...television	...Fernsehen	**fehrn**-zay-hehn
...telephone	...Telefon	tehl-eh-**fohn**
...air conditioning	...Klimaanlage	**klee**-mah-ahn-lah-geh

SLEEPING

...kitchenette	...Kleinküche	**klīn**-kewkh-eh
Is there an elevator?	Gibt es einen Fahrstuhl?	gipt ehs **ī**-nehn **far**-shtool
Do you have a swimming pool?	Haben Sie einen Pool?	**hah**-behn zee **ī**-nehn pool
I arrive Monday, depart Wednesday.	Ich komme am Montag, und reise am Mittwoch ab.	ikh **koh**-meh ahm **mohn**-tahg oont **rī**-zeh ahm **mit**-vohkh ahp
We arrive Monday, depart Wednesday.	Wir kommen am Montag, und reisen am Mittwoch ab.	veer **koh**-mehn ahm **mohn**-tahg oont **rī**-zehn ahm **mit**-vohkh ahp
I'm desperate.	Ich bin am Verzweifeln.	ikh bin ahm fehr-**tsvī**-fehln
We're desperate.	Wir sind am Verzweifeln.	veer zint ahm fehr-**tsvī**-fehln
I'll sleep anywhere.	Ich kann irgendwo schlafen.	ikh kahn **ir**-gehnd-voh **shlah**-fehn
We'll sleep anywhere.	Wir können irgendwo schlafen.	veer **kurn**-nehn **ir**-gehnd-voh **shlah**-fehn
I have a sleeping bag.	Ich habe einen Schlafsack.	ikh **hah**-beh **ī**-nehn **shlahf**-zahk
We have sleeping bags.	Wir haben Schlafsäcke.	veer **hah**-behn **shlahf**-zehk-eh
Will you please call another hotel for me?	Rufen Sie bitte in einem anderen Hotel für mich an?	**roo**-fehn zee **bit**-teh in **ī**-nehm **ahn**-der-ehn hoh-**tehl** fewr meekh ahn

Families

Do you have a...?	Haben Sie ein...?	**hah**-behn zee īn
...family room	...Familienzimmer	fah-**mee**-lee-ehn-**tsim**-mer
...family discount	...Familienrabatt	fah-**mee**-lee-ehn-rah-**baht**
...discount for children	...Rabatt für Kinder	rah-**baht** fewr **kin**-der
I have / We have...	Ich habe / Wir haben...	ikh **hah**-beh / veer **hah**-behn

...one child, ___ months / years old.	...ein Kind, ___ Monate / Jahre alt.	īn kint, ___ moh-**nah**-teh / **yar**-eh ahlt
...two children, ___ and ___ years old.	...zwei Kinder, ___ und ___ Jahre alt.	tsvī **kin**-der, ___ oont ___ **yar**-eh ahlt
I'd like...	Ich hätte gern...	ikh **heht**-teh gehrn
We'd like...	Wir hätten gern...	veer **heht**-tehn gehrn
...a crib.	...ein Kinderbett.	īn **kin**-der-beht
...a small extra bed.	...ein kleines Extrabett.	īn **klī**-nehs **ehk**-strah-beht
...bunk beds.	...Kojen.	**koh**-yehn
babysitting service	Kinderaufsicht	**kin**-der-**owf**-zikht
Is a... nearby?	Ist ein... in der Nähe?	ist īn... in dehr **nay**-heh
...park	...Park	park
...playground	...Spielplatz	**shpeel**-plahts
...swimming pool	...Schwimmbad	**shvim**-baht

For fun, Germans call little boys *Lausbub* (kid with lice) and little girls *Göre* (brat).

Mobility Issues

Stairs are... for me / us / my husband / my wife.	Treppen sind für mich / uns / meinen Mann / meine Frau...	**treh**-pehn zint fewr mikh / oons / **mī**-nehn mahn / **mī**-neh frow
...impossible	...unmöglich.	oon-**murg**-likh
...difficult	...schwierig.	**shvee**-rig
Do you have...?	Haben Sie...?	**hah**-behn zee
...an elevator	...einen Lift	**ī**-nehn lift
...a ground floor room	...ein Zimmer im Erdgeschoß	īn **tsim**-mer im **ehrd**-geh-shohs
...a wheelchair-accessible room	...ein rollstuhl-gängiges Zimmer	īn **rohl**-shtool-**gayng**-ig-ehs **tsim**-mer

Confirming, Changing, and Canceling Reservations

You can use this template for your telephone call.

I have a reservation.	Ich habe eine Reservierung.	ikh **hah**-beh **ī**-neh reh-zer-**feer**-oong
We have a reservation.	Wir haben eine Reservierung.	veer **hah**-behn **ī**-neh reh-zer-**feer**-oong
My name is ___.	Ich heiße ___.	ikh **hī**-seh ___
I'd like to... my reservation.	Ich möchte meine Reservierung...	ikh **murkh**-teh **mī**-neh reh-zer-**feer**-oong
...confirm	...bestätigen	beh-**shtay**-teh-gehn
...reconfirm	...nochmals bestätigen.	**nohkh**-mahls beh-**shtay**-tig-ehn
...cancel	...annullieren	ah-nool-**eer**-ehn
...change	...ändern	**ehn**-dern
The reservation is / was for...	Die Reservierung ist / war für...	dee reh-zer-**feer**-oong ist / var fewr
...one person	...eine Person	**ī**-neh pehr-**zohn**
...two people	...zwei Personen	tsvī pehr-**zoh**-nehn
...today / tomorrow	...heute / morgen	**hoy**-teh / **mor**-gehn
...the day after tomorrow	...übermorgen	**ew**-ber-**mor**-gehn
...August 13	dreizehnten August	**drī**-tsayn-tehn ow-**goost**
...one night / two nights	...eine Nacht / zwei Nächte	**ī**-neh nahkht / tsvī **naykh**-teh
Did you find my / our reservation?	Haben Sie meine / unsere Reservierung gefunden?	**hah**-behn zee **mī**-neh / **oon**-zer-eh reh-zer-**feer**-oong geh-**foon**-dehn
What is your cancellation policy?	Wie ist es mit einer Annulierung?	vee ist ehs mit **ī**-ner ah-nool-**eer**-oong
Will I be billed for the first night if I can't make it?	Werde ich für die erste Nacht belastet, wenn ich nicht kommen kann?	**vehr**-deh ikh fewr dee **ehr**-steh nahkht beh-**lah**-steht vehn ikh nikht **koh**-mehn kahn

I'd like to arrive instead on ___.	Ich möchte lieber am ___ kommen.	ikh **murkh**-teh **lee**-ber ahm ___ **koh**-mehn
We'd like to arrive instead on ___.	Wir möchten lieber am ___ kommen.	veer **murkh**-tehn **lee**-ber ahm ___ **koh**-mehn
Is everything O.K.?	Ist alles in Ordnung?	ist **ahl**-lehs in **ord**-noong
Thank you. See you then.	Vielen Dank. Bis dann.	**fee**-lehn dahngk bis dahn
I'm sorry, I need to cancel.	Ich bedauere, aber ich muß annullieren.	ikh beh-**dow**-eh-reh **ah**-ber ikh moos ah-nool-**eer**-ehn

Nailing Down the Price

How much is...?	Wie viel kostet...?	vee feel **kohs**-teht
...a room for ___ people	...ein Zimmer für ___ Personen	īn **tsim**-mer fewr ___ pehr-**zoh**-nehn
...your cheapest room	...Ihr billigstes Zimmer	eer **bil**-lig-stehs **tsim**-mer
Breakfast included?	Frühstück inklusive?	**frew**-shtewk in-kloo-**zee**-veh
Is half-pension required?	Ist Halbpension Bedingung?	ist **halb**-pehn-see-ohn beh-**ding**-oong
Complete price?	Vollpreis?	**fohl**-prīs
Is it cheaper if I stay three nights?	Ist es billiger, wenn ich drei Nächte bleibe?	ist ehs **bil**-lig-er vehn ikh drī **naykh**-teh **blī**-beh
I'll stay three nights.	Ich werde drei Nächte bleiben.	ikh **vehr**-deh drī **naykh**-teh **blī**-behn
We will stay three nights.	Wir werden drei Nächte bleiben.	veer **vehr**-dehn drī **naykh**-teh **blī**-behn
Is it cheaper if I pay cash?	Ist es billiger, wenn ich bar zahle?	ist ehs **bil**-lig-er vehn ikh bar **tsah**-leh
What is the cost per week?	Was ist der Wochenpreis?	vahs ist dehr **vohkh**-ehn-prīs

Choosing a Room

| Can I see the room? | Kann ich das Zimmer sehen? | kahn ikh dahs **tsim**-mer **zay**-hehn |

Can we see the room?	Können wir das Zimmer sehen?	**kurn**-nehn veer dahs **tsim**-mer **zay**-hehn
Show me / us another room?	Zeigen Sie mir / uns ein anderes Zimmer?	**tsi**-gehn zee meer / oons īn **ahn**-der-ehs **tsim**-mer
Do you have something...?	Haben Sie etwas...?	**hah**-behn zee **eht**-vahs
...larger / smaller	...größeres / kleineres	**grur**-ser-ehs / **klī**-ner-ehs
...better / cheaper	...besseres / billiges	**behs**-ser-ehs / **bil**-lig-er-ehs
...brighter	...helleres	**hehl**-ler-ehs
...in the back	...nach hinten hinaus	nahkh **hin**-tehn hin-**ows**
...quieter	...ruhigeres	**roo**-i-ger-ehs
Sorry, it's not right for me / us.	Tut mir leid, es ist nicht das Richtige für mich / uns.	toot meer līt ehs ist nikht dahs **rikh**-tig-eh fewr mikh / oons
I'll take it.	Ich nehme es.	ikh **nay**-meh ehs
We'll take it.	Wir nehmen es.	veer **nay**-mehn ehs
My key, please.	Mein Schlüssel, bitte.	mīn **shlew**-sehl **bit**-teh
Sleep well.	Schlafen Sie gut.	**shlah**-fehn zee goot
Good night.	Gute Nacht.	**goo**-teh nahkht

Breakfast

When does breakfast start?	Wann beginnt das Frühstück?	vahn beh-**gint** dahs **frew**-shtewk
When does breakfast end?	Wann endet das Frühstück?	vahn **ehn**-deht dahs **frew**-shtewk
Where is breakfast served?	Wo wird Frühstück serviert?	voh virt **frew**-shtewk zer-**veert**

Breakfast is normally included in the price of your room. For a list of breakfast words, see pages 78–79.

SLEEPING

Hotel Help

I'd like...	Ich hätte gern...	ikh **heht**-teh gehrn
We'd like...	Wir hätten gern...	veer **heht**-tehn gehrn
...a / another	...ein / noch ein	īn / nohkh īn
...towel.	...Handtuch.	**hahnd**-tookh
...clean bath towel(s).	...sauberes Badetuch / saubere Badetücher.	**zow**-ber-ehs **bah**-deh-tookh / **zow**-ber-eh **bah**-deh-tewkh-er
...pillow.	...Kissen.	**kis**-sehn
...clean sheets.	...saubere Bettwäsche.	**zow**-ber-eh **beht**-veh-sheh
...blanket.	...Decke.	**dehk**-eh
...glass.	...Glas.	glahs
...sink stopper.	...Abflußstöpsel.	**ahp**-floos-shturp-zehl
...soap.	...Seife.	**zī**-feh
...toilet paper.	...Klopapier.	**kloh**-pah-peer
...electrical adapter.	...Stromwandler.	**strohm**-vahnd-ler
...brighter light bulb.	...hellere Glühbirne.	**hehl**-eh-reh **gloo**-bir-neh
...lamp.	...Lampe.	**lahm**-peh
...chair.	...Stuhl.	shtool
...table.	...Tisch.	tish
...Internet access.	...Internetanschluß.	**in**-tehr-neht-**ahn**-shloos
...different room.	...anderes Zimmer.	**ahn**-der-ehs **tsim**-mer
...silence.	...Ruhe.	**roo**-heh
...to speak to the manager.	...mit dem Chef sprechen.	mit daym shehf **shprekh**-ehn
I've fallen and I can't get up.	Ich bin gefallen und kann nicht aufstehen.	ikh bin geh-**fahl**-lehn oont kahn nikht **owf**-shtay-hehn
How can I make the room...?	Wie kann ich das Zimmer... machen?	vee kahn ikh dahs **tsim**-mer...**mahkh**-ehn
...cooler / warmer?	...kühler / wärmer?	**kewl**-er / **vehrm**-er
Where can I wash / hang my laundry?	Wo kann ich meine Wäsche waschen / aufhängen?	voh kahn ikh **mī**-neh **vehsh**-eh **vahsh**-ehn / **owf**-hehng-ehn

Is a... laundry nearby?	Ist ein Waschsalon... in der Nähe?	ist in **vahsh**-sah-lohn in dehr **nay**-heh
...self-service	...mit Selbstbedienung	...mit zehlpst-beh-**dee**-noong
...full service	...mit Dienstleistung	mit **deenst**-līs-toong
I'd like / We'd like...	Ich möchte / Wir möchten...	ikh **murkh**-teh / veer **murkh**-tehn
...to stay another night.	...noch eine Nacht bleiben.	nokh **ī**-neh nahkht **blī**-behn
Where can I park?	Wo soll ich parken?	voh zohl ikh **par**-kehn
What time do you lock up?	Um wie viel Uhr schließen Sie ab?	oom vee feel oor **shlee**-sehn zee ahp
Please wake me at 7:00.	Wecken Sie mich um sieben Uhr, bitte.	**vehk**-ehn zee mikh oom **zee**-behn oor **bit**-teh
Where do you go to eat lunch / eat dinner / drink coffee?	Wo gehen Sie zum Mittag essen / Abend essen / Kaffee trinken?	voh **gay**-hehn zee tsoom **mit**-tahg **eh**-sehn / **ah**-behnt **eh**-sehn / kah-**fay trink**-ehn

Hotel Hassles

Come with me.	Kommen Sie mit mir.	**koh**-mehn zee mit meer
There is a problem in my room.	Es gibt ein Problem mit meinem Zimmer.	ehs gipt in proh-**blaym** mit **mī**-nehm **tsim**-mer
It smells bad.	Es stinkt.	ehs shtinkt
bedbugs	Wanzen	**vahn**-tsehn
mice	Mäuse	**moy**-zeh
cockroaches	Kakerlaken	**kah**-ker-**lahk**-ehn
prostitutes	Freudenmädchen	**froy**-dehn-**mayd**-tyehn
I'm covered with bug bites.	Ich bin mit Wanzenbissen übersät.	ikh bin mit **vahn**-tsehn-**bis**-sehn ew-ber-**zayt**
The bed is too soft / hard.	Das Bett ist zu weich / hart.	dahs beht ist tsoo vīkh / hart
I can't sleep.	Ich kann nicht schlafen.	ikh kahn nikht **shlah**-fehn

SLEEPING

The room is too...	*Das Zimmer ist zu...*	dahs **tsim**-mer ist tsoo
...hot / cold.	*...heiß / kalt.*	hīs / kahlt
...noisy / dirty.	*...laut / schmutzig.*	lowt / **shmoot**-sig
I can't	*Ich kann... nicht*	ikh kahn... nikht
open / shut	*öffnen / schliessen*	**urf**-nehn / **shlees**-ehn
the door /	*die Tür /*	dee tewr /
the window.	*das Fenster*	dahs **fehn**-ster
Air conditioner...	*Klimaanlage...*	**klee**-mah-ahn-lah-geh
Lamp...	*Lampe...*	**lahm**-peh
Lightbulb...	*Birne...*	**bir**-neh
Electrical outlet...	*Steckdose...*	**shtehk**-doh-zeh
Key...	*Schlüssel...*	**shlew**-sehl
Lock...	*Schloß...*	shlohs
Window...	*Fenster...*	**fehn**-ster
Faucet...	*Wasserhahn...*	**vah**-ser-hahn
Sink...	*Waschbecken...*	**vahsh**-behk-ehn
Toilet...	*Toilette...*	toh-**leh**-teh
Shower...	*Dusche...*	**doo**-sheh
...doesn't work.	*...ist kaputt.*	ist kah-**poot**
There is no	*Es gibt kein*	ehs gipt kīn
hot water.	*warmes Wasser.*	**var**-mehs **vahs**-ser
When is the	*Wann wird das*	vahn virt dahs
water hot?	*Wasser warm?*	**vahs**-ser varm

Checking Out

When is check-	*Wann muß ich das*	vahn mus ikh dahs
out time?	*Zimmer verlassen?*	**tsim**-mer fehr-**lah**-sehn
I'll leave...	*Ich fahre... ab.*	ikh **fah**-reh... ahp
We'll leave...	*Wir fahren... ab.*	veer **fah**-rehn... ahp
...today / tomorrow	*...heute / morgen*	**hoy**-teh / **mor**-gehn
...very early	*...sehr früh*	zehr frew
Can I pay now?	*Kann ich jetzt zahlen?*	kahn ikh yetzt **tsah**-lehn
Can we pay now?	*Können wir jetzt*	**kurn**-nehn veer yetzt
	zahlen?	**tsah**-lehn
Bill, please.	*Rechnung, bitte.*	**rehkh**-noong **bit**-teh
Credit card O.K.?	*Kreditkarte O.K.?*	kreh-**deet**-kar-teh "O.K."

Everything was great.	*Alles war gut.*	**ahl**-lehs var goot
I slept like a bear.	*Ich habe wie ein Bär geschlafen.*	ikh **hah**-beh vee īn bayr geh-**shlahf**-ehn
Will you call my next hotel...?	*Können Sie mein nächstes Hotel anrufen...?*	**kurn**-nehn zee mīn **nehkh**-stehs hoh-**tehl** **ahn**-roo-fehn
...for tonight	*...für heute Abend*	fewr **hoy**-teh **ah**-behnt
...to make a reservation	*...zum reservieren*	tsoom reh-ser-**veer**-ehn
...to confirm a reservation	*...zum bestätigen*	tsoom beh-**shtay**-teh-gehn
I will pay for the call.	*Ich bezahle für den Anruf.*	ikh beh-**tsah**-leh fewr dayn **ahn**-roof
Can I...?	*Kann ich...?*	kahn ikh
Can we...?	*Können wir...?*	**kurn**-nehn veer
...leave baggage here until ___	*...das Gepäck hier lassen bis ___*	dahs geh-**pehk** heer **lah**-sehn bis

I never tip beyond the included service charges in hotels or for hotel services.

Camping

camping	*Camping*	**kahm**-ping
campsite	*Zeltstelle*	**tsehlt**-shtehl-leh
tent	*Zelt*	tsehlt
The nearest campground?	*Der nächste Campingplatz?*	dehr **nehkh**-steh **kahm**-ping-plahts
Can I...?	*Kann ich...?*	kahn ikh
Can we...?	*Können wir...?*	**kurn**-nehn veer
...camp here for one night	*...hier eine Nacht zelten*	heer **ī**-neh nahkht **tsehl**-tehn
Are showers included?	*Duschen eingeschlossen?*	**doo**-shehn **īn**-geh-shlohs-sehn

EATING

RESTAURANTS

Types of Restaurants

Here are several types of eateries and some variations you'll find per country:

Restaurant—Primarily fine dining with formal service
Ratskeller—Atmospheric restaurant cellar with food of varying
  quality
Gasthaus, Gasthof, or *Wirtschaft*—Country inn serving fine meals
Gaststätte or *Gaststube*—Informal restaurant
Heurigen—Austrian wine bar that serves food (see "Wine," page 98)
Kneipe—German bar
Weinstübli or *Bierstübli*—Wine bar or tavern in Switzerland
Café or *Konditorei*—Pastry and coffee shop that sometimes serves
  light lunches (Mittagessen)
Schnell Imbiß—Small fast-food stand

Finding a Restaurant

Where's a good...	*Wo ist hier ein gutes...*	voh ist heer īn **goo**-tehs...
restaurant nearby?	*Restaurant?*	rehs-tow-**rahnt**
...cheap	*...billiges*	**bil**-lig-ehs
...local-style	*...einheimisches*	īn-**hī**-mish-ehs
...untouristy	*...nicht für Touristen*	nikht fewr too-**ris**-tehn
	gedachtes	geh-**dahkh**-tehs

...vegetarian	*...vegetarisches*	vehg-eht-**ar**-ish-ehs
...fast food	*...Schnellimbiß*	shnehl-**im**-bis
...self-service	*...Selbstbedienungs-*	zehlpst-beh-**dee**-noongs-
buffet	*Buffet*	boo-fay
...Italian	*...italienisches*	i-tahl-**yehn**-ish-ehs
...Turkish	*...türkisches*	**tewrk**-ish-ehs
...Chinese	*...chinesisches*	khee-**nayz**-ish-ehs
beer garden	*Biergarten*	**beer**-gar-tehn
with terrace	*mit Terrasse*	mit tehr-**rahs**-seh
with a salad bar	*mit Salatbar*	mit **zah**-laht-bar
with candles	*bei Kerzenlicht*	bī **kehr**-tzehn-likht
romantic	*romantisch*	roh-**mahn**-tish
moderate price	*günstig*	**gewn**-stig
splurge	*zum Verwöhnen*	tsoom fehr-**vur**-nehn
Is it better than	*Ist es besser als*	ist ehs behs-ser ahls
McDonald's?	*McDonald's?*	"McDonald's"

German restaurants close one day a week. It's called *Ruhetag* (quiet day). Before tracking down a recommended restaurant, call to make sure it's open.

Getting a Table

When does this	*Wann ist hier*	vahn ist heer
open / close?	*geöffnet /*	geh-**urf**-neht /
	geschlossen?	geh-**shlohs**-sehn
Are you open...?	*Sind Sie... geöffnet?*	zint see... geh-**urf**-neht
...today / tomorrow	*...heute / morgen*	**hoy**-teh / **mor**-gehn
...for lunch / dinner	*...zum Mittagessen /*	tsoom **mit**-tahg-eh-sehn /
	Abendessen	**ah**-behnt-eh-sehn
Are reservations	*Soll mann*	zohl mahn
recommended?	*reservieren?*	reh-zer-**feer**-ehn
I'd like...	*Ich hätte gern...*	ikh **heh**-teh gehrn
We'd like...	*Wir hätten gern...*	veer **heh**-tehn gehrn
...a table for	*...einen Tisch für*	**ī**-nehn tish fewr
one / two.	*ein / zwei.*	īn / tsvī
...to reserve a table	*...einen Tisch für*	**ī**-nehn tish fewr
for two people...	*zwei reserviert...*	tsvī reh-ser-**veert**

Key Phrases: Restaurants

Where's a good restaurant nearby?	*Wo ist hier ein gutes Restaurant?*	voh ist heer **īn** **goo**-tehs rehs-tow-**rahnt**
I'd like...	*Ich hätte gern...*	ikh **heh**-teh gehrn
We'd like...	*Wir hätten gern...*	veer **heh**-tehn gehrn
...a table for one / two.	*...einen Tisch für ein / zwei.*	**ī**-nehn tish fewr īn / tsvī
...non-smoking (if possible).	*...nichtraucher (wenn möglich).*	**nikht**-rowkh-er (vehn **mur**-glikh)
Is this seat free?	*Ist hier frei?*	ist heer frī
Menu (in English), please.	*Speisekarte (auf Englisch), bitte.*	**shpī**-zeh-kar-teh (owf **ehng**-lish) **bit**-teh
Bill, please.	*Rechnung, bitte.*	**rehkh**-noong **bit**-teh
Credit card O.K.?	*Kreditkarte O.K.?*	kreh-**deet**-kar-teh "O.K."

...for today / tomorrow	*...für heute / morgen*	fewr **hoy**-teh / **mor**-gehn
...at 8 P.M.	*...um zwanzig Uhr*	oom **tsvahn**-tsig oor
My name is ___.	*Ich heiße ___.*	ikh **hī**-seh
I have a reservation for ___ people.	*Ich habe eine Reservierung für ___ Personen.*	ikh **hah**-beh **ī**-neh reh-zer-**feer**-oong fewr___ pehr-**zohn**-ehn
I'd like to sit...	*Ich möchte... sitzen.*	ikh **murkh**-teh... **zit**-sehn
We'd like to sit...	*Wir möchten... sitzen.*	veer **murkh**-tehn... **zit**-sehn
...inside / outside.	*...drinn / draussen*	drin / **drow**-sehn
...by the window.	*...beim Fenster*	bīm **fehn**-ster
...with a view.	*...mit Aussicht*	mit **ows**-zikht
...where it's quiet.	*...im Ruhigen*	im **roo**-hig-ehn
non-smoking (if possible).	*Nichtraucher (wenn möglich).*	**nikht**-rowkh-er (vehn **mur**-glikh)
Is this table free?	*Ist dieser Tisch frei?*	ist **dee**-zer tish frī
Can I sit here?	*Kann ich hier sitzen?*	kahn ikh heer **zit**-sehn

EATING

| Can we sit here? | Können wir hier sitzen? | **kurn**-ehn veer heer **zit**-sehn |

Germans eat meals about when we do. In many bars and restaurants, you'll see tables with little signs that say *Stammtisch* ("This table reserved for our regulars"). Don't sit there unless you're invited by a local.

The Menu

menu	Karte, Speisekarte	**kar**-teh, **shpī**-zeh-**kar**-teh
fixed-price meal	Touristenmenü	too-**ris**-tehn-meh-**new**
menu of the day	Tageskarte	**tah**-gehs-kar-teh
fast service special	Schnellbedienung	shnehl-beh-**dee**-noong
self-service	Selbstbedienung	sehlbst-beh-**dee**-noong
specialty of the house	Spezialität des Hauses	**shpayt**-see-ahl-ee-**tayt** dehs **how**-zehs
half portion	halbe Portion	**hahl**-beh por-tsee-**ohn**
breakfast	Frühstück	**frew**-shtewk
lunch	Mittagessen	**mit**-tahg-eh-sehn
dinner	Abendessen	**ah**-behnt-eh-sehn
appetizers	Vorspeise	**for**-shpī-zeh
cold plates	kalte Gerichte	**kahl**-teh geh-**rikh**-teh
sandwiches	Brotzeiten	**broht**-tsī-tehn
bread	Brot	broht
salad	Salat	zah-**laht**
soup	Suppe	**zup**-peh
first course	erster Gang	**ehr**-ster gahng
main course	Hauptgerichte	**howpt**-geh-rikh-teh
meat	Fleisch	flīsh
poultry	Geflügel	geh-**flew**-gehl
fish	Fisch	fish
seafood	Meeresfrüchte	**meh**-rehs-frewkh-teh
children's plate	Kinderteller	**kin**-der-tehl-ler
side dishes	Beilagen	**bī**-lah-gehn
vegetables	Gemüse	geh-**mew**-zeh
cheese	Käse	**kay**-zeh
dessert	Nachspeise	**nahkh**-shpī-zeh

munchies	*zum Knabbern*	tsoom **knahb**-bern
beverages	*Getränke*	geh-**trehnk**-eh
drink menu	*Getränkekarte*	geh-**trehnk**-eh-**kar**-teh
beer	*Bier*	beer
wine	*Wein*	vīn
cover charge	*Eintritt*	**īn**-trit
service included	*Trinkgeld*	**trink**-gehlt
	inklusive	in-kloo-**zee**-veh
service not	*Trinkgeld nicht*	**trink**-gehlt nikht
included	*inklusive*	in-kloo-**zee**-veh
hot / cold	*warm / kalt*	varm / kahlt
with / and /	*mit / und /*	mit / oont /
or / without	*oder / ohne*	**oh**-der / **oh**-neh

Save money by ordering a *halbe Portion* (half portion) or a *Tageskarte* (menu of the day).

Ordering

waiter	*Kellner*	**kehl**-ner
waitress	*Kellnerin*	**kehl**-ner-in
I'm ready to order.	*Ich möchte*	ikh **murkh**-teh
	bestellen.	beh-**shtehl**-lehn
We're ready	*Wir möchten*	veer **murkh**-tehn
to order.	*bestellen.*	beh-**shtehl**-lehn
I'd like...	*Ich möchte...*	ikh **murkh**-teh
We'd like...	*Wir möchten...*	veer **murkh**-tehn
...just a drink.	*...nur etwas zu*	noor **eht**-vahs tsoo
	trinken.	**trink**-ehn
...a snack.	*...eine Kleinigkeit.*	**ī**-neh **klī**-nig-kīt
...just a salad.	*...nur einen Salat.*	noor **ī**-nehn zah-**laht**
...a half portion.	*...eine halbe*	**ī**-neh **hahl**-beh
	Portion.	por-tsee-**ohn**
...to see the menu.	*...die Karte sehen.*	dee **kar**-teh **zay**-hehn
...to order.	*...bestellen.*	beh-**shtehl**-lehn
...to pay.	*...zahlen.*	**tsahl**-ehn
...to throw up.	*...mich übergeben.*	mikh **ew**-ber-gay-behn

Do you have...?	Haben Sie...?	**hah**-behn zee
...an English menu	...eine Speisekarte auf Englisch	**ī**-neh **shpī**-zeh-kar-teh in **ehng**-lish
...a lunch special	...ein Mittagsmenü	īn **mit**-tahgs-meh-**new**
What do you recommend?	Was schlagen Sie vor?	vahs **shlah**-gehn zee for
What's your favorite dish?	Was ist Ihr Lieblingsessen?	vahs ist eer **leeb**-lings-eh-sehn
Is it...?	Ist es...?	ist ehs
...good	...gut	goot
...expensive	...teuer	**toy**-er
...light	...leicht	līkht
...filling	...sättigend	**seht**-tee-gehnd
What is...?	Was ist...?	vahs ist
...that	...das	dahs
...local	...typisch	**tew**-pish
...fresh	...frisch	frish
...cheap	...billig	**bil**-lig
What is fast?	Was geht schnell?	vahs gayt shnehl
Can we split this and have an extra plate?	Können wir das teilen und noch einen Teller haben?	**kurn**-nehn veer dahs **tī**-lehn oont nohkh **ī**-nehn **tehl**-ler **hah**-behn
I've changed my mind.	Ich habe es mir anders überlegt.	ikh **hah**-beh ehs meer **ahn**-ders ew-ber-**laygt**
Nothing with eyeballs.	Nichts mit Augen.	nihkts mit **ow**-gehn
Can I substitute (anything) for the __?	Kann ich (etwas anderes) statt __ haben?	kahn ikh (**eht**-vahs **ahn**-der-ehs) shtaht __ **hah**-behn
Can I / Can we get it to go?	Kann ich / Können wir das mitnehmen?	kahn ikh / **kurn**-nehn veer dahs **mit**-nay-mehn
To go?	Zum Mitnehmen?	tsoom **mit**-nay-mehn

To get the waiter's attention, ask *"Bitte?"* (Please?). This is the sequence of a typical restaurant experience: The waiter gives you a menu (*Speisekarte*) and then asks if you'd like something to drink

EATING

(*Etwas zu trinken?*). When ready to take your order, the waiter simply says, "*Bitte?*" After the meal, he asks if the meal tasted good (*Hat's gut geschmeckt?*), if you'd like dessert (*Möchten Sie eine Nachspeise?*), and if you'd like anything else (*Sonst noch etwas?*). You ask for the bill (*Die Rechnung, bitte*).

Tableware and Condiments

plate	*Teller*	**tehl**-ler
extra plate	*Extrateller*	**ehk**-strah-tehl-ler
napkin	*Serviette*	zer-vee-**eht**-teh
silverware	*Besteck*	beh-**shtehk**
knife	*Messer*	**mehs**-ser
fork	*Gabel*	**gah**-behl
spoon	*Löffel*	**lurf**-fehl
cup	*Tasse*	**tah**-seh
glass	*Glas*	glahs
carafe	*Karaffe*	kah-**rah**-feh
water	*Wasser*	**vah**-ser
bread	*Brot*	broht
large pretzel	*Brezel*	**breht**-sehl
butter	*Butter*	**boo**-ter
margarine	*Margarine*	mar-gah-**ree**-neh
salt / pepper	*Salz / Pfeffer*	zahlts / **pfehf**-fer
sugar	*Zucker*	**tsoo**-ker
artificial sweetener	*Süßstoff*	**sews**-shtohf
honey	*Honig*	**hoh**-nig
mustard...	*Senf...*	zehnf
...mild / sharp / sweet	*...mild / scharf / süß*	meelt / sharf / zews
ketchup	*Ketchup*	"ketchup"
mayonnaise	*Mayonnaise*	mah-yoh-**nay**-zeh
toothpick	*Zahnstocher*	**tsahn**-shtohkh-er

The Food Arrives

Is it included with the meal?	*Ist das im Essen inclusive?*	ist dahs im **eh**-sehn in-kloo-**zee**-veh
I did not order this.	*Dies habe ich nicht bestellt.*	deez **hah**-beh ikh nikht beh-**shtehlt**

We did not order this.	Dies haben wir nicht bestellt.	deez **hah**-behn veer nikht beh-**shtehlt**
Please heat this up?	Bitte aufwärmen?	**bit**-teh **owf**-vehr-mehn
A little.	Ein bißchen.	īn **bis**-yehn
More. / Another.	Mehr. / Noch ein.	mehr / nohkh īn
The same.	Das gleiche.	dahs **glīkh**-eh
Enough.	Genug.	geh-**noog**
Finished.	Fertig.	**fehr**-tig
I'm full.	Ich bin satt.	ikh bin zaht

After bringing the meal, your server might wish you a cheery "*Guten Appetit!*" (pronounced **goo**-tehn ah-peh-**teet**).

Complaints

This is...	Dies ist...	deez ist
...dirty.	...schmutzig.	**shmut**-tsig
...greasy.	...fettig.	**feht**-tig
...salty.	...salzig.	**zahl**-tsig
...undercooked.	...zu wenig gekocht.	tsoo **vay**-nig geh-**kohkht**
...overcooked.	...zu lang gekocht.	tsoo lahng geh-**kohkht**
...inedible.	...nicht eßbar.	nikht **ehs**-bar
...cold.	...kalt.	kahlt
Do any of your customers return?	Kommen Ihre Kunden je zurück?	**koh**-mehn **eer**-eh **koon**-dehn yay tsoo-**rewk**
Yuck!	Igitt!	ee-**git**

Compliments

Yummy!	Mmmh!	mmm
Delicious!	Lecker!	**lehk**-er
Excellent!	Ausgezeichnet!	ows-geh-**tsīkh**-neht
It tastes very good!	Schmeckt sehr gut!	shmehkt zehr goot
I love German / this food.	Ich liebe deutsches / dieses Essen.	ikh **lee**-beh **doy**-chehs / **dee**-zehs **eh**-sehn
Better than mom's cooking.	Besser als bei Muttern.	**behs**-ser ahls bī **moo**-tern
My compliments to the chef!	Kompliment an den Koch!	kohmp-li-**mehnt** ahn dayn kohkh

Paying for Your Meal

The bill, please.	*Die Rechnung, bitte.*	dee **rehkh**-noong **bit**-teh
Together.	*Zusammen.*	tsoo-**zah**-mehn
Separate checks.	*Getrennte Rechnung.*	geh-**trehn**-teh **rehkh**-noong
Credit card O.K.?	*Kreditkarte O.K.?*	kreh-**deet**-kar-teh "O.K."
This is not correct.	*Dies stimmt nicht.*	deez shtimt nikht
Please explain.	*Erklären Sie, bitte.*	ehr-**klehr**-ehn zee **bit**-teh
Can you explain / itemize the bill?	*Können Sie die Rechnung einzeln / erklären?*	**kurn**-nehn zee dee **rehkh**-noong **īn**-tsehln / ehr-**klehr**-ehn
What if I wash the dishes?	*Und wenn ich die Teller wasche?*	oont vehn ikh dee **tehl**-ler **vah**-sheh
Is tipping expected?	*Wird ein Trinkgeld erwartet?*	virt īn **trink**-gehlt ehr-**var**-teht
What percent?	*Wie viel Prozent?*	vee feel proh-**tsehnt**
tip	*Trinkgeld*	**trink**-gehlt
Keep the change.	*Stimmt so.*	shtimt zoh
This is for you.	*Dies ist für Sie.*	deez ist fewr zee
Could I have a receipt, please?	*Kann ich bitte einen Beleg haben?*	kahn ikh **bit**-teh **ī**-nehn beh-**lehg hah**-behn

When you're ready for the bill, ask for the ***Rechnung*** (reckoning). The service charge is nearly always included. Tipping is not expected beyond that, though it's polite to round up to the next big coin. If you're uncertain whether to tip, ask another customer if tipping is expected (***Wird ein Trinkgeld erwartet?***). Rather than leave the tip on the table, it's better style to say the total amount you want to pay (including the tip) when you give the waiter your money.

In Austria, a cover charge (***Gedeck***) is added at finer dining establishments. If the restaurant doesn't include a cover charge, the bread placed on your table usually costs extra. Ask to make sure you're not charged for food you don't want: "***Ist es inbegriffen?***" (Is it included?).

SPECIAL CONCERNS

In a Hurry

I'm in a hurry.	Ich bin in Eile.	ikh bin in **ī**-leh
We're in a hurry.	Wir sind in Eile.	veer zint in **ī**-leh
Will the food be ready soon?	Ist das Essen bald bereit?	ist dahs **eh**-sehn bahlt beh-**rīt**
I need / We need to be served quickly. Is that O.K.?	Ich muß / Wir müssen schnell bedient werden. Geht das?	ikh mus / veer **mews**-sehn shnehl beh-**deent** **vehr**-dehn. gayt dahs
I must / We must leave in 30 minutes / one hour.	Ich muß / Wir müssen in dreißig Minuten / einer Stunde gehen.	ikh mus / veer **mews**-sehn in **drī**-sig mee-**noo**-tehn / **ī**-ner **shtoon**-deh **gay**-hehn

Dietary Restrictions

I'm allergic to...	Ich bin allergisch auf...	ikh bin ah-**lehr**-gish **owf**
I / he / she cannot eat...	Ich / er / sie darf kein...essen.	ikh / ehr / zee darf kīn... **eh**-sehn
...dairy products.	...Milchprodukte	**milkh**-proh-dook-teh
...wheat.	...Weizen	vī-tsehn
...meat / pork.	...Fleisch / Schweinefleisch	flīsh / **shvī**-neh-flīsh
...salt / sugar.	...Salz / Zucker	zahlts / **tsoo**-ker
...shellfish.	...Meeresfrüchte	**meh**-rehs-**frewkh**-teh
...spicy foods.	...scharfe Gewürze	**shar**-feh geh-**vewr**-tseh
...nuts.	...Nüsse	**new**-seh
I'm a diabetic.*	Ich bin Diabetiker.*	ikh bin dee-ah-**beht**-ik-er
I'd like a...	Ich hätte gern ein...	ikh **heh**-teh gehrn īn
We'd like a...	Wir hätten gern ein...	veer **heh**-tehn gehrn īn
...low-fat meal.	...wenig fettiges Gericht.	**veh**-nig **feht**-tig-ehs geh-**rikht**
...kosher meal.	...koscher Gericht.	**kohsh**-er geh-**rikht**
No salt / sugar.	Kein Salz / Zucker.	kīn zahlts / **tsoo**-ker
I eat only insects.	Ich esse nur Insekten.	ikh **ehs**-seh noor in-**zehkt**-ehn

No fat.	*Ohne Fett.*	**oh**-neh feht
Minimal fat.	*Mit wenig Fett.*	mit **vay**-nig feht
Low cholesterol.	*Niedriges Cholesterin.*	**nee**-dri-gehs koh-**lehs**-ter-in
No caffeine.	*Koffeinfrei.*	koh-fay-**een**-frī
No alcohol.	*Kein Alkohol.*	kīn **ahl**-koh-hohl
Organic.	*Biologisch.*	bee-oh-**loh**-gish
I'm a...	*Ich bin...*	ikh bin
...vegetarian.	*...Vegetarier.**	veh-geh-**tar**-ee-er
...strict vegetarian.	*...strenger Vegetarier.**	**shtrehng**-er veh-geh-**tar**-ee-er
...carnivore.	*...Fleischesser.*	**flīsh**-ehs-ser
...big eater.	*...grosser Esser.*	**groh**-ser **ehs**-ser
Is any meat or animal fat used in this?	*Hat es Fleisch oder tierische Fette drin?*	haht ehs flīsh **oh**-der **teer**-ish-eh **feht**-teh drin

* If you're female, add "in" to the end of these words if you're describing yourself, like this: *Diabetikerin* and *Vegetarierin*.

Children

Do you have...?	*Haben Sie...?*	**hah**-behn zee
...a children's portion	*...eine Kinderportion*	**ī**-neh **kin**-der-por-tsee-**ohn**
...a half portion	*...eine halbe Portion*	**ī**-neh **hahl**-beh por-tsee-**ohn**
...a high chair / booster seat	*...einen Kinderhocker/ Kindersitz*	**ī**-nehn **kin**-der-**hoh**-ker **kin**-der-zits
plain noodles / rice	*Nudeln / Reis ohne alles*	**noo**-dehln / rīs **oh**-neh **ahl**-lehs
with butter	*mit Butter*	mit **boo**-ter
no sauce	*ohne Sauce*	**oh**-neh **zoh**-seh
sauce / dressing on the side	*Sauce / Salatsoße separat*	**zoh**-seh / zah-**laht**-zoh-seh zeh-par-**aht**
pizza	*Pizza*	"pizza"
...cheese only	*...nur Käse*	noor **kay**-zeh
...pepperoni and cheese	*...Salami und Käse*	zah-**lah**-mee oont **kay**-zeh

EATING

jelly sandwich	Marmeladenbrot	mar-meh-**lah**-dehn-broht
toasted...	getoastet...	geh-**tohst**-eht
grilled...	gegrillt...	geh-**grilt**
...cheese sandwich	...Käsebrot	**kay**-zeh-broht
hot dog	frankfurter	**frahnk**-foort-er
hamburger	Hamburger	**hahm**-boor-ger
cheeseburger	Cheeseburger	**cheez**-boor-ger
French fries	Pommes frites,	pohm frits,
	Pommes	**poh**-mehs
ketchup	Ketchup	"ketchup"
crackers	Kekse,	**kehk**-seh,
	Salzgebäck	**zahlts**-geh-behk
Nothing spicy.	Nicht scharf	nikht sharf
	gewürzt.	geh-**vewrtst**
Not too hot.	Nicht zu heiß.	nikht tsoo hīs
Don't let the food	Speisen auf	**shpī**-zehn owf
mix together on	Teller nicht	**tehl**-ler nikht
the plate.	vermischen.	fehr-**mish**-ehn
He will / She will /	Er wird / Sie wird /	ehr virt / zee virt /
They will share	Sie werden unser	zee **vehr**-dehn **oon**-ser
our meal.	Essen teilen.	**eh**-sehn **tī**-lehn
Please bring the	Bitte schnell	**bit**-teh shnehl
food quickly.	servieren.	zer-**veer**-ehn
Can I / Can we	Kann ich / Können	kahn ikh / **kurn**-nehn
have an extra...?	wir ein	veer īn
	zusätzliche...	tsoo-**zehts**-likh-eh...
	haben?	**hah**-behn
...plate	...Teller	**tehl**-ler
...cup	...Schale, Becher	**shah**-leh, **behkh**-er
...spoon / fork	...Löffel / Gabel	**lurf**-fehl / **gah**-behl
Can I / Can we	Kann ich / Können	kahn ikh / **kurn**-nehn
have two extra...?	wir zwei	veer tsvī
	zusätzliche...	tsoo-**zehts**-likh-eh...
	haben?	**hah**-behn
...plates	...Teller	**tehl**-ler
...cups	...Schalen, Becher	**shah**-lehn, **behkh**-er
...spoons / forks	...Löffel / Gabeln	**lurf**-fehl / **gah**-behln

A small milk (in a plastic cup).	Eine kleine Portion Milch (in einem plastikbecher).	ī-neh klī-neh por-tsee-ohn milkh (in ī-nehm plah-steek-behkh-er)
Straw(s).	Halm(e).	**hahlm**(-eh)
More napkins, please.	Mehr Servietten, bitte.	mehr zer-vee-**eht**-tehn **bit**-teh
Sorry for the mess.	Entschuldigen Sie die Unordnung.	ehnt-**shool**-dig-oong zee dee oon-**ord**-noong

WHAT'S COOKING?

Breakfast

breakfast	Frühstück	**frew**-shtewk
bread	Brot	broht
roll	Brötchen, Semmel	**brurt**-syehn, **zehm**-mehl
toast	Toast	tohst
butter	Butter	**boo**-ter
jelly	Marmelade	mar-meh-**lah**-deh
pastry	Kuchen, Gebäck	**kookh**-ehn, geh-**behk**
croissant	Gipfel	**gip**-fehl
omelet	Omelett	**ohm**-leht
egg / eggs	Ei / Eier	ī / **ī**-er
fried eggs	Spiegeleier	**shpee**-gehl-ī-er
scrambled eggs	Rühreier	**rew**-rī-er
soft boiled / hard boiled	weichgekocht / hartgekocht	**vīkh**-geh-kohkht / **hart**-geh-kohkht
ham	Schinken	**shink**-ehn
bacon	Speck	shpehk
cheese	Käse	**kay**-zeh
yogurt	Joghurt	**yoh**-gurt
cereal	Cornflakes	"cornflakes"
granola cereal	Müsli	**mews**-lee
milk	Milch	milkh
fruit juice	Fruchtsaft	**frookht**-zahft
orange juice (fresh)	Orangensaft (frischgepreßt)	oh-**rahn**-zhehn-zahft (frish-geh-**prehst**)

Key Phrases: What's Cooking?

food	Essen	**eh**-sehn
breakfast	Frühstück	**frew**-shtewk
lunch	Mittagessen	**mit**-tahg-eh-sehn
dinner	Abendessen	**ah**-behnt-eh-sehn
bread	Brot	broht
cheese	Käse	**kay**-zeh
soup	Suppe	**zup**-peh
salad	Salat	zah-**laht**
meat	Fleisch	flīsh
chicken	Hähnchen	**hayn**-syehn
fish	Fisch	fish
fruit	Obst	ohpst
vegetables	Gemüse	geh-**mew**-zeh
dessert	Nachspeise	**nahkh**-shpī-zeh
Delicious!	Lecker!	**lehk**-er

hot chocolate	heiße Schokolade	**hī**-seh shoh-koh-**lah**-deh
coffee / tea	Kaffee / Tee	kah-**fay** / tay
(see Drinking, page 95)		
Breakfast included?	Frühstück inklusive?	**frew**-shtewk in-kloo-**zee**-veh

Germans have an endearing and fun-to-mimic habit of greeting others in the breakfast room with a slow, miserable, "*Morgen*" (Morning). *Frühstück* is almost always included with your room and is your chance to fuel up for the day with pots of coffee, bread, rolls, cheese, ham, eggs, and sometimes local specialties. For a hearty cereal, try *Bircher Müsli*, a healthy mix of oats, nuts, yogurt, and fruit. If breakfast is optional, take a walk to the *Bäckerei-Konditorei* (bakery). Germany and Austria are famous for this special cultural attraction—more varieties of bread, pastries, and cakes than you ever imagined, baked fresh every morning and throughout the day. Sometimes a café is part of a *Konditorei*.

Best of the Wurst

Wurst mit...	voorst mit	sausage with...
...Kraut	krowt	...sauerkraut
...Brot und Senf	broht oont zehnf	...bread and mustard
Blutwurst	**bloot**-voorst	made from (gulp!) blood
Beinwurst	**bīn**-voorst	sausage made of smoked pork, herbs, and wine
Bockwurst	**bohk**-voorst	thick pork sausage (white)
Bosna	**bohs**-nah	sausage with onions and curry
Bratwurst	**braht**-voorst	thick pork sausage, grilled or fried
Burewurst	**boo**-reh-voorst	bratwurst boiled instead of grilled
Currywurst	**kuh**-ree-voorst	burewurst flavored with curry
Cervelat	sehr-veh-**la**	mild Swiss veal sausage
Cervelat Salat	sehr-veh-**la** zah-**laht**	served cold with onions, cheese, and salad dressing

Snacks, Quick Lunches, and Appetizers

Bündnerfleisch	**bewnt**-ner-flīsh	air-dried beef, thinly sliced
Wurstplatte, Schlachtplatte ("slaughterplate")	**voorst**-plah-teh, **shlahkht**-plah-teh	assorted cold cuts (sausages, ham, liver paté, cow's tongue...)
Sauerkrautplatte	**zow**-er-krowt-**plah**-teh	assorted cold cuts with sauerkraut
Käsebrot	**kay**-zeh-broht	bread with cheese
Frikadelle	frik-ah-**dehl**-leh	large meatball / hamburger
Bauernomelette	**bow**-ern-ohm-leht	omelet with bacon and onion

EATING

Debreziner	deh-breh-**tseen**-er	thin, spicy sausage served in Austria
Jagdwurst	**yagt**-voorst	smoked pork with garlic and mustard
Käsekrainer	**kay**-zeh-krī-ner	sausage and cheese mixed
Leberkäse	**lay**-ber-kay-zeh	meatloaf of pork liver
Leberwurst	**lay**-ber-voorst	liverwurst
Mettwurst	**meht**-voorst	spicy, soft sausage spread
Nürnberger	**newrn**-behr-ger	fried, spiced pork and veal sausage
Stolzer Heinrich	**shtohlts**-er **hīn**-rikh	Bavarian fried pork sausage in beer sauce
Tirolerwurst	tee-**roh**-ler-voorst	Austrian smoked sausage
Weisswurst	**vīs**-voorst	very tender white boiled veal (Munich)
Wienerli / Frankfurter	**veen**-er-lee / **frahnk**-foort-er	thin frankfurter (hot dog)
Zwiebelwurst	**tsvee**-behl-voorst	liver and onion sausage

Rollmops	**rohl**-mohps	pickled herring
Brezel	**breht**-sehl	pretzel
Toast mit Schinken und Käse	tohst mit **shink**-ehn oont **kay**-zeh	toast with ham and cheese

Say Cheese

cheese	*Käse*	**kay**-zeh
mild / sharp	*mild / scharf*	meelt / sharf
cheese plate	*Käseplatte, Käseteller*	**kay**-zeh-**plah**-teh, **kay**-zeh-**tehl**-ler
Can I try a taste?	*Kann ich es probieren?*	kahn ikh ehs **proh**-beer-ehn

Cheese Specialties

Allgäuer Bergkäse	**ahl**-goy-er **behrg**-kay-zeh	hard, mild cheese, with holes
Altenburger	**ahlt**-ehn-boorg-er	soft, mild goat cheese
Appenzeller	**ah**-pehn-tsehl-ler	hard, sharp, tangy Swiss cow's milk cheese
Edelpilzkäse	**ay**-dehl-pilts-**kay**-zeh	mild blue cheese
Emmentaler	**ehm**-mehn-tah-ler	hard, mild Swiss cheese
Frischkäse	**frish**-kay-zeh	soft curd cheese with fresh herbs
Gorgonzola	gor-gohn-**tsoh**-lah	aged, blue-veined cheese
Gruyère	groo-**yehr**	strong-flavored, hard Swiss cheese
Limburger	**lim**-boorg-er	strong-smelling, herbed, soft cheese
Münster	**mewn**-ster	strong-tasting, hard cheese w/ caraway seed
Quark	kvark	smooth curd cheese, like thick yogurt
Tilsiter	**til**-sit-er	mild, semi-hard, and tangy cheese

EATING

The holes in Swiss cheese are made during fermentation—the more symmetrical the holes, the more expert the fermentation. Two of Switzerland's best-known specialties are cheese-based. *Käse Fondue* is Emmentaler and Gruyère cheese melted with white wine and garlic.

Eat this tasty, cheesy treat by dipping cubes of bread into it. Lose your bread in the pot and you have to kiss all the men (or women) at the table. *Raclette* is melted cheese from the Valais region. A special appliance slowly melts the bottom of the brick of cheese. Just scrape off a mound and eat it with potatoes, pickled onions, and gherkins.

Sandwiches

I'd like a sandwich.	*Ich hätte gern ein Sandwich.*	ikh **heh**-teh gehrn īn **zahnd**-vich

We'd like two sandwiches.	Wir hätten gern zwei Sandwiche.	veer **heh**-tehn gehrn tvsī **zahnd**-vich-eh
toasted	getoastet	geh-**tohst**-eht
cheese	Käse	**kay**-zeh
chicken	Hähnchen	**hayn**-syehn
egg salad	Eiersalat	**ī**-er-zah-laht
fish	Fisch	fish
ham	Schinken	**shink**-ehn
jelly	Marmelade	mar-meh-**lah**-deh
peanut butter	Erdnußbutter	**ehrd**-noos-boo-ter
pork sandwich	Schweinefleisch Sandwich	**shvīn**-flīsh **zahnd**-vich
salami	Salami	zah-**lah**-mee
tuna	Thunfisch	**toon**-fish
turkey	Truthahn, Pute	**troot**-hahn, **poo**-teh
lettuce	Kopfsalat	**kohpf**-zah-laht
mayonnaise	Mayonnaise	mah-yoh-**nay**-zeh
tomatoes	Tomaten	toh-**mah**-tehn
mustard	Senf	zehnf
onions	Zwiebeln	**tsvee**-behln
Does this come cold or warm?	Wird das kalt oder warm serviert?	virt dahs kahlt **oh**-der varm zer-**veert**
Heated, please.	Erwärmt, bitte.	ehr-**vehrmt bit**-teh

If You Knead Bread

bread	Brot	broht
dark bread	dunkles Brot	**doon**-klehs broht
three-grain bread	Dreikornbrot	**drī**-korn-broht
rye bread	Roggenmischbrot	**roh**-gehn-mish-broht
dark rye bread	Schwarzbrot	**shvarts**-broht
whole grain bread	Vollkornbrot	**fohl**-korn-broht
light bread	Weißbrot	**vīs**-broht
wimpy white bread	Toast	tohst
French bread	Baguette	bah-**geht**
roll (Germany, Austria)	Brötchen, Semmel	**brurt**-khehn, **zehm**-mehl
roll (Switz)	Brötli	**brurt**-lee

There are hundreds of different kinds of local breads in Germany, Austria, and Switzerland. Add a visit to the neighborhood *Bäckerei* to your touring schedule and look for their specialties (*Spezialitäten*). *Stollen* (pron. shtohl-lehn) is a sweet Christmas bread with raisins and nuts, topped with powdered sugar.

Soups and Salads

soup (of the day)	Suppe (des Tages)	**zup**-peh (dehs **tahg**-ehs)
chicken broth...	Hühnerbrühe...	**hew**-ner-brew-heh
beef broth...	Rinderbrühe...	**rin**-der-brew-heh
...with noodles	...mit Nudeln	mit **noo**-dehln
...with rice	...mit Reis	mit rīs
stew	Eintopf	**īn**-tohpf
vegetable soup	Gemüsesuppe	geh-**mew**-zeh-zup-peh
spicy goulash soup	Gulaschsuppe	**goo**-lahsh-zup-peh
liver dumpling soup	Leberknödel-suppe	**lay**-ber-kuh-nur-dehl-zup-peh
split pea soup	Erbsensuppe	**ehrb**-sehn-zup-peh
oxtail soup	Ochsenschwanz-suppe	**okh**-sehn-shvants-zup-peh
cabbage and sausage soup	Bauernsuppe	**bow**-ern-zup-peh
Serbian-style bean soup	Serbische Bohnen-suppe	**zehr**-bi-sheh **boh**-nehn-zup-peh
salad	Salat	zah-**laht**
green salad	grüner Salat	**grew**-ner zah-**laht**
mixed salad	gemischter Salat	geh-**mish**-ter zah-**laht**
potato salad	Kartoffelsalat	kar-**tohf**-fehl-zah-laht
Greek salad	griechischer Salat	**greekh**-ish-er zah-**laht**
chef's salad...	gemischter Salat des Hauses...	geh-**mish**-ter zah-**laht** dehs **how**-zehs
...with ham and cheese	...mit Schinken und Käse	mit **shink**-ehn oont **kay**-zeh
...with egg	...mit Ei	mit ī
plate of various salads	Salatteller	zah-**laht**-tehl-ler

EATING

small pieces of cold cuts mixed with pickles and mayonnaise	Fleischsalat	**flīsh**-zah-laht
vegetable platter	Gemüseplatte, Gemüseteller	geh-**mew**-zeh-plah-teh, geh-**mew**-zeh-tehl-ler
lettuce	Salat	zah-**laht**
tomato	Tomate	toh-**mah**-teh
onion	Zwiebel	**tsvee**-behl
cucumber	Gurken	**gur**-kehn
oil / vinegar	Öl / Essig	url / **ehs**-sig
salad dressing	Salatsoße	zah-**laht**-zoh-seh
dressing on the side	Salatsoße separat	zah-**laht**-zoh-seh zeh-par-**aht**
What is in this salad?	Was ist in diesem Salat?	vahs ist in **dee**-zehm zah-**laht**

In Germany, soup is often served as a first course to the large midday meal (*Mittagessen*). Typical German salads usually consist of a single ingredient with dressing, such as *Gurkensalat* (sliced cucumber marinated in a sweet vinaigrette) and *Tomatensalat* (tomatoes in vinaigrette with dill). For a meaty salad, try a Fleischsalat (**flīsh**-zah-laht)—chopped cold cuts mixed with pickles and mayonnaise.

The *Salatbar* (salad bar) is becoming a global phenomenon. You'll normally be charged by the size of the plate for one load. Choose a *Teller* (plate) that is *kleiner* (small), *mittlerer* (medium), or *großer* (large). Budget travelers eat a cheap and healthy lunch by grabbing a small plate and stacking it high.

Seafood

seafood	Meeresfrüchte	**meh**-rehs-**frewkh**-teh
assorted seafood	gemischte Meeresfrüchte	geh-**mish**-teh **meh**-rehs-**frewkh**-teh
fish	Fisch	fish
clams	Muscheln	**moo**-shehln
cod	Dorsch	dorsh
herring	Hering	**hehr**-ing

pike	Hecht	hehkht
salmon	Lachs	lahkhs
trout	Forelle	foh-**rehl**-leh
tuna	Thunfisch	**toon**-fish
What's fresh today?	Was ist heute frisch?	vahs ist **hoy**-teh frish
Do you eat this part?	Ißt man diesen Teil?	ist mahn **dee**-zehn tīl
Just the head, please	Nur den Kopf, bitte.	noor dayn kohpf **bit**-teh

Poultry

poultry	Geflügel	geh-**flew**-gehl
chicken	Hähnchen	**hayn**-syehn
roast chicken	Brathähnchen	**braht**-hayn-syehn
duck	Ente	**ehn**-teh
turkey	Truthahn, Pute	**troot**-hahn, **poo**-teh
How long has this been dead?	Wie lange ist dieses Tier schon tot?	vee **lahng**-eh ist **dee**-zehs teer shohn toht

Meat

meat	Fleisch	flīsh
bacon	Speck	shpehk
beef	Rindfleisch	**rint**-flīsh
beef steak	Beefsteak	**beef**-shtayk
brains	Hirn	hehrn
bunny	Kaninchen	kah-**neen**-syehn
cutlet	Kotelett	**koht**-leht
ham	Schinken	**shink**-ehn
lamb	Lamm	lahm
liver	Leber	**lay**-ber
mixed grill	Grillteller	**gril**-tehl-ler
organs	Innereien	in-neh-**rī**-ehn
pork	Schweinefleisch	**shvī**-neh-flīsh
roast beef	Rinderbraten	**rin**-der-brah-tehn
sausage	Wurst	voorst
tripe	Kutteln	**kut**-tehln
veal	Kalbfleisch	**kahlp**-flīsh

Avoiding Mis-Steaks

tenderloin	*Filet mignon*	"filet mignon"
T-bone	*T-bone*	**tay**-bohn
tenderloin of T-bone	*Lendenstück*	**lehn**-dehn-shtewk
raw	*roh*	roh
very rare	*blutig*	**bloo**-tig
rare	*rot*	roht
medium	*halbgar*	**hahlp**-gar
well-done	*gar,*	gar,
	durchgebraten	**durkh**-geh-brah-tehn
very well-done	*ganz gar*	gahnts gar
almost burnt	*fast verkohlt*	fahst fehr-**kohlt**

Main Course Specialties

Fleischtorte	**flīsh**-tor-teh	meat pie
Geschnetzeltes	geh-**shneht**-sehl-tehs	strips of veal or chicken braised in a rich sauce and served with noodles or Rösti (Switz.)
Gulasch (suppe)	**goo**-lahsh (**zup**-peh)	spicy stew
Hasenpfeffer / Rehpfeffer	**hah**-zehn-**pfeh**-fer / **ray**-pfeh-fer	spicy rabbit / deer stew with mushrooms and onions (Aus. and Switz.)
Kohlroulade	**kohl**-roo-lah-deh	cabbage leaves stuffed with minced meat
Matjesfilet auf Hausfrauenart	maht-yehs-fi-**lay** owf **hows**-frow-ehn-art	herring filets sautéed with apples, onions, and sour cream (Ger.)
Maultaschen	**mowl**-tahsh-ehn	German ravioli filled with various fillings like veal, cheese, and spinach
Ratsherrentopf	**rahts**-hehr-rehn-tohpf	stew of roasted meat with potatoes

Rösti	**rur**-shtiee	Swiss hashbrowns often mixed with cheese, ham eggs, and/or vegetables
Schweinebraten	**shvīn**-eh-brah-tehn	roasted pork with gravy
Spargel	**shpar**-gehl	big, white asparagus in season in May, served as a cream soup or on a plate with cream sauce
Tafelspitz	**tah**-fehl-shpits	boiled beef with apple and horseradish sauce (Aus. and Switz.)
Tiroler Bauernschmaus	tee-**roh**-ler **bow**-ern-shmows	several types of meat served w/ sauerkraut, potatoes, and dumplings
Wiener Schnitzel	**vee**-ner **shnit**-sehl	breaded, fried veal cutlet—Viennese style

During fall hunting season in the Alps, venison (*Wildbret*) and chamois (*Gämse*, a goat-like antelope) are often featured on the menu.

Eating Italian

Italian restaurants provide a good budget break from *Wurst* und *Kraut*. Here are the words you'll find on the menu: *Spaghetti, Pizza, Tomaten, Schinken* (ham), *Käse* (cheese), *Champignons* (mushrooms), *Paprika* (peppers), *Ei* (egg), *Pepperoni* (small hot peppers), *Zwiebeln* (onions), *Artischocken* (artichokes), *Basilikum* (basil), *Meeresfrüchte* (seafood), *Muscheln* (clams), and *Vegetaria* (vegetarian).

How Food is Prepared

assorted	*gemischte*	geh-**mish**-teh
baked	*gebacken*	geh-**bah**-kehn
boiled	*gekocht*	geh-**kohkht**
braised	*geschmort*	geh-**shmort**

EATING

Styles of Cooking

Art	style of cooking
Bauern	farmer-style, with potatoes (good and hearty)
Französisch	French
Hausfrauen	housewife-style, with apples, onions, and sour cream
Hausgemacht	homemade
Italienisch	Italian
Jäger	hunter-style, with mushrooms and gravy
Wiener	Viennese, breaded and fried

broiled	*ofengegrillt*	**ohf**-ehn-geh-grilt
cold	*kalt*	kahlt
cooked	*gekocht*	geh-**kohkht**
deep-fried	*frittiert*	frit-**eert**
fillet	*Filet*	fi-**lay**
fresh	*frisch*	frish
fried	*gebraten*	geh-**brah**-tehn
grilled	*gegrillt*	geh-**grilt**
homemade	*hausgemacht*	**hows**-geh-mahkht
hot	*heiß*	hīs
in cream sauce	*in Rahmsauce*	in **rahm**-zoh-seh
medium	*halbgar*	**hahlp**-gar
microwave	*Mikrowelle*	**mee**-kroh-vehl-leh
mild	*mild*	meelt
mixed	*gemischte*	geh-**mish**-teh
poached	*pochierte*	pohkh-ee-**ehr**-teh
rare	*rot*	roht
raw	*roh*	roh
roast	*Braten*	**brah**-tehn
roasted	*geröstet*	geh-**rurs**-teht
sautéed	*pfannengebraten*	**pfahn**-nehn-geh **braht**-ehn
smoked	*geräuchert*	geh-**roykh**-ert
sour	*sauer*	**zow**-er

EATING

spicy hot	scharf	sharf
steamed	gedünstet	geh-**dewn**-steht
stuffed	gefüllt	geh-**fewlt**
sweet	süß	zews
topped with cheese	mit Käseschicht	mit **kay**-zeh-shnit
well-done	gar	gar
with rice	mit Reis	mit rīs

Side Dishes

green salad	grüner Salat	**grew**-ner zah-**laht**
mixed salad	gemischter Salat	geh-**mish**-ter zah-**laht**
potato salad	Kartoffelsalat	kar-**tohf**-fehl-zah-laht
potatoes	Kartoffeln	kar-**tohf**-fehln
roasted potatoes	Bratkartoffeln	**braht**-kar-tohf-fehln
mashed potatoes	Kartoffelbrei,	kar-**tohf**-fehl-brī
	Kartoffelstock	kar-**tohf**-fehl-shtohk
French fries	Pommes frites,	pom frits,
	Pommes	**poh**-mehs
potato pancake	Reibekuchen	**rī**-beh-kookh-ehn
hashbrowns	Rösti	**rur**-shtiee
rice	Reis	rīs
liver / bread...	Leber / Semmel...	**lay**-ber / **zehm**-mehl
...dumplings	...knödel	kuh-**nur**-dehl
sauerkraut	Sauerkraut	**zow**-er-krowt
noodles	Nudeln	**noo**-dehln
spaghetti	Spaghetti	shpah-**geh**-tee
boiled German-	Spätzle	**shpehts**-leh
style noodles		

Veggies

vegetables	Gemüse	geh-**mew**-zeh
mixed vegetables	gemischtes	geh-**mish**-tehs
	Gemüse	geh-**mew**-zeh
with vegetables	mit Gemüse	mit geh-**mew**-zeh
artichoke	Artischocke	art-i-**shoh**-keh
asparagus	Spargel	**shpar**-gehl

beans	*Bohnen*	**boh**-nehn
beets	*Rüben*	**rew**-behn
broccoli	*Brokkoli*	**brohk**-koh-lee
cabbage	*Kohl*	kohl
carrots	*Karotten*	kah-**roht**-tehn
cauliflower	*Blumenkohl*	**bloo**-mehn-kohl
corn	*Mais*	mīs
cucumber	*Gurken*	**goor**-kehn
eggplant	*Auberginen*	oh-ber-**zhee**-nehn
garlic	*Knoblauch*	kuh-**noh**-blowkh
green beans	*grüne Bohnen*	**grew**-neh **boh**-nehn
leeks	*Lauch*	lowkh
lentils	*Linsen*	**lin**-zehn
mushrooms	*Pilze*	**pilt**-seh
olives	*Oliven*	oh-**leev**-ehn
onions	*Zwiebeln*	**tsvee**-behln
peas	*Erbsen*	**ehrb**-zehn
pepper...	*Paprika...*	**pah**-pree-kah
...green / red / yellow	*...grün / rot / gelb*	grewn / roht / gehlp
pickles	*Essiggurken*	**ehs**-sig-goor-kehn
potatoes	*Kartoffeln*	kar-**tof**-fehln
radishes	*Radieschen*	rah-**dee**-syehn
spinach	*Spinat*	shpee-**naht**
tomatoes	*Tomaten*	toh-**mah**-tehn
zucchini	*Zucchini*	tsoo-**kee**-nee

Fruits

apple	*Apfel*	**ahp**-fehl
apricot	*Aprikose*	ahp-ri-**koh**-zeh
banana	*Banane*	bah-**nah**-neh
berries	*Beeren*	**behr**-ehn
blackberries	*Brombeeren*	**brohm**-behr-ehn
canteloupe	*Melone*	meh-**loh**-neh
cherry	*Kirsche*	**keer**-sheh
cranberries	*Preiselbeeren*	**prī**-sehl-behr-ehn
date	*Dattel*	**daht**-tehl
fig	*Feige*	**fī**-geh

fruit	*Obst*	ohpst
grapefruit	*Pampelmuse,*	pahm-pehl-**moo**-zeh,
	Grapefruit	**grahp**-froot
grapes	*Trauben*	**trow**-behn
lemon	*Zitrone*	tsee-**troh**-neh
orange	*Apfelsine,*	ahp-fehl-**zee**-neh,
	Orange	oh-**rahn**-zheh
peach	*Pfirsich*	**pfeer**-zikh
pear	*Birne*	**beer**-neh
pineapple	*Ananas*	**ahn**-ahn-ahs
plum	*Pflaume,*	**pflow**-meh,
	Zwetsche	**tsveht**-sheh
prune	*Backpflaume*	**bahk**-pflow-meh
raspberries	*Himbeeren*	**him**-behr-ehn
red currants	*Johannis-*	yoh-**hahn**-nis-
	beeren	behr-ehn
strawberries	*Erdbeeren*	**ehrt**-behr-ehn
tangerine	*Mandarine*	mahn-dah-**ree**-neh
watermelon	*Wassermelone*	**vah**-ser-meh-loh-neh

Nuts

nut	*Nuß*	noos
almond	*Mandel*	**mahn**-dehl
chestnut	*Kastanie*	kahs-**tahn**-yeh
coconut	*Kokosnuß*	**koh**-kohs-noos
hazelnut	*Haselnuß*	**hah**-zehl-noos
peanut	*Erdnuß*	**ehrd**-noos
pistachio	*Pistazien*	pis-**tahts**-ee-ehn
walnut	*Walnuß*	**vahl**-noos

Teutonic Treats

dessert	*Nachspeise,*	**nahkh**-shpī-zeh,
	Nachtisch	**nahkh**-tish
strudel	*Strudel*	**shtroo**-dehl
cake	*Kuchen*	**kookh**-ehn
a piece of cake	*ein Stück Kuchen*	īn stewk **kookh**-ehn

sherbet	*Sorbet*	zor-**beht**
fruit cup	*Früchtebecher*	**frewkh**-teh-behkh-er
fruit salad	*Obstsalat*	**ohpst**-zah-laht
tart	*Törtchen*	**turt**-shyehn
pie	*Torte*	**tor**-teh
cream	*Sahne, Rahm*	**zah**-neh, rahm
whipped cream	*Schlagsahne*	**shlahg**-zah-neh
chocolate	*Schokolade*	shoh-koh-**lah**-deh
chocolate mousse	*Mousse*	moos
pudding	*Pudding*	"pudding"
pastry	*Gebäck*	geh-**behk**
cookies	*Kekse*	**kayk**-zeh
candy	*Bonbons*	**bon**-bonz
low calorie	*kalorienarm*	kah-loh-**ree**-ehn-arm
homemade	*hausgemacht*	**hows**-geh-mahkht
We'll split one.	*Wir teilen eine.*	veer **tī**-lehn **ī**-neh
Two forks / spoons, please.	*Zwei Gabeln / Löffel, bitte.*	tsvī **gah**-behln / **lurf**-fehl **bit**-teh
I shouldn't, but...	*Ich sollte nicht, aber...*	ikh **zohl**-teh nikht **ah**-ber
Delicious!	*Köstlich! Lecker!*	**kurst**-likh / **lehk**-er
Heavenly.	*Himmlisch.*	**him**-lish
Death by chocolate.	*Tod durch Schokolade.*	tohd durkh shoh-koh-**lah**-deh
Better than sex.	*Besser als Sex.*	**behs**-ser ahls zehx
A moment on the lips, forever on the hips.	*Ein Weilchen auf der Zunge, ewig auf der Hüfte.*	īn **vīl**-shyehn owf dehr **tsoong**-eh **eh**-vig owf dehr **hewf**-teh
I'm in seventh heaven.	*Ich bin im siebten Himmel.*	ikh bin im **zeeb**-tehn **him**-mehl

Ice Cream

ice cream	*Eis*	īs
scoop	*Kugel*	**koog**-ehl
cone	*Waffel*	**vah**-fehl
small bowl	*Schale*	**shah**-leh
chocolate	*Schokolade*	shoh-koh-**lah**-deh

vanilla	*Vanille*	vah-**nil**-leh
strawberry	*Erdbeer*	**ehrt**-behr
lemon	*Zitrone*	tsee-**troh**-neh
rum-raisin	*Malaga*	**mah**-lah-gah
hazelnut	*Haselnuß*	**hah**-zehl-noos
Can I taste it?	*Kann ich probieren?*	kahn ikh **proh**-beer-ehn

Dessert Specialties

Apfelstrudel	**ahp**-fehl-**shtroo**-dehl	apples and raisins in puff pastry
Berliner	behr-**lee**-ner	raspberry-filled doughnut
Cremeschnitte	**krehm**-shnit-eh	flaky pastry layered w/ cream, topped w/ vanilla and chocolate icing
Germknödel	**gehrm**-ku-nur-dehl	sourdough dumplings
Kaiserschmarren	**kīz**-er-shmah-rehn	shredded pancakes w/ raisins, sugar, and cinnamon
Linzertorte	**lints**-er-tor-teh	almond cake w/ raspberry (Austria)
Mandelgipfel	**mahn**-dehl-gip-fehl	almond-filled croissant
Mohnkuchen	**mohn**-kookh-ehn	poppy-seed cake
Mohr im Hemd	mor im hehmt	chocolate pudding w/ chocolate sauce
Nürnberger Lebkuchen	**newrn**-behr-ger **layb**-kookh-ehn	gingerbread in every shape and size (German Christmas specialty)
Pfannkuchen	**pfahn**-kookh-ehn	thin pancakes often served w/ berries and powdered sugar
Rissoles	**ree**-zohl	pear tarts
Rote Grütze	**roh**-teh **grew**-tseh	raspberry and currant pudding topped w/ cream
Sachertorte	**zahkh**-er-tor-teh	chocolate cake layered w/ chocolate cream

EATING

Salzburger Nockerl	**zalts**-boorg-er **nohk**-erl	fluffy baked pudding/flan
Schwarzwälder Kirschtorte	**shvarts**-vehl-der **keersh**-tor-teh	Black Forest cake– chocolate with cherries, cream, and rum
Streußelkuchen	**shtroy**-sehl- kookh-ehn	coffee cake squares w/ crumbled topping
Vermicell	vehr-mee-**sehl**	noodle-shaped chestnut mousse w/ rum and cream (Swiss)
Zwetschgenknödel	**tsvehtsh**-gehn- ku-nur-dehl	plum dumplings boiled, then fried in bread crumbs

Two great dessert specialties are Vienna's famous super-chocolate cake, *Sachertorte,* and Germany's Black Forest cherry cake, called *Schwarzwälder Kirschtorte.* This diet-killing chocolate cake with cherries and rum can be found all over Germany. For a little bit of Italy, try *Gelato* (Italian ice cream) at a *gelateria* (a.k.a. *Eiscafé*).

In Germany at Christmas time, look for the spiced gingerbread, *Lebkuchen,* packaged inside tins shaped like cottages, bells, animals, and fanciful Christmas designs.

The Swiss changed the world in 1875 with their invention of milk chocolate. Nestlé, Suchard, and Lindt are the major producers and sometimes offer factory tours—and samples, of course. *Nußnougat Crème* (milk chocolate hazelnut) is a popular spread all over Europe, especially the Italian brand, Nutella. Anything dipped in Nutella becomes a tasty cultural experience.

DRINKING

Water and Juice

mineral water...	*Mineralwasser...*	min-eh-**rahl**-vah-ser
...with / without gas	*...mit / ohne Gas*	mit / **oh**-neh gahs
mixed with mineral water	*gespritzt*	geh-**shpritst**

EATING

Key Phrases: Drinking

drink	*Getränk*	geh-**traynk**
(mineral) water	*(Mineral-) Wasser*	(min-eh-**rahl**-) **vah**-ser
tap water	*Leitungswasser*	**lī**-toongs-vah-ser
milk	*Milch*	milkh
juice	*Saft*	zahft
coffee	*Kaffee*	kah-**fay**
tea	*Tee*	tay
wine	*Wein*	vīn
beer	*Bier*	beer
Cheers!	*Prost!*	prohst

tap water	*Leitungswasser*	**lī**-toongs-vah-ser
fruit juice	*Fruchtsaft*	**frookht**-zahft
100% juice	*reiner Fruchtsaft*	**rī**-ner **frookht**-zahft
orange juice	*Orangensaft*	oh-**rahn**-zhehn-zahft
freshly squeezed	*frischgepreßt*	frish-geh-**prehst**
apple juice	*Apfelsaft*	**ahp**-fehl-zahft
grapefruit juice	*Grapefruitsaft*	**grahp**-froot-zahft
clear soda	*Limonade*	lee-moh-**nah**-deh
with / without...	*mit / ohne...*	mit / **oh**-neh
...sugar	*...Zucker*	**tsoo**-ker
...ice	*...Eis*	īs
glass / cup	*Glas / Tasse*	glahs / **tah**-seh
small / large	*kleine / große*	**klī**-neh / **groh**-seh
bottle	*Flasche*	**flah**-sheh
Is the water safe to drink?	*Ist das Trinkwasser?*	ist dahs **trink**-vahs-ser

On a menu, you'll find drinks listed under *Getränkekarte* (drink menu). If you ask for *Wasser* in a restaurant, you'll be served mineral water. Germans rarely drink tap water at the table; develop a taste for the inexpensive and classier *Mineralwasser*. Bubbly mineral water might be listed on menus or in stores as "*mit*

Kohlensäure" (with carbon dioxide) or *"mit Sprudel"* (with bubbles). But when you're requesting it, the easy-to-remember *"mit Gas"* will do the trick. To get water without bubbles, look for *"ohne Kohlensäure / Sprudel / Gas."* If you have your heart set on free tap water, ask for *Leitungswasser* and be persistent.

Soda-lovers seek out the Fanta/Coke blend called *Mezzo Mix* or *Spezi. Rivella* is a dairy-based Swiss soft drink. To get a diet drink, use the word "light" instead of "diet" (for instance, Diet Coke is called "Coke Light").

Milk

milk	Milch	milkh
whole milk	Vollmilch	**fohl**-milkh
skim milk	Magermilch	**mah**-ger-milkh
fresh milk	frische Milch	**frish**-eh milkh
acidophilus	Acidophilus, Kefir	ah-**see**-doh-fi-lus, **keh**-feer
buttermilk	Buttermilch	**boo**-ter-milkh
chocolate milk	Schokomilch	**shoh**-koh-milkh
hot chocolate	heiße Schokolade, Kakao	**hī**-seh shoh-koh-**lah**-deh, kah-**kow**
Ovaltine (grain-based hot drink)	Ovomaltine	oh-voh-mahl-**tee**-neh
milkshake	Milchshake	**milkh**-shayk

Coffee and Tea

coffee	Kaffee	kah-**fay**
espresso	Espresso	ehs-**prehs**-soh
cappuccino	Cappuccino	kah-poo-**chee**-noh
decaffeinated	koffeinfrei, Haag	koh-fay-**in**-frī, hahg
instant coffee	Pulverkaffee, Nescafe	pool-ver-kah-**fay**, "Nescafe"
black	schwarz	shvarts
with cream / milk	mit Sahne / Milch	mit **zah**-neh / milkh
with sugar	mit Zucker	mit **tsoo**-ker
iced coffee or coffee w/ ice cream	Eiskaffee	**īs**-kah-fay

Austrian Coffee Lingo

In Austria, coffee has a language of its own.

Brauner	**brown**-er	coffee w/ small pitcher of milk
Melange	meh-**lahnzh**	coffee with lots of milk
Mokka, Schwarzer	**moh**-kah, **shvart**-ser	black espresso
Obers	**oh**-bers	cream
Masagran	**mahs**-ah-grahn	iced coffee with maraschino liqueur
Wiener Eiskaffee	**veen**-er **īs**-kah-fay	coffee w/ vanilla ice-cream and whipped cream
Maria Theresia	mah-**ree**-ah teh-**ray**-zee-ah	coffee with orange liqueur

hot water	*heißes Wasser*	**hī**-sehs **vah**-ser
tea / lemon	*Tee / Zitrone*	tay / tsee-**troh**-neh
tea bag	*Teebeutel*	**tay**-boy-tehl
iced tea	*Eistee*	**īs**-tay
herbal tea	*Kräutertee*	**kroy**-ter-tay
peppermint tea	*Pfefferminztee*	**pfeh**-fer-mints-tay
fruit tea	*Früchte Tee*	**frewkh**-teh tay
little pot	*Kännchen*	**kehn**-shyehn
Another cup.	*Noch eine Tasse.*	nohkh **ī**-neh **tah**-seh

Wine

I would like...	*Ich hätte gern...*	ikh **heh**-teh gehrn
We would like...	*Wir hätten gern...*	veer **heh**-tehn gehrn
...a glass...	*...ein Glas...*	īn glahs
...an eighth liter...	*...ein Achtel...*	īn **ahkh**-tehl
...a quarter liter...	*...ein Viertel...*	īn **feer**-tehl
...a carafe...	*...eine Karaffe...*	**ī**-neh kah-**rah**-feh

EATING

...a half bottle...	...eine halbe Flasche...	ī-neh **hahl**-beh **flah**-sheh
...a bottle...	...eine Flasche...	ī-neh **flah**-sheh
...a five-liter jug...	...einen fünf-Liter Krug...	ī-nehn **fewnf**-lee-ter kroog
...a barrel...	...ein Faß...	īn fahs
...a vat...	...ein Riesenfaß...	īn **rī**-zehn-fahs
...of red wine.	...Rotwein.	**roht**-vīn
...of white wine.	...Weißwein.	**vīs**-vīn
...the wine list.	...die Weinkarte.	dee **vīn**-kar-teh

Three-quarters of German, Austrian, and Swiss wines are white. As you travel through wine-growing regions, you'll see *Probieren* signs inviting you in for a free (or nearly free) wine tasting.

White wines to look for in Germany are *Riesling* (fruity and fragrant), *Müller Thurgau* (best when young, smooth, and sweet), *Gewürztraminer* (intense and spicy), and *Grauburgunder* (soft, full-bodied white—known as *Pinot Gris* or *Grigio* in other countries). In Austria, consider *Grüner Veltliner* (dry, light), *Riesling, Pinot Blanc* (semi-dry, fruity nose), and *Heuriger* wine (new wine). In Switzerland, try the tart, white *Fendant* and the lovely, fruity *St. Saphorin* from the slopes above Lake Geneva.

Typically, you order a glass of wine by saying *Ein Viertel* (a quarter liter) or *Ein Achtel* (an eighth liter). In Switzerland, a *Pfiff* is two deciliters of red wine, and a *Bocalino* is a small, decorated ceramic jug with two deciliters of a light Swiss red wine called *Dole*.

Wine Words

wine	Wein	vīn
red wine	Rotwein	**roht**-vīn
white wine	Weißwein	**vīs**-vīn
rosé	Rosé	roh-**zay**
table wine	Tafelwein	**tah**-fehl-vīn
house wine	Hausmarke	**hows**-mar-keh
local	einheimisch	**īn**-hī-mish

of the region	*regional*	reh-gee-ohn-**ahl**
sparkling	*sprudelnd*	**shproo**-dehlnt
fruity	*fruchtig*	**frookh**-tig
light / heavy	*leicht / schwer*	līkht / shvehr
sweet	*süß, lieblich*	zews, **leeb**-likh
medium	*halbsüß*	**hahlp**-zews
semi-dry	*halbtrocken*	**hahlp**-trohk-ehn
dry	*trocken*	**trohk**-ehn
very dry	*sehr trocken*	zehr **trohk**-ehn
full-bodied	*vollmundig*	fohl-**moon**-dig
mature	*trinkreif*	**trink**-rīf
wine spritzer	*Wein gespritzt*	vīn geh-**shpritst**
cork	*Korken*	**kor**-kehn
corkscrew	*Korkenzieher*	**kor**-kehn-tsee-her
grapes	*Weintrauben*	**vīn**-trow-behn
vintage	*Weinlese*	**vīn**-lay-zeh
vineyard	*Weinberg*	**vīn**-behrg
wine-tasting	*Weinprobe*	**vīn**-proh-beh
What is a good year (vintage)?	*Welcher Jahrgang (Weinlese) ist gut?*	**vehlkh**-er **yar**-gahng (**vīn**-lay-zeh) ist goot
What do you recommend?	*Was empfehlen Sie?*	vahs ehmp-**fay**-lehn zee

Unfermented wine is called *Most*. Partially fermented wine is called *Federweißer* (pron. **feh**-der-vī-ser) in Germany, *Suuser* (pron. **zoo**-ser) in Switzerland, and *Sturm* (pron. **shtoorm**) in Austria. *Staubiger* (pron. **shtow**-big-er) is a cloudy, fully fermented Austrian wine.

Wine Labels

As with most European countries, Germany has a strict set of rules dictating how quality wine is produced: the higher the percentage of natural grape sugar, the higher the alcohol content, the higher the rating. You can identify the origin of German wine by the color or shape of the bottle: brown (Rhine), green (Mosel), or jug-shaped (Franconian). The *Weinsiegel* (wine seal) on the neck of the bottle is also color-coded—yellow for dry, green for semi-dry, and red for sweet. Switzerland and Austria produce less wine than Germany but follow similar standards. Listed below are terms to help you decipher all of the information on a German, Austrian, or Swiss wine label.

Kabinett	lightest and usually driest wine
Spätlese, Auslese, Beerenauslese, Trockenbeerenauslese, Eiswein	late harvest wines (listed in order of grape sugar content from high to highest)
Qualitätswein	mid-quality wine
QmP (Qualitätswein mit Prädikat)	highest quality wine
QbA (Qualitätswein bestimmter Anbaugebiete)	quality wine of a specific region
Sekt	sparkling champagne-like wine
Heuriger	new wine (Austria)
Landwein	country wine, dry to semi-dry
Tafelwein	table wine–lowest category

Beer

beer	*Bier*	beer
bar	*Kneipe (Germany), Beisl (Austria), Baiz (Switzerland)*	ku-**nī**-peh, **bī**-zehl, bīts
from the tap	*vom Faß*	fom fahs
bottle	*Flasche*	**flah**-sheh
light—but not "lite"	*Helles*	**hehl**-lehs
dark	*Dunkles*	**doonk**-lehs
local / imported	*einheimisch / importiert*	**īn**-hī-mish / im-por-tee-**ehrt**
small / large	*kleines / großes*	**klī**-nehs / **groh**-sehs
half-liter	*Halbes*	**hahl**-behs
liter (Bavarian)	*Maß*	mahs
low calorie	*Light*	"light"
cold	*kalt*	kahlt
colder	*kälter*	**kehl**-ter

Germany is Europe's beer capital. Its beer is regulated by the German Purity law (**Reinheitsgebot**), the oldest food and beverage law in the world. Only four ingredients may be used in German beer: malt, yeast, hops, and water. Pils is a bottom-fermented, full beer and **Weizen** is wheat-based. **Malzbier** is the non-alcoholic malt beer that children drink. The barely alcoholic **Nährbier**, considered healthy and caloric, is for fattening up skinny kids. **Radler** (which means biker) is a refreshing mix of beer and lemon soda, invented in Munich for cyclists on hot days. A **Berliner Weisse mit Schuß** is a wheat beer with a shot of fruit syrup. **Bockbier**, from Bavaria, is a strong amber called "liquid bread" and is consumed mostly at Easter and Christmas. **Märzen** is a light beer brewed in March (**März**), then stored for **Oktoberfest**.

Drink menus list exactly how many deciliters you'll get in your glass. A "5 dl" beer is half a liter, or about a pint. When you order beer, ask for "**Ein Halbes**" for a half liter or "**Ein Maß**" for a whole liter (about a quart). Some beer halls serve beer only by the liter! Children are welcome in beer halls.

In Austria, order "**ein Bier**" and you get a light, basic beer in a standard beer mug. Order a **Pils** and you get a more flavorful, stronger beer in a tulip glass. A **Dunkel** is the darkest, served in a straight, tall glass. In the German-speaking regions of Switzerland, a **Stange** is a **Pils** in a tall, fluted glass. The popular **Weizenbier**, which is poured slowly to build its frothy head thick and high, is served in a large rounded-top glass with a wedge of lemon.

Bar Talk

Let's go out for a drink.	Komm, wir gehen aus für ein Drink.	kohm veer **gay**-hehn ows fewr īn drink
May I buy you a drink?	Kann ich dir ein Drink spendieren?	kahn ikh deer īn drink shpehn-**deer**-ehn
My treat.	Ich lade ein.	ikh **lah**-deh īn
The next one's on me.	Die nächste Runde geht auf mich.	dee **nehkh**-steh **roon**-deh gayt owf mikh
What would you like?	Was hättest du gern?	vahs **heh**-tehst doo gehrn
I'll have a ___.	Ich nehme ein ___.	ikh **nay**-meh īn

I don't drink.	Ich trinke keinen Alcohol.	ikh **trink**-eh **kīn**-ehn **ahl**-koh-hohl
alcohol-free	alkoholfrei	**ahl**-koh-hohl-**frī**
What is the local specialty?	Was ist die Spezialität hier?	vahs ist dee **shpayt**-see-ahl-ee-**tayt** heer
What is a good man's / woman's drink?	Was ist ein gutes Männer-/Damen-Getränk?	vahs ist īn **goo**-tehs **meh**-ner / dah-mehn geh-**trehnk**
Straight.	Pur.	poor
With / Without...	Mit / Ohne...	mit / **oh**-neh
...alcohol.	...Alkohol.	**ahl**-koh-hohl
...ice.	...Eis.	īs
One more.	Noch eins.	nokh īns
Cheers!	Prost!	prohst
To your health!	Auf Ihre Gesundheit!	owf **eer**-eh geh-**zoond**-hīt
To you!	Zum Wohl!	tsoom vohl
Long life!	Langes Leben!	**lahng**-ehs **lay**-behn
I'm...	Ich bin...	ikh bin
...tipsy.	...beschwippst.	beh-**shvipst**
...a little drunk.	...ein bißchen betrunken.	īn **bis**-yehn beh-**troonk**-ehn
...wasted.	...völlig blau. ("completely blue")	**furl**-lig blow
...a boozehound.	...Schnapshund.	**shnahps**-hoont
I'm hung over.	Ich hab' ein Kater. ("I have a tomcat.")	ikh hahp īn **kah**-ter

EATING

The bartender will often throw a coaster (**Bierdeckel**) down at your place and keep track of your bill by keeping a stroke tally on the coaster. To get your bill, hand the bartender your coaster.

Spirits

| Apfelwein (especially popular in Frankfurt) | **ahp**-fehl-vīn | apple wine |
| Appenzeller Alpenbitter | **ah**-pehn-tsehl-ler **ahl**-pehn-bit-ter | digestif made from 65 different flowers and roots |

Aprikosenlikör	ahp-ri-koh-zehn-li-kur	apricot liqueur
Eierlikör	ī-er-li-kur	eggnog-like liqueur
Glühwein	glew-vīn	hot spiced wine
Jägermeister	**yay**-ger-mī-ster	anise- and herb-flavored digestive
Jägertee ("hunter's tea")	**yay**-ger-tay	half tea and half brandy with rum
Kirsch	keersh	firewater from crushed cherry pits
Korn, Marc	korn, mark	grain-based Schnaps
Obstler	**ohpst**-ler	fruit brandy
Pflümli	**pflewm**-lee	plum Schnaps (Switzerland)
Schnaps	shnahps	high-alcohol brandy (firewater!)

For drinks at reasonable prices, do what the locals do. Visit an atmospheric *Weinstube* (wine bar) or *Biergarten* (beer garden) to have a drink and chat with friends.

PICNICKING

At the Grocery

Self-service?	*Selbstbedienung?*	**zehlpst**-beh-dee-noong
Ripe for today?	*Jetzt reif?*	yehtst rīf
Does this need to be cooked?	*Muß man das kochen?*	mus mahn dahs **kohkh**-ehn
Can I taste it?	*Kann ich probieren?*	kahn ikh proh-**beer**-ehn
Fifty grams.	*Fünfzig Gramm.*	**fewnf**-tsig grahm
One hundred grams.	*Hundert Gramm.*	**hoon**-dert grahm
More. / Less.	*Mehr. / Weniger.*	mehr / **vay**-nig-er
A piece.	*Ein Stück.*	īn shtewk
A slice.	*Eine Scheibe.*	ī-neh **shī**-beh
Four slices.	*Vier Scheiben.*	feer **shī**-behn
Sliced.	*In Scheiben.*	in **shī**-behn
Half.	*Halb.*	hahlp
A small bag.	*Eine kleine Tüte.*	ī-neh **klīn**-eh **tew**-teh

EATING

A bag, please.	Eine Tüte, bitte.	īn **tew**-teh **bit**-teh
Can you make me / us...?	Können Sie mir / uns... machen?	**kurn**-nehn zee meer / oons... **mahkh**-ehn
...a sandwich	...ein Sandwich	īn **zahnd**-vich
...two sandwiches	...zwei Sandwiche	tsvī **zahnd**-vich-eh
To take out.	Zum Mitnehmen.	tsoom **mit**-nay-mehn
Can I use the microwave?	Kann ich die Mikrowelle benutzen?	kahn ikh dee mee-kroh-**vehl**-leh beh-**noot**-sehn
May I borrow a...?	Kann ich ein... leihen?	kahn ikh īn... **lī**-hehn
Do you have a...?	Haben Sie ein...?	**hah**-behn zee īn
Where can I buy / find a...?	Wo kann ich ein... kaufen / finden?	voh kahn ikh īn... **kow**-fehn / **fin**-dehn
...corkscrew	...Korkenzieher	**kor**-kehn-tsee-her
...can opener	...Dosenöffner	**doh**-zehn-urf-ner
Is there a park nearby?	Gibt es einen Park in der Nähe?	gipt ehs ī-nehn park in dehr **nay**-heh
Where is a good place to picnic?	Wo ist gut picknicken?	voh ist goot **pik**-nik-ehn
Is picnicking allowed here?	Darf man hier picknicken?	darf mahn heer **pik**-nik-ehn

Tasty Picnic Words

EATING

picnic	Picknick	**pik**-nik
open air market	Markt	markt
grocery store	Lebensmittel-geschäft	**lay**-behns-mit-tehl-geh-**shehft**
supermarket	Supermarkt	**zoo**-per-markt
delicatessen	Feinkostgeschäft	**fīn**-kohst-geh-**shehft**
bakery	Bäckerei	behk-eh-**rī**
pastry shop	Konditorei, Patisserie	kohn-dee-toh-**rī**, pah-tis-er-**ee**
cheese shop	Käserei	kay-zeh-**rī**
sandwich	Sandwich	**zahnd**-vich
bread	Brot	broht
roll	Brötchen, Semmel	**brurt**-shyehn, **zehm**-mehl

ham	*Schinken*	**shink**-ehn
sausage	*Wurst*	voorst
cheese	*Käse*	**kay**-zeh
mustard...	*Senf...*	zehnf
mayonnaise...	*Mayonnaise...*	mah-yoh-**nay**-zeh
...in a tube	*...in der Tube*	in dehr **too**-beh
mild / sharp / sweet	*mild / scharf / süß*	meelt / sharf / zews
yogurt	*Joghurt*	"yogurt"
fruit	*Obst*	ohpst
juice	*Saft*	zaft
cold drinks	*kalte Getränke*	**kahl**-teh geh-**trehnk**-eh
plastic...	*Plastik...*	**plah**-steek
...spoon / fork	*...Löffel / Gabel*	**lurf**-fehl / **gah**-behl
paper...	*Papier...*	pah-**peer**
...plate / cup	*...teller / becher*	**tehl**-ler / **behkh**-er

Assemble your picnic at a *Markt* (open-air market) or *Supermarkt* (supermarket)—or get a fast snack at an *Obst* (fruit stand) or *Imbiß* (fast-food stand).

At the grocery, you buy meat and cheese by the gram. One hundred grams is about a quarter pound, enough for two sandwiches. To weigh and price your produce, put it on the scale, push the photo or number (keyed to the bin it came from), and then stick your sticker on the food. To get real juice, look for 100% or *kein Zucker* on the label. *Drink* or *Trink* is soda. *Bio* means organically grown, and a *Bioladen* (*Bioläderli* in Switzerland) is a store that sells organic products.

MENU DECODER

GERMAN/ENGLISH

This handy German-English decoder (followed by an English-German decoder) won't list every word on the menu, but it'll get you *Bratwurst* (pork sausage) instead of *Blutwurst* (blood sausage).

Abendessen	dinner
Achtel	eighth liter
Allgäuer Bergkäse	hard, mild cheese with holes
Altenburger	soft, mild goat cheese
Ananas	pineapple
Apfel	apple
Apfelsaft	apple juice
Apfelsine	orange
Apfelstrudel	apples and raisins in puff pastry
Appenzeller	sharp, hard Swiss cheese
Appenzeller Alpenbitter	digestif (alcohol) made from flower and roots
Aprikose	apricot
Artischocke	artichoke
Aubergine	eggplant
Bäckerei	bakery
Backpflaume	prune
Banane	banana
Bauern	farmer-style (from the garden)

MENU DECODER

German / English

Bauernsuppe	cabbage and sausage soup
Becher	small glass
Bedienung	service
Beere	berry
Beilagen	side dishes
Beinwurst	smoked pork, herb sausage
Berliner	raspberry-filled doughnut
Bier	beer
biologisch/bio	organic
Birne	pear
Blumenkohl	cauliflower
Blutwurst	blood sausage
Bockbier	Bavarian amber beer
Bockwurst	white pork sausage
Bohnen	beans
Braten	roast
Brathähnchen	roast chicken
Bratwurst	pork sausage
Brezel	pretzel
Brokkoli	broccoli
Brombeere	blackberry
Brot	bread
Brötchen	roll
Brotzeit	snack
Bündnerfleisch	air-cured beef
Burewurst	boiled *Bratwurst*
Butterhörnchen	croissant
Champignon	mushroom
chinesisch	Chinese
Churer Fleischtorte	meat pie (Switz.)
Cremeschnitte	Napoleon
Currywurst	curry-flavored *Burewurst*
Dattel	date
Debreziner	spicy Hungarian sausage
Dorsch	cod
Dreikornbrot	three-grain bread
dunkel	dark

durchgebraten	well-done
Edelpilzkäse	mild blue cheese
Ei	egg
Eier	eggs
Eierlikör	eggnog-like liqueur
einheimisch	local
Eintopf	stew
Eintritt	cover charge
Eis	ice cream; ice
Eiskaffee	iced coffee, coffee with ice cream
Eistee	iced tea
Emmentaler	hard, mild Swiss cheese
Ente	duck
Erbsen	peas
Erbsensuppe	split pea soup
Erdbeere	strawberry
Erdnuß	peanut
erster Gang	first course
Essen	food
Essig	vinegar
Essiggurken	pickles
Feige	fig
Feinkostgeschäft	delicatessen
Fett	fat
Fisch	fish
Flasche	bottle
Fleisch	meat
Fleischsalat	cubed deli-meat salad
Forelle	trout
französisch	French
Frikadelle	large meatball, hamburger
frisch	fresh
frischgepreßt	freshly squeezed
Frischkäse	soft curd cheese with herbs
Frittaten	sliced pancakes
frittiert	deep-fried
Früchtebecher	fruit cup

fruchtig	fruity (wine)
Fruchtsaft	fruit juice
Frühstück	breakfast
Gang	course
ganz gar	very well-done
gar	well-done
Gas	carbonation
Gasthaus, Gasthof	country inn and restaurant
Gaststätte, Gaststube	informal restaurant
Gebäck	pastry
gebraten	baked
gedünstet	steamed
Geflügel	poultry
gefüllt	stuffed
gegrillt	grilled
gekocht	cooked
gemischt	mixed
gemischter Salat	mixed salad
Gemüse	vegetables
Gemüseplatte/-teller	vegetable platter
Gemüsesuppe	vegetable soup
geräuchert	smoked
Germknödel	sourdough dumplings
geröstet	roasted
geschmort	braised
Geschnetzeltes	meat slivers in a rich sauce with noodles or Rösti
gespritzt	with mineral water
Getränke	beverages
Getränkekarte	drink menu
Glas	glass
Glühwein	hot spiced wine
Graubrot	whole wheat bread
Grillteller	mixed grill
groß	big
grün	green
grüner Salat	green salad

Gruyère	strong-flavored Swiss cheese
Gulasch	spicy stew (goulash)
Gurken	cucumber
Gutsabfüllung	estate bottled (wine)
Hähnchen	chicken
halb	half
halbgar	medium
halbsüß	semi-sweet, medium (wine)
halbtrocken	semi-dry (wine)
hartgekocht	hard-boiled
Haselnuß	hazelnut
Hauptspeise	main course
Haus	house
Hausfrauen Art	housewife-style (apples, onions, and sour cream)
hausgemacht	homemade
heiß	hot
heiße Schockolade	hot chocolate
helles	light (beer)
Hering	herring
Heurigen	young wine; wine bar with food
Himbeere	raspberry
Honig	honey
Hühnerbrühe	chicken broth
importiert	imported
inklusive	included
Innereien	organs
italienisch	Italian
Jagdwurst	smoked pork, garlic, and mustard sausage
Jäger	hunter-style (with mushrooms and gravy)
Jägermeister	anise and herb digestif
Jägertee	tea with brandy and rum
Joghurt	yogurt
Johannisbeere	red currant
Kaffee	coffee
Kaiserschmarren	shredded pancakes with raisins, sugar, and cinnamon

Kakao	cocoa
Kalbfleisch	veal
kalt	cold
Kaninchen	bunny
Kännchen	small pot of tea
Karaffe	carafe
Karotte	carrot
Karte	menu
Kartoffel	potato
Kartoffelsalat	potato salad
Käse	cheese
Käse Fondue	melted Swiss cheeses eaten with cubes of bread
Käsebrot	cheese with bread
Käsekrainer	sausage mixed with cheese
Käseplatte/-teller	cheese platter
Käserei	cheese shop
Kastanie	chestnut
Kekse	cookies
Kinderteller	children's portion
Kirsche	cherry
klein	small
Kleinigkeit	snack
Kneipe	bar, tavern
Knoblauch	garlic
Knödel	dumpling
Kohl	cabbage
Kohlensäure	carbonation
Kohlroulade	stuffed cabbage leaves
Kokosnuß	coconut
Konditerei	pastry shop
Korkenzieher	corkscrew
koscher	kosher
köstlich	delicious
Kotelett	cutlet
Kraut	sauerkraut
Kräutertee	herbal tea

Kugel	scoop
Kutteln	tripe
Lamm	lamb
Leber	liver
Leberkäse	pork liver meatloaf
Leberknödelsuppe	liver dumpling soup
Leberwurst	liverwurst
Lebkuchen	gingerbread
leicht	light
lieblich	sweet (wine)
Limburger	strong-smelling, soft cheese with herbs
limonade	clear soda or lemonade
Linsen	lentils
Linzertorte	almond cake with raspberry
Mais	corn
Malaga	rum-raisin flavor
Malzbier	non-alcoholic kids' beer
Mandarine	tangerine
Mandel	almond
Mandelgipfli	almond croissant (Switz.)
Marmelade	jelly
Maß	liter of beer
Matjesfilet	herring filets
Maultaschen	ravioli
Meeresfrüchte	seafood
Melone	cantaloupe
Mettwurst	spicy, soft sausage spread
Miesmuscheln	mussels
Mikrowelle	microwave
Milch	milk
mild	mild
Mineralwasser	mineral water
mit	with
Mittagessen	lunch
Mohnkuchen	poppy-seed cake
Mohr im Hemd	chocolate pudding with chocolate sauce
Möhre	carrot

German	English
Muscheln	clams
Müsli	granola cereal
Nachspeise	dessert
Nachtisch	dessert
Nudel	noodle
Obst	fruit
Obstler	fruit brandy
Obstsalat	fruit salad
Ochsenschwanzsuppe	oxtail soup
oder	or
ohne	without
Öl	oil
Oliven	olives
Omelett	omelet
Orangensaft	orange juice
Pampelmuse	grapefruit
Paprika	bell pepper
Pfannekuchen	pancakes
Pfeffer	pepper
Pfefferminz	peppermint
Pfirsich	peach
Pflaume	plum
Pflümli	plum *Schnaps*
Pistazien	pistachio
pochieren	poached
Pommes (frites)	French fries
Preiselbeere	cranberry
Pute	turkey
Quark	smooth curd cheese
Quittung	receipt
Raclette	melted cheese with vegetable side dishes (Switz.)
Radiesch	radish
Radler	beer and lemon soda
Rahmsauce	cream sauce
Ratsheerentopf	roasted meats and potato stew
Ratskeller	cellar restaurant

Rinderbraten	roast beef
Rinderbrühe	beef broth
Rindfleisch	beef
Rissoles	pear tarts
Roggenmischbrot	rye bread
roh	raw
Rollmops	pickled herring
Rösti	hash browns (Switz.)
Rote Grütze	raspberry and currant pudding
Rotwein	red wine
Rotweiß	with ketchup and mayonnaise (Wurst)
Rüben	beets
Rühreier	scrambled eggs
Sachertorte	chocolate cake layered with chocolate cream
Sahne	cream
Salat	salad
Salatsoße	salad dressing
Salatteller	plate of various salads
Salz	salt
Salzburger Nockerl	fluffy, baked pudding/flan
sättigend	filling
Sauce	sauce
Sauerbraten	braised beef
Schalentiere	shellfish
scharf	spicy
Scheibe	slice
Schinken	ham
Schlachtplatte	assorted cold meats
Schlagsahne	whipped cream
schnell	fast
Schnellimbiß	fast-food stand
Schnitzel	thinly sliced pork or veal
Schokolade	chocolate
Schwarzbrot	dark rye bread
Schwarzwälder Kirschtorte	Black Forest cake—chocolate, cherries, and cream

Schweinebraten	roasted pork with gravy
Schweinefleisch	pork
sehr	very
Semmel	roll
Senf	mustard
Serbische Bohnensuppe	bean soup (Aus.)
Sorbet	sherbet
Soße	sauce
Spargel	asparagus (usually white)
Spätzle	German-style noodles
Speck	bacon
Spezialität	specialty
Spiegeleier	fried eggs
Spinat	spinach
Sprudel	carbonation (bubbles)
sprudelnd	sparkling
Stollen	Christmas bread with fruit and nuts
Stolzer Heinrich	pork sausage fried in beer
Streußelkuchen	coffeecake squares
Stück	piece
Suppe	soup
süß	sweet
Tafelspitz	boiled beef with apples and horseradish
Tafelwein	table wine
Tage	day
Tageskarte, Tagesgericht	menu of the day
Tasse	cup
Tee	tea
Teller	plate
Thunfisch	tuna
Tilsiter	mild, tangy, firm cheese
Tiroler Bauernschmaus	various meats with sauerkraut, potatoes, and dumplings
Tirolerwurst	Austrian smoked sausage
Tomaten	tomatoes
Törtchen	tart
Torte	cake

Traube	grape
trocken	dry
Truthahn	turkey
typisch	local
und	and
Vanille	vanilla
Vegetarier	vegetarian
Vermicell	noodle-shaped chestnut mousse
Viertel	quarter liter
Vollkornbrot	dark bread, whole wheat
vollmundig	full-bodied (wine)
vom Faß	on tap (beer)
Vorspeise	appetizers
Waffel	cone
Walnuß	walnut
Wasser	water
Wassermelone	watermelon
weichgekocht	soft-boiled
Wein	wine
Weinberg	vineyard
Weinkarte	wine list
Weinlese	vintage (wine)
Weinprobe	wine tasting
Weintrauben	grapes (wine)
weiß	white
Weißbrot	light bread
Weißwein	white wine
Weißwurst	boiled veal sausage
Weizen	wheat
Weizenbier	wheat beer
Wiener	Viennese style—breaded and fried
Wiener Schnitzel	breaded, pan-fried veal
Wienerli	thin frankfurter (hot dog)
Wurst	sausage
Zahnstocher	toothpick
Zitrone	lemon
Zucchini	zucchini

Zucker	sugar
zum Mitnehmen	"to go"
Zwetschge	plum
Zwetschgenknödel	fried plum dumplings
Zwiebel	onion
Zwiebelbraten	pot roast with onions
Zwiebelwurst	liver and onion sausage

ENGLISH/GERMAN

almond	mandel
and	und
appetizers	Vorspeise
apple	Apfel
apple juice	Apfelsaft
apricot	Aprikose
artichoke	Artischocke
asparagus	Spargel
bacon	Speck
baked	gebraten
bakery	Bäckerei
banana	Banane
bar	Kneipe
beans	Bohnen
beef	Rindfleisch
beef broth	Rinderbrühe
beef, braised	Sauerbraten
beef, roast	Rinderbraten
beer	Bier
beer and lemon soda	Radler
beer on tap	Bier vom Faß
beer, dark	dunkles
beer, light	helles
beer, non-alcoholic kids'	Malzbier
beer, wheat	Weizenbier
beets	Rüben
bell pepper	Paprika
berry	Beere
beverages	Getränke
big	groß
blackberry	Brombeere
bottle	Flasche
bread	Brot
bread, dark rye	Schwarzbrot

bread, dark whole wheat	Vollkornbrot
bread, light	Weißbrot
bread, rye	Roggenmischbrot
bread, three-grain	Dreikornbrot
bread, whole wheat	Graubrot
breakfast	Frühstück
broccoli	Brokkoli
bunny	Kaninchen
cabbage	Kohl
cabbage leaves, stuffed	Kohlroulade
cake	Torte
cake, Black Forest	Schwarzwälder Kirschtorte
cake, chocolate, layered with chocolate cream	Sachertorte
cake, poppy-seed	Mohnkuchen
cantaloupe	Melone
carafe	Karaffe
carbonation	Gas, Kohlensäure, Sprudel
carrot	Karotte, Möhre
cauliflower	Blumenkohl
cheese	Käse
cheese platter	Käseplatte, Käseteller
cheese shop	Käserei
cheese with bread	Käsebrot
cherry	Kirsche
chestnut	Kastanie
chicken	Hähnchen
chicken broth	Hühnerbrühe
chicken, roast	Brathähnchen
children's portion	Kinderteller
Chinese	chinesisch
chocolate	Schokolade
clams	Muscheln
cocoa	Kakao
coconut	Kokosnuß
cod	Dorsch
coffee	Kaffee

coffee with ice cream or iced coffee	Eiskaffee
cold	kalt
cone	Waffel
cooked	gekocht
cookies	Kekse
corkscrew	Korkenzieher
corn	Mais
course	Gang
course, first	erster Gang
course, main	Hauptspeise
cover charge	Eintritt
cranberry	Preiselbeere
cream	Sahne
cream sauce	Rahmsauce
cream, whipped	Schlagsahne
croissant	Butterhörnchen
cucumber	Gurken
cup	Tasse
cutlet	Kotelett
dark	dunkel
date	Dattel
day	Tage
delicatessen	Feinkostgeschäft
delicious	köstlich, lecker
dessert	Nachspeise, Nachtisch
dinner	Abendessen
doughnut (raspberry-filled)	Berliner
drinks (menu)	Getränke(-karte)
dry	trocken
duck	Ente
dumpling	Knödel
dumplings, fried plum	Zwetschgenknödel
dumplings, sourdough	Germknödel
egg	Ei
eggs	Eier
eggs, fried	Spiegeleier

eggs, scrambled	Rühreier
eggplant	Aubergine
fast	schnell
fast-food stand	Schnellimbiß
fat	Fett
fig	Feige
filling	sättigend
fish	Fisch
food	Essen
French	französisch
French fries	Pommes (frites)
fresh	frisch
freshly squeezed	frischgepreßt
fried or deep-fried	frittiert
fruit	Obst
fruit cup	Früchtebecher
fruity (wine)	fruchtig
full-bodied (wine)	vollmundig
garlic	Knoblauch
gingerbread	Lebkuchen
glass	Glas
glass, small	Becher
goulash (spicy stew)	Gulasch
granola cereal	Müsli
grape	Traube
grapefruit	Pampelmuse
grapes for wine	Weintrauben
green	grün
grill, mixed	Grillteller
grilled	gegrillt
half	halb
ham	Schinken
hard-boiled	hartgekocht
hashbrowns (Switz.)	Rösti
hazelnut	Haselnuß
herring	Hering
herring filets	Matjesfilet

herring, pickled	Rollmops
homemade	hausgemacht
honey	Honig
hot	heiß
hot chocolate	heiße Schockolade
house	Haus
ice cream	Eis
iced tea	Eistee
imported	importiert
included	inklusive
Italian	italienisch
jelly	Marmelade
juice, apple	Apfelsaft
juice, fruit	Fruchtsaft
juice, orange	Orangensaft
kosher	koscher
lamb	Lamm
lemon	Zitrone
lemonade (usually clear soda)	limonade
lentils	Linsen
light	leicht
light (beer)	helles
liter	Liter
liter of beer	Maß
liter, half	Halbes
liter, quarter	Viertel
liter, eighth	Achtel
liver	Leber
liverwurst	Leberwurst
local	einheimisch, typisch
lunch	Mittagessen
meat	Fleisch
medium (meat)	halbgar
menu	Karte
menu of the day	Tageskarte, Tagesgericht
microwave	Mikrowelle
mild	mild

English / German

MENU DECODER

milk	Milch
mineral water	Mineralwasser
mineral water, mixed with	gespritzt
mixed	gemischt
mushroom	Champignon
mussels	Miesmuscheln
mustard	Senf
noodle	Nudel
noodles, German-style	Spätzle
oil	Öl
olives	Oliven
omelet	Omelett
on tap (beer)	vom Faß
onion	Zwiebel
onion pot roast	Zwiebelbraten
or	oder
orange	Orange, Apfelsine
orange juice	Orangensaft
organic	biologisch, bio
organs	Innereien
pancakes	Pfannekuchen
pancakes, shredded, with raisins, sugar, and cinnamon	Kaiserschmarren
pancakes, sliced	Frittaten
pastry	Gebäck
pastry shop	Konditerei
peach	Pfirsich
peanut	Erdnuß
pear	Birne
pear tarts	Rissoles
peas	Erbsen
pepper	Pfeffer
peppermint	Pfefferminz
pickles	Essiggurken
piece	Stück
pineapple	Ananas
pistachio	Pistazien

plate	Teller
plum	Pflaume, Zwetschge
poached	pochieren
pork	Schweinefleisch
pork, roasted, with gravy	Schweinebraten
potato	Kartoffel
poultry	Geflügel
pretzel	Brezel
prune	Backpflaume
rabbit	Kaninchen
radish	Radiesch
raspberry	Himbeere
ravioli	Maultaschen
raw	roh
receipt	Quittung
red currant	Johannisbeere
restaurant	Restaurant
restaurant, cellar	Ratskeller
restaurant, country inn	Gasthaus, Gasthof
restaurant, informal	Gaststätte, Gaststube
roast	Braten
roasted	geröstet
roll	Brötchen, Semmel
salad	Salat
salad dressing	Salatsoße
salad, cubed deli-meat	Fleischsalat
salad, fruit	Obstsalat
salad, green	grüner Salat
salad, mixed	gemischter Salat
salad, potato	Kartoffelsalat
salads, plate of various	Salatteller
salt	Salz
sauce	Soße, Sauce
sauce, cream	Rahmsauce
sauerkraut	Kraut
sausage	Wurst
sausage, blood	Blutwurst

sausage, boiled Bratwurst	Burewurst
sausage, boiled veal	Weißwurst
sausage, pork	Bratwurst
sausage, pork, fried in beer	Stolzer Heinrich
sausage, spicy Hungarian	Debreziner
sausage, thin frankfurter (hot dog)	Wienerli
sausage, white pork	Bockwurst
scoop	Kugel
seafood	Meeresfrüchte
semi-dry (wine)	halbtrocken
service	Bedienung
shellfish	Schalentiere
sherbet	Sorbet
side dishes	Beilagen
slice	Scheibe
small	klein
smoked	geräuchert
snack	Brotzeit, Kleinigkeit
soft-boiled	weichgekocht
soup	Suppe
soup, cabbage and sausage	Bauernsuppe
soup, oxtail	Ochsenschwanzsuppe
soup, split pea	Erbsensuppe
soup, vegetable	Gemüsesuppe
sparkling	sprudelnd
specialty	Spezialität
spicy	scharf
spinach	Spinat
steamed	gedünstet
stew	Eintopf
stew, spicy (goulash)	Gulasch
strawberry	Erdbeere
stuffed	gefüllt
sugar	Zucker
sweet	süß
sweet (wine)	süß, lieblich

tangerine	Mandarine
tart	Törtchen
tea	Tee
tea with brandy and rum	Jägertee
tea, herbal	Kräutertee
tea, iced	Eistee
tea, small pot	Kännchen
"to go"	zum Mitnehmen
tomatoes	Tomaten
toothpick	Zahnstocher
tripe	Kutteln
trout	Forelle
tuna	Thunfisch
turkey	Pute (north), Truthahn (south)
vanilla	Vanille
veal	Kalbfleisch
veal or pork, thinly sliced	Schnitzel
veal, breaded, pan-fried	Wiener Schnitzel
vegetable plate	Gemüseplatte, Gemüseteller
vegetables	Gemüse
vegetarian	Vegetarier
very	sehr
vinegar	Essig
vineyard	Weinberg
vintage (wine)	Weinlese
walnut	Walnuß
water	Wasser
watermelon	Wassermelone
well-done	gar, durchgebraten
well-done, very	ganz gar
wheat	Weizen
whipped cream	Schlagsahne
white	weiß
wine	Wein
dry	trocken
fruity	fruchtig
full-bodied	vollmundig

semi-dry	halbtrocken
semi-sweet (medium)	halbsüß
sweet	süß, lieblich
wine grapes	Weintrauben
wine list	Weinkarte
wine tasting	Weinprobe
wine vintage	Weinlese
wine, hot spiced	Glühwein
wine, red	Rotwein
wine, table	Tafelwein
wine, white	Weißwein
wine, young	Heurigen
with	mit
without	ohne
yogurt	Joghurt
zucchini	Zucchini

ACTIVITIES

SIGHTSEEING

Where?

Where is...?	*Wo ist...?*	voh ist
...the tourist information office	*...das Touristeninformationsbüro*	dahs too-**ris**-tehn-in-for-maht-see-**ohns**-bew-roh
...the best view	*...der beste Ausblick*	dehr **behs**-teh **ows**-blick
...the main square	*...der Hauptplatz*	dehr **howpt**-plahts
...the old town center	*...die Altstadt*	dee **ahlt**-shtaht
...the town hall	*...das Rathaus*	dahs **raht**-hows
...the museum	*...das Museum*	dahs moo-**zay**-um
...the castle	*...die Burg*	dee boorg
...the palace	*...das Schloß*	dahs shlohs
...the ruins	*...die Ruine*	dee roo-**ee**-neh
...an amusement park	*...einen Vergnügungspark*	ī-nehn fehrg-**new**-goongs-park
...the entrance / exit	*...der Eingang / Ausgang*	dehr **īn**-gahng / **ows**-gahng
...the toilet	*...die Toilette*	dee toh-**leh**-teh
Nearby is there a...?	*Gibt es in der Nähe ein...?*	gipt ehs in dehr **nay**-heh īn
...fair (rides, games)	*...Kirmes*	**keer**-mehs
...festival (music)	*...Festival*	fehs-tee-**vahl**

129

Key Phrases: Sightseeing

Where is...?	*Wo ist...?*	voh ist
How much is it?	*Wie viel kostet das?*	vee feel **kohs**-teht dahs
What time does this...?	*Um wie viel Uhr ist hier...?*	oom vee feel oor ist heer
...open / close	*...geöffnet / geschlossen*	geh-**urf**-neht / geh-**shloh**-sehn
Do you have a guided tour?	*Haben Sie eine geführte Tour?*	**hah**-behn zee **ī**-neh geh-**fewr**-teh toor
When is the next tour in English?	*Wann ist die nächste Tour auf Englisch?*	vahn ist dee **nehkh**-steh toor owf **ehng**-lish

At the Sight

Do you have...?	*Haben Sie...?*	**hah**-behn zee
...information...	*...Auskunft...*	**ows**-koonft
...a guidebook...	*...einen Stadtführer / ein Reisebuch...*	**ī**-nehn **shtaht**-fewr-er / īn **rī**-zeh-bookh
...in English	*...auf Englisch*	owf **ehng**-lish
Is it free?	*Ist es umsonst?*	ist ehs oom-**zohnst**
How much is it?	*Wie viel kostet das?*	vee feel **kohs**-teht dahs
Is the ticket good all day?	*Gilt der Schein den ganzen Tag lang?*	gilt dehr shīn dayn **gahn**-tsehn tahg lahng
Can I get back in?	*Kann ich wieder hinein?*	kahn ikh **vee**-der hin-**īn**
What time does this open / close?	*Um wie viel Uhr ist hier geöffnet / geschlossen?*	oom vee feel oor ist heer geh-**urf**-neht / geh-**shloh**-sehn
When is the last entry?	*Wann ist letzter Einlaß?*	vahn ist **lehts**-ter **īn**-lahs

Please

PLEASE let me / us in!	*BITTE, lassen Sie mich / uns hinein!*	**bit**-teh **lah**-sehn zee mikh / oons hin-**īn**

I've / We've traveled all the way from ___.	Ich bin / Wir sind extra aus ___ gekommen.	ikh bin / veer zint **ehk**-strah ows ___ geh-**koh**-mehn
I must / We must leave tomorrow.	Ich muß / Wir müssen morgen abreisen.	ikh mus / veer **mew**-sehn **mor**-gehn **ahp**-rī-zehn
I promise I'll / we'll be fast.	Ich verspreche, mich / uns zu beeilen.	ikh fehr-**shprehkh**-eh mikh / oons tsoo beh-**ī**-lehn
I promised my mother on her deathbed that I'd see this.	Ich habe meiner Mutter am Sterbebett versprochen, das zu sehen.	ikh **hah**-beh **mī**-ner **moo**-ter ahm **shtehr**-beh-beht fehr-**shprohkh**-ehn dahs tsoo **zay**-hehn
I've always wanted to see this.	Ich wollte das schon immer sehen.	ikh **vohl**-teh dahs shohn **im**-mehr **zay**-hen

Tours

Do you have...?	Haben Sie...?	**hah**-behn zee
...an audioguide	...einen Tonbandführer	**ī**-nehn **tohn**-bahnt-fewr-er
...a guided tour...	...eine geführte Tour...	**ī**-neh geh-**fewr**-teh toor
...a city walking tour...	...eine geführte Stadtbesichtigung...	**ī**-neh geh-**fewr**-teh shtaht-beh-**zikh**-tig-oong
...in English	...auf Englisch	owf **ehng**-lish
When is the next tour in English?	Wann ist die nächste Führung auf Englisch?	vahn ist dee **nehkh**-steh **few**-roong owf **ehng**-lish
Is it free?	Ist es umsonst?	ist ehs oom-**zohnst**
How much is it?	Wie viel kostet das?	vee feel **kohs**-teht dahs
How long does it last?	Wie lange dauert es?	vee **lahng**-eh **dow**-ert ehs
Can I / Can we join a tour in progress?	Kann ich / Können wir mit der angefangenen Führung gehen?	kahn ikh / **kurn**-nehn veer mit dehr ahn-geh-**fahng**-ehn-ehn **few**-roong **gay**-hehn

ACTIVITIES

Entrance Signs

Erwachsene	adults
kombinierter Eintritt	combo-ticket
Führung	guided tour
Ausstellung	exhibit
Standort	you are here (on map)

Discounts

You may be eligible for a discount at tourist sights, in hotels, or on buses and trains—ask.

Is there a discount for...?	*Gibt es eine Ermäßigung für...?*	gipt ehs **ī**-neh ehr-**may**-see-goong fewr
...youth	*...Kinder*	**kin**-der
...students	*...Studenten*	shtoo-**dehn**-tehn
...families	*...Familien*	fah-**meel**-yehn
...seniors	*...Senioren*	zehn-**yor**-ehn
...groups	*...Gruppen*	**groop**-ehn
I am...	*Ich bin...*	ikh bin
He / She is...	*Er / Sie ist...*	ehr / zee ist
...___ years old.	*...___ Jahre alt.*	___ **yah**-reh ahlt
...extremely old.	*...extrem alt.*	ehx-**trehm ahlt**

In the Museum

Where is...?	*Wo ist...?*	voh ist
I'd like to see...	*Ich möchte gerne ___ sehen.*	ikh **murkh**-teh **gehr**-neh ___ **zay**-hehn
We'd like to see...	*Wir möchten gerne ___ sehen.*	veer **murkh**-tehn **gehr**-neh ___ **zay**-hehn
Photo / Video O.K.?	*Fotografieren / Videofilmen O.K.?*	foh-toh-grah-**feer**-ehn / **vee**-deh-oh-fil-mehn "O.K."
No flash.	*Kein Blitz.*	kīn blits
No tripod.	*Stativ verboten.*	shtah-**teef** fehr-**boh**-tehn
I like it.	*Es gefällt mir.*	ehs geh-**fehlt** meer
It's so...	*Es ist so...*	ehs ist zoh
...beautiful.	*...schön.*	shurn

...ugly.	...häßlich.	**hehs**-likh
...strange.	...seltsam.	**zehlt**-tsahm
...boring.	...langweilig.	**lahng**-vī-lig
...interesting.	...interessant.	in-tehr-ehs-**sahnt**
...pretentious.	...angeberisch.	**ahn**-gay-ber-ish
...thought-provoking.	...Gedanken anregend.	geh-**dahnk**-ehn **ahn**-ray-gehnt
...B.S.	...Blödsinn.	**blurd**-zin
I don't get it.	Kapier' ich nicht.	kah-**peer** ik nikht
Is it upside down?	Ist es verkehrt?	ist ehs fehr-**kehrt**
Who did this?	Wer hat das gemacht?	vehr haht dahs geh-**mahkht**
How old is this?	Wie alt ist das?	vee ahlt ist dahs
Wow!	Fantastisch! Toll!	fahn-**tahs**-tish / tohl
My feet have had it!	Meine Füße sind ganz plattgelaufen!	**mī**-neh **few**-seh zint gahnts **plaht**-geh-lowf-ehn
I'm exhausted!	Ich bin fix und fertig!	ikh bin fix oont **fehr**-tig
We're exhausted!	Wir sind fix und fertig!	veer zint fix oont **fehr**-tig

Be careful when planning your sightseeing. Many museums close one day a week, and many stop selling tickets 45 minutes or so before they close. Some sights are tourable only by groups with a guide. Individuals usually end up with the next German escort. To get an English tour, call in advance to see if one's scheduled. Individuals can often tag along with a large tour group.

Art and Architecture

art	Kunst	koonst
artist	Künstler	**kewnst**-ler
painting	Gemälde	geh-**mayl**-deh
self-portrait	Selbstporträt / Eigenbildnis	**zehlpst**-por-trayt / **ī**-gehn-bilt-nis
sculptor	Bildhauer	**bilt**-how-er
sculpture	Skulptur	skoolp-**toor**

architect	Architekt	**arkh**-i-tehkt
architecture	Architektur	arkh-i-tehk-**toor**
original	Original	oh-rig-ee-**nahl**
restored	restauriert	rehs-tow-**reert**
B.C.	vor Christus (v. Chr.)	for **kris**-tus
A.D.	nach Christus (n. Chr.)	nahkh **kris**-tus
century	Jahrhundert	yar-**hoon**-dert
style	Stil	shteel
copy by ___	Kopie von ___	koh-**pee** fohn
after the style of ___	im Stil von ___	im shteel fohn
from the	aus der	ows dehr
school of ___	Schule von ___	**shoo**-leh fohn
abstract	abstrakt	ahp-**strahkt**
ancient	altertümlich	ahl-ter-**tewm**-likh
Art Nouveau	Jugendstil	**yoo**-gehnd-shteel
Baroque	barock	bah-**rohk**
classical (music)	klassisch	**klah**-sish
classical period	klassizistisch	klah-sits-**is**-tish
Gothic	gothisch	**goh**-tish
Impressionist	impressionistisch	im-preh-see-oh-**nis**-tish
medieval	mittelalterlich	**mit**-tehl-ahl-ter-likh
modern	modern	moh-**dehrn**
Neoclassical	neoklassizistisch	**nay**-oh-klah-sits-**is**-tish
Renaissance	Renaissance	**rehn**-ah-sahns
Romanesque	romanisch	roh-**mahn**-ish
Romantic	Romantisch	roh-**mahn**-tik

Castles and Palaces

castle	Burg	boorg
palace	Schloß	shlohs
treasury	Schatzkammer	**shots**-kah-mer
hall	Saal	zahl
kitchen	Küche	**kewkh**-eh
cellar	Keller	**kehl**-ler
dungeon	Verlies	fehr-**lees**
castle keep	Wehr	vehr

moat	*Burggraben*	**boorg**-grah-behn
fortified wall	*Burgmauer*	**boorg**-mow-er
tower	*Turm*	toorm
fountain, well	*Brunnen*	**broon**-nehn
garden	*Garten*	**gar**-tehn
king / emperor	*König / Kaiser*	**kur**-nig / **kī**-zer
queen / empress	*Königin/ Kaiserin*	**kur**-nig-in / **kī**-zer-in
knight	*Ritter*	**rit**-ter

You'll see the words **Burg** (castle) and **Berg** (mountain) linked to the end of names (such as Rothenburg and Ehrenberg). Salzburg means "salt-castle."

Religious Words

cathedral	*Kathedrale, Dom*	kah-teh-**drah**-leh, dohm
church	*Kirche*	**keerkh**-eh
monastery	*Kloster*	**klohs**-ter
mosque	*Moschee*	moh-**shay**
synagogue	*Synagoge*	zin-ah-**goh**-geh
chapel	*Kapelle*	kah-**pehl**-leh
altar	*Altar*	ahl-**tar**
bells	*Glocken*	**glohk**-ehn
choir	*Chor*	kor
cloister	*Kloster*	**kloh**-ster
cross	*Kreuz*	kroyts
crypt	*Krypte*	**krip**-teh
dome	*Kuppel*	**kup**-pehl
organ	*Orgel*	**org**-ehl
pulpit	*Kanzel*	**kahnts**-ehl
relic	*Reliquie*	reh-**leek**-vee-eh
treasury	*Schatzkammer*	**shahts**-kah-mer
saint	*Heiliger*	**hī**-lig-er
God	*Gott*	goht
Christian	*christlich*	**krist**-likh
Protestant	*evangelisch*	eh-vahn-**gay**-lish
Catholic	*katholisch*	kah-**toh**-lish

Jewish	jüdisch	**yew**-dish
Muslim	muselmanisch	moo-sehl-**mah**-nish
agnostic	agnostisch	ahg-**nohs**-tish
atheist	atheistisch	ah-tay-**is**-tish
When is the service?	Wann ist der Gottesdienst?	vahn ist dehr **goh**-tehs-deenst
Are there church concerts?	Gibt es Kirchenkonzerte?	gipt ehs **keerkh**-ehn-kohn-**tsehr**-teh

SHOPPING

German Shops

Where is a...?	Wo ist ein...?	voh ist īn
antique shop	Antiquitätenladen	ahn-tee-kvee-**tay**-tehn-**lah**-dehn
art gallery	Kunstgalerie	koonst-gah-leh-**ree**
bakery	Bäckerei	behk-eh-**rī**
barber shop	Herrenfrisör	hehr-rehn-friz-**ur**
beauty salon	Frisiersalon, Haarsalon	friz-**eer**-zah-lohn, **har**-zah-lohn
book shop	Buchladen	**bookh**-lah-dehn
camera shop	Photoladen	**foh**-toh-lah-dehn
cell phone shop	Handyladen	**han**-dee-lah-dehn
cheese shop	Käserei	kay-zeh-**rī**
clothing boutique	Kleiderladen	**klī**-der-lah-dehn
coffee shop	Kaffeeladen	**kah**-fay-lah-dehn
delicatessen	Feinkostgeschäft	**fīn**-kohst-geh-**shehft**
department store	Kaufhaus	**kowf**-hows
flea market	Flohmarkt	**floh**-markt
flower market	Blumenmarkt	**bloo**-mehn-markt
grocery store	Lebensmittelgeschäft	**lay**-behns-mit-tehl-geh-**shehft**
hardware store	Eisenwarengeschäft	**ī**-zehn-**vah**-rehn-geh-**shehft**
Internet café	Internetcafé	**in**-tehr-neht-kah-**fay**

ACTIVITIES

Key Phrases: Shopping

Where can I buy___?	*Wo kann ich___ kaufen?*	voh kahn ik **kow**-fehn
Where is a...?	*Wo ist ein...?*	voh ist īn
...grocery store	*...Lebensmittel- geschäft*	**lay**-behns-mit-tehl- geh-**shehft**
...department store	*...Kaufhaus*	**kowf**-hows
...Internet café	*...Internetcafé*	**in**-tehr-neht-kah-**fay**
...launderette	*...Waschsalon*	**vahsh**-zah-lohn
...pharmacy	*...Apotheke*	ah-poh-**tay**-keh
How much is it?	*Wie viel kostet das?*	vee feel **kohs**-teht dahs
I'm just browsing.	*Ich sehe mich nur um.*	ikh **zay**-heh mikh noor oom

---

jewelry shop	*Schmuckladen*	**shmook**-lah-dehn
launderette	*Waschsalon*	**vahsh**-zah-lohn
newsstand	*Kiosk, Zeitungs- stand*	**kee**-ohsk, **tsī**-toongs- shtahnt
office supplies	*Bürobedarf*	**bew**-roh-beh-darf
open-air market	*Markt*	markt
optician	*Optiker*	**ohp**-ti-ker
pastry shop	*Konditorei, Zuckerbäcker*	kohn-dee-toh-**rī**, **tsoo**-ker-bayk-er
pharmacy	*Apotheke*	ah-poh-**tay**-keh
photocopy shop	*Copyshop*	"copy shop"
shopping mall	*Einkaufszentrum*	**īn**-kowfs-tsehn-troom
souvenir shop	*Souvenirladen*	zoo-veh-**neer**-lah-den
supermarket	*Supermarkt*	**zoo**-per-markt
sweets shop	*Süßwaren- geschäft*	**zoos**-vah-rehn- geh-**shehft**
toy store	*Spielzeugladen*	**shpeel**-tsoyg-lah-dehn
travel agency	*Reiseagentur*	**rī**-zeh-ah-gehn-tur
used bookstore	*Bücher aus zweiter Hand, Antiquariat*	**bookh**-er ows **tsvī**-ter hahnt, ahn-teek-vah-**ree**-aht

...with books in	...mit englischen	mit **ehng**-lish-ehn
English	Büchern	**bewkh**-ern
wine shop	Weinhandlung	**vīn**-hahnt-loong

Many businesses close from 12:00 to 15:00 on weekday afternoons and all day on Sundays. Typical hours are Monday through Friday 9:00 to 18:00 or 20:00, Saturday 9:00 to 13:00.

Shop Till You Drop

opening hours	Öffnungszeiten	urf-noongs-**tsī**-tehn
sale	Schlussverkauf	**shloos**-fehr-kowf
special	Angebot	**ahn**-geh-boht
good value	preiswert	**prīs**-vehrt
I'd like...	Ich hätte gern...	ikh **heh**-teh gehrn
We'd like...	Wir hätten gern...	veer **heh**-tehn gehrn
Where can I buy ___?	Wo kann ich ___ kaufen?	voh kahn ikh ___ **kow**-fehn
Where can we buy ___?	Wo können wir ___ kaufen?	voh **kurn**-ehn veer ___ **kow**-fehn
How much is it?	Wie viel kostet das?	vee feel **kohs**-teht dahs
I'm just browsing.	Ich sehe mich nur um.	ikh **zay**-heh mikh noor oom
We're just browsing.	Wir sehen uns nur um.	veer **zay**-hehn oons noor oom
Do you have something cheaper?	Haben Sie etwas Billigeres?	**hah**-behn zee **eht**-vahs **bil**-lig-er-ehs
Better quality, please.	Bessere Qualität, bitte.	**behs**-ser-er kvah-lee-**tayt** **bit**-teh
genuine / imitation	echt / imitation	ehkht / im-i-taht-see-**ohn**
Can I see more?	Kann ich mehr sehen?	kahn ikh mehr **zay**-hehn
Can we see more?	Können wir mehr sehen?	**kurn**-ehn veer mehr **zay**-hehn
This one.	Dieses.	**dee**-zehs
Can I try it on?	Kann ich es anprobieren?	kahn ikh ehs **ahn**-proh-beer-ehn

Do you have a mirror?	*Haben Sie einen Spiegel?*	**hah**-behn zee **ī**-nehn **shpee**-gehl
Too...	*Zu...*	tsoo
...big.	*...groß.*	grohs
...small.	*...klein.*	klīn
...expensive.	*...teuer.*	**toy**-er
It's too...	*Es ist zu...*	ehs ist tsoo
...short / long.	*...kurz / lang.*	koorts / lahng
...tight / loose.	*...eng / weit.*	ehng / vīt
...dark / light.	*...dunkel / hell.*	**doon**-kehl / hehl
What is it made of?	*Was ist das für Material?*	vahs ist dahs fewr mah-tehr-ee-**ahl**
Is it machine washable?	*Ist es waschmaschinenfest?*	ist ehs **vahsh**-mah-sheen-ehn-fehst
Will it shrink?	*Läuft es ein?*	loyft ehs īn
Is it color-fast?	*Ist es farbenfest?*	ist ehs **far**-behn-fehst
Credit card O.K.?	*Kreditkarte O.K.?*	kreh-**deet**-kar-teh "O.K."
Can you ship this?	*Können Sie das versenden?*	**kurn**-nehn zee dahs fehr-**zehn**-dehn
Tax-free?	*Steuerfrei?*	**shtoy**-er-frī
I'll think about it.	*Ich denke drüber nach.*	ikh **dehnk**-eh **drew**-ber nahkh
What time do you close?	*Um wie viel Uhr schließen Sie?*	oom vee feel oor **shlee**-sehn zee
What time do you open tomorrow?	*Wann öffnen Sie morgen?*	vahn **urf**-nehn zee **mor**-gehn

Street Markets

Did you make this?	*Haben Sie das gemacht?*	**hah**-behn zee dahs geh-**mahkht**
Is that your lowest price?	*Ist das der günstigste Preis?*	ist dahs dehr **gewn**-stig-steh prīs
Cheaper?	*Billiger?*	**bil**-ig-er
Good price.	*Guter Preis.*	**goo**-ter prīs
My last offer.	*Mein letztes Angebot.*	mīn **lehts**-tehs **ahn**-geh-boht
I'll take it.	*Ich nehme es.*	ikh **nay**-meh ehs

We'll take it.	Wir nehmen es.	veer **nay**-mehn ehs
I'm nearly broke.	Ich bin fast pleite.	ikh bin fahst **plī**-teh
We're nearly broke.	Wir sind fast pleite.	veer zint fahst **plī**-teh
My male friend...	Mein Freund...	mīn froynd
My female friend...	Meine Freundin...	**mī**-neh **froyn**-din
My husband...	Mein Mann...	mīn mahn
My wife...	Meine Frau...	**mī**-neh frow
...has the money.	...hat das Geld.	haht dahs gehlt

Clothes

For...	Für...	fewr
...a baby.	...ein Baby.	īn **bay**-bee
...a male / a female child.	...einen Buben / ein Mädchen.	**ī**-nehn **boo**-behn / īn **mayd**-khehn
...a male / a female teenager.	...einen Jungen / ein Fräulein.	**ī**-nehn **yoong**-ehn / īn **froy**-līn
...a man.	...einen Herren.	**ī**-nehn **hehr**-ehn
...a woman.	...eine Dame.	**ī**-neh **dah**-meh
bathrobe	Bademantel	**bah**-deh-mahn-tehl
bib	Latz	lahts
belt	Gurt	goort
bra	BH (Büstenhalter)	bay hah (**bewst**-ehn-hahl-ter)
clothing	Kleider	**klī**-der
dress	Kleid	klīt
flip-flops	Strandsandalen	**shtrahnt**-zahn-dah-lehn
gloves	Handschuhe	**hahnt**-shoo-heh
hat	Hut	hoot
jacket	Jacke	**yah**-keh
jeans	Jeans	"jeans"
nightgown	Nachthemd	**nahkht**-hehmt
nylons	Strümpfe	**shtrewmp**-feh
pajamas	Pyjama	pew-**jah**-mah
pants	Hosen	**hoh**-zehn
raincoat	Regenmantel	**ray**-gehn-mahn-tehl
sandals	Sandalen	zahn-**dah**-lehn

scarf	Schal	shahl
shirt...	Hemd...	hehmt
...long-sleeved	...mit langen Ärmeln	mit **lahng**-ehn **ehr**-mehln
...short-sleeved	...mit kurzen Ärmeln	mit **koorts**-ehn **ehr**-mehln
...sleeveless	...ohne Ärmel	**oh**-neh **ehr**-mehl
shoelaces	Schnürsenkel	**shnewr**-zehn-kehl
shoes	Schuhe	**shoo**-heh
shorts	kurze Hosen	**koorts**-eh **hoh**-zehn
skirt	Rock	rohk
sleeper (for baby)	Kindereinteiler	**kin**-der-**in**-tī-ler
slip	Unterrock	**oon**-ter-rohk
slippers	Pantoffeln	pahn-**tohf**-ehln
socks	Socken	**zohk**-ehn
sweater	Pullover, Pulli	"pullover," **poo**-lee
swimsuit	Badeanzug	**bah**-deh-ahn-tsoog
tennis shoes	Tennisschuhe	**teh**-nis-shoo-heh
tights	strümpfe	**shtrewmp**-feh
T-shirt	T-shirt, Hemdchen	**tay**-shirt, **hehmt**-shyehn
underwear	Unterhosen	**oon**-ter-hoh-zehn
vest	Weste	**veh**-steh

Colors

black	schwarz	shvarts
blue	blau	blow (rhymes with cow)
brown	braun	brown
gray	grau	grow (rhymes with cow)
green	grün	grewn
orange	orange	oh-**rahn**-zheh
pink	rosa	**roh**-sah
purple	lila	**lee**-lah
red	rot	roht
white	weiß	vīs
yellow	gelb	gehlp
dark / light	dunkel / hell	**doon**-kehl / hehl

A lighter...	Eine hellere...	**ī**-neh **hehl**-er-eh
A brighter...	Eine farbigere...	**ī**-neh **far**-big-er-eh
A darker...	Eine dunklere...	**ī**-neh **doon**-kler-eh
...shade.	...Schattierung.	shaht-**eer**-oong

Materials

brass	Messing	**mehs**-sing
bronze	Bronze	**brohn**-seh
ceramic	Keramik	keh-**rah**-mik
copper	Kupfer	**koop**-fer
cotton	Baumwolle	**bowm**-voh-leh
glass	Glas	glahs
gold	Gold	gohlt
lace	Spitze	**shpit**-seh
leather	Leder	**lay**-der
linen	Leinen	**lī**-nehn
marble	Marmor	**mar**-mor
metal	Metall	meh-**tahl**
nylon	Nylon	**nee**-lohn
paper	Papier	pah-**peer**
pewter	Zinn	tsin
plastic	Plastik	**plah**-stik
polyester	Polyester	poh-lee-**ehs**-ter
porcelain	Porzellan	por-tsehl-**lahn**
silk	Seide	**zī**-deh
silver	Silber	**zil**-ber
velvet	Samt	zahmt
wood	Holz	hohlts
wool	Wolle	**voh**-leh

Jewelry

jewelry	Schmuck	shmook
bracelet	Armband	**arm**-bahnt
brooch	Brosche	**broh**-sheh
earrings	Ohrringe	**or**-ring-eh
necklace	Halsband	**hahls**-bahnt
ring	Ring	ring

Is this...?	Ist das...?	ist dahs
...sterling silver	...echt Silber	ehkht **zil**-ber
...real gold	...echt Gold	ehkht gohlt
...stolen	...gestohlen	geh-**shtoh**-lehn

SPORTS

Bicycling

bicycle	Fahrrad, Velo (Switz.)	**far**-raht, **feh**-loh
mountain bike	Mountainbike	"mountain bike"
I'd like to rent a bicycle.	Ich möchte ein Fahrrad mieten.	ikh **murkh**-teh īn **far**-raht **mee**-tehn
We'd like to rent two bicycles.	Wir möchten zwei Fahrräder mieten.	veer **murkh**-tehn tsvī **far**-ray-der **mee**-tehn
How much per...?	Wie viel pro...?	vee feel proh
...hour	...Stunde	**shtoon**-deh
...half day	...halben Tag	**hahl**-behn tahg
...day	...Tag	tahg
Is a deposit required?	Brauchen Sie eine Anzahlung?	**browkh**-ehn zee ī-neh **ahn**-tsahl-oong
deposit	Anzahlung	**ahn**-tsahl-oong
helmet	Helm	hehlm
lock	Schloß	shlohs
air / no air	Luft / keine Luft	looft / **kī**-neh looft
tire	Reifen	**rī**-fehn
pump	Pumpe	**poom**-peh
map	Karte	**kar**-teh
How many gears?	Wie viele Gänge?	vee **fee**-leh **gayng**-eh
What is a...	Was ist eine...	vahs ist ī-neh...
route of about ___ kilometers?	Strecke von etwas ___ Kilometer?	**shtreh**-keh fohn **eht**-vahs ___ kee-loh-**may**-ter
...good	...gute	**goo**-teh
...scenic	...schöne	**shurn**-eh
...interesting	...interessante	in-tehr-ehs-**sahn**-teh
...easy	...leichte	**līkh**-teh

How many minutes / hours by bicycle?	Wie viele Minuten / Stunden mit dem Rad?	vee **fee**-leh mee-**noo**-tehn / **shtoon**-dehn mit daym raht
I (don't) like hills.	Ich mag (keine) Hügel.	ikh mahg (**kī**-neh) **hew**-gehl
I brake for bakeries.	Ich bremse für Bäckereien.	ikh **brehm**-zeh fewr behk-eh-**rī**-ehn

Swimming and Boating

Where can I rent a...?	Wo kann ich ein... mieten?	voh kahn ikh īn... **mee**-tehn
Where can we rent a...?	Wo können wir ein... mieten?	voh **kurn**-ehn veer īn... **mee**-tehn
...paddleboat	...Wasserfahrrad	**vah**-ser-fah-raht
...rowboat	...Ruderboot	**roo**-der-boot
...boat	...Boot	boot
...sailboat	...Segelboot	**zay**-gehl-boot
How much per...?	Wie viel pro...?	vee feel proh
...hour	...Stunde	**shtoon**-deh
...half day	...halben Tag	**hahl**-behn tahg
...day	...Tag	tahg
beach	Strand	shtrahnt
nude beach	FKK-Strand	ehf-kah-**kah**-shtrahnt
Where's good beach?	Wo ist ein guter Strand?	voh ist īn **goo**-ter shtrahnt
Is it safe for swimming?	Ist Schwimmen ohne Gefahr?	ist **shvim**-mehn **oh**-neh geh-**far**
flip-flops	Sandalen	zahn-**dah**-lehn
pool	Schwimmbad	**shvim**-baht
snorkel and mask	Schnorchel und Maske	**shnorkh**-ehl oont **mah**-skeh
sunglasses	Sonnenbrille	**zohn**-nehn-bril-leh
sunscreen	Sonnenschutz	**zohn**-nehn-shoots
surfboard	Surfboard	"surfboard"
surfer	Wellenreiter	**veh**-lehn-rī-ter
swimsuit	Badeanzug	**bah**-deh-ahn-tsoog

ACTIVITIES

towel	*Badetuch*	**bah**-deh-tookh
waterskiing	*Wasserskifahren*	**vah**-ser-shi-**far**-ehn
windsurfing	*Windsurfen*	**vint**-zoorf-ehn

Germans are pioneers in the field of nudity—they're internationally known for letting it all hang out. Pretty much any beach in Germany can be topless, but if you want a true nude beach, look for *FKK,* which stands for *Freikörper Kultur* (Free Body Culture). You'll also stumble into plenty of nude sunbathers (more men than women) on sunny days at any big-city park or riverbank.

Sports Talk

sports	*Sport*	shport
game	*Spiel*	shpeel
team	*Mannschaft*	**mahn**-shahft
championship	*Meisterschaft*	**mī**-ster-shahft
soccer	*Fußball*	**foos**-bahl
basketball	*Basketball,*	**bahs**-keht-bahl,
	Korbballspiel	**kor**-bahl-shpeel
hockey	*Hockey*	**hoh**-kee
American football	*Football*	**foot**-bahl
tennis	*Tennis*	**teh**-nees
golf	*Golf*	gohlf
skiing	*Skifahren*	**shee**-far-ehn
gymnastics	*Gymnastik*	gewm-**nah**-steek
Olympics	*Olympiade*	oh-lewm-pee-**ah**-deh
gold / silver / bronze...	*Gold- / Silber- / Ehren...*	gohlt / **zil**-ber / **eh**-rehn
...medal	*...Medaille*	**meh**-dahl-yeh
What sport	*Sportler / Team*	**shport**-ler / "team"
athlete / team do	*haben Sie am*	**hah**-behn zee ahm
you like?	*liebsten?*	**leeb**-stehn
Where can I see	*Wo kann ich ein*	voh kahn ikh īn
a game?	*Spiel sehen?*	shpeel **zay**-hehn
jogging	*Jogging*	"jogging"
Where's a good	*Wo geht man*	voh gayt mahn
place to jog?	*gut Jogging?*	goot "jogging"

ACTIVITIES

ENTERTAINMENT

What's happening tonight?	Was ist heute abend los?	vahs ist **hoy**-teh **ah**-behnt lohs
What do you recommend?	Was empfehlen Sie?	vahs ehmp-**fay**-lehn zee
Where is it?	Wo ist es?	voh ist ehs
How do I get there?	Wie komme ich hin?	vee **koh**-meh ikh hin
How do we get there?	Wie kommen wir hin?	vee **koh**-mehn veer hin
Is it free?	Ist es umsonst?	ist ehs oom-**zohnst**
Are there seats available?	Gibt es noch Platz?	gipt ehs nohkh plahts
Where can I buy a ticket?	Wo kann ich eine Karte kaufen?	voh kahn ikh **ī**-neh **kar**-teh **kowf**-ehn
Do you have tickets for today / tonight?	Haben Sie Karten für heute / heute Abend?	**hah**-behn zee **kar**-tehn fewr **hoy**-teh / **hoy**-teh **ah**-behnt
When does it start?	Wann fängt es an?	vahn fehngt ehs ahn
When does it end?	Wann endet es?	vahn **ehn**-deht ehs
Where's the best place to dance nearby?	Wo geht man hier am besten Tanzen?	voh gayt mahn heer ahm **behs**-tehn **tahn**-tsehn
Where do people stroll?	Wo geht man hier Promenieren?	voh gayt mahn heer proh-meh-**neer**-ehn

Entertaining Words

movie...	Film...	film
...original version	...im Original	im oh-rig-ee-**nahl**
...in English	...auf Englisch	owf **ehng**-lish
...with subtitles	...mit Untertiteln	mit **oon**-ter-tee-tehln
...dubbed	...synchronisiert	zewn-kroh-nee-**zeert**
music...	Musik...	moo-**zeek**
...live	...live	"live"
...classical	...klassisch	**klahs**-sish
...opera	...Oper	**oh**-per

...symphony	...Symphonie	zewm-foh-**nee**
...choir	...Chor	kor
folk music	Volksmusik	**fohlks**-moo-zeek
rock / jazz / blues	Rock-N-Roll / Jazz / Blues	"rock-n-roll" / "jazz" / "blues"
male singer	Sänger	**zehng**-er
female singer	Sängerin	**zehng**-er-in
concert	Konzert	kohn-**tsehrt**
show	Vorführung	**for**-few-roong
dancing	Tanzen	**tahn**-tsehn
folk dancing	Volkstanz	**fohlks**-tahnts
disco	Disko	**dis**-koh
bar with live music	Bar mit Live-Musik	bar mit "live" moo-**zeek**
nightclub	Nachtklub	**nahkht**-kloob
(no) cover charge	(kein) Eintritt	(kīn) **in**-trit
sold out	ausverkauft	**ows**-fehr-kowft

Oktoberfest, the famous Munich beer festival, fills Bavaria's capital with the sounds of *"Prost!",* carnival rides, sizzling *Bratwurst,* and oompah bands. The party starts the third Saturday in September and lasts for 16 days. The *Salzburger Festspiele* (Salzburg's music festival) treats visitors to the sound of music from late July to the end of August.

CONNECT

PHONING

I'd like to buy a...	Ich möchte eine... kaufen.	ikh **murkh**-teh ī-neh... **kow**-fehn
...telephone card.	...Telefonkarte	tehl-eh-**fohn**-kar-teh
...cheap international telephone card.	...billige internationale Telefonkarte	**bil**-lig-geh in-tehr-naht-see-oh-**nah**-leh tehl-eh-**fohn**-kar-teh
Where is the nearest phone?	Wo ist das nächste Telefon?	voh ist dahs **nehkh**-steh tehl-eh-**fohn**
It doesn't work.	Es ist außer Betrieb.	ehs ist **ow**-ser beh-**treep**
May I use your phone?	Darf ich Ihr Telefon benutzen?	darf ikh eer tehl-eh-**fohn** beh-**noot**-sehn
Can you talk for me?	Können Sie für mich sprechen?	**kurn**-nehn zee fewr mikh **shprehkh**-ehn
It's busy.	Beßetzt.	beh-**zehtst**
Will you try again?	Noch einmal versuchen?	nohkh **īn**-mahl fehr-**zookh**-ehn
My name is ___.	Ich heiße ___.	ikh **hī**-seh
Sorry, I speak only a little German.	Tut mir leid, ich spreche nur ein bißchen deutsch.	toot meer līt ikh **shprehkh**-eh noor īn **bis**-yehn doych
Speak slowly and clearly.	Sprechen Sie langsam und deutlich.	**shprehkh**-ehn zee **lahng**-zahm oont **doyt**-likh
Wait a moment.	Moment mal.	moh-**mehnt** mahl

Telephone Words

telephone	*Telefon*	tehl-eh-**fohn**
telephone card	*Telefonkarte*	tehl-eh-**fohn**-kar-teh
cheap international telephone card	*billige internationale Telefonkarte*	**bil**-lig-geh in-tehr-naht-see-oh-**nah**-leh tehl-eh-**fohn**-kar-teh
PIN code	*Geheimnummer*	geh-**him**-noo-mer
phone booth	*Telefonkabine*	tehl-eh-**fohn**-kah-bee-neh
out of service	*außer Betrieb*	**ow**-ser beh-**treep**
post office	*Post*	pohst
operator	*Vermittlung*	fehr-**mit**-loong
international assistance	*internationale Auskunft*	in-tehr-naht-see-oh-**nah**-leh **ows**-koonft
international call	*Auslandsgespräch*	**ows**-lahnts-geh-shpraykh
collect call	*R-gespräch*	**ehr**-geh-shpraykh
credit card call	*Kreditkartenge-spräch*	kreh-**deet**-kar-tehn-geh-shpraykh
toll-free	*gebührenfrei*	geh-**bew**-rehn-frī
fax	*Fax*	fahx
country code	*Landesvorwahl*	**lahn**-dehs-for-vahl
area code	*Vorwahl*	**for**-vahl
extension	*Intern*	in-**tehrn**
telephone book	*Telefonbuch*	tehl-eh-**fohn**-bookh
yellow pages	*gelbe Seiten*	**gehl**-beh **zī**-tehn

In German-speaking countries, it's polite to identify yourself by name at the beginning of every phone conversation. For domestic calls, make your calls from phone booths with an insertable card (sold at newsstands, handier than coins—except in Austria, where coin phones are more common). For international calls, ask at the newsstand for the cheapest deal for calling home (***Was ist die billigste Möglichkeit für den Anruf Amerika/Kanada?***)—you'll get a PIN code and access number, either printed on your receipt, or on a scratch-off card.

At phone booths, you'll encounter these words: ***Kartentelefon*** (accepts cards, sometimes coins), ***Ganzein-schieben*** (insert completely), **Bitte wählen** (please dial), and **Guthaben** (the value left on your card). If the number you're calling is out of service, you'll hear a recording: *"Kein Anschluß unter dieser Nummer."* For more tips, see "Let's Talk Telephones" on page 260 in the appendix.

Cell Phones

Where is a cell phone shop?	Wo is ein Handyladen?	voh ist īn **han**-dee-lah-dehn
I'd like...	Ich möchte...	ikh **murkh**-teh
We'd like...	Wir möchten...	veer **murkh**-tehn
...a cell phone.	...ein Handy.	īn "handy"
...a chip.	...eine Chipkarte.	**ī**-neh **chip**-kar-teh
...to buy more time.	...mehr Sprechzeit kaufen.	mehr **shprehkh**-tsīt **kow**-fehn
How do you...?	Wie kann man...?	vee kahn mahn
...make calls	...telefonieren	teh-leh-fohn-**eer**-ehn
...receive calls	...abnehmen	**ahp**-nay-mehn
Will this work outside this country?	Geht das im Ausland?	gayt dahs im **ows**-lahnt
Where can I buy a chip for this this phone / this service?	Wo kann ich einen Microchip kaufen für dieses Telefon / diesen Dienst?	voh kahn ikh **ī**-nehn **meek**-roh-chip **kow**-fehn fewr **dee**-zehs teh-leh-**fohn** / **dee**-zehn deenst

Many travelers now buy cell phones in Europe to make both local and international calls. You'll pay under $40–75 for a "locked" phone that works only in the country you buy it in (includes about $20 worth of calls). You can buy additional time at a newsstand or cell phone shop. An "unlocked" phone is more expensive, but it works all over Europe: when you cross a border, buy a SIM card at a cell phone shop and insert the pop-out chip, which comes with a new phone number. Pricier tri-band phones (**Triband Handys**) also work in North America.

CONNECT

EMAIL AND THE WEB

My email address is ___.	Meine E-Mail-Adresse ist ___.	**mī**-neh "email" ah-**dreh**-seh ist
What's your email address?	Was ist Ihre E-Mail-Adresse?	vahs ist **ee**-reh "email" ah-**dreh**-seh
May I use this computer to check my email?	Darf ich diesen Computer benutzen um mein E-Mail nachzulesen?	darf ikh **dee**-zehn kohm-**pew**-ter beh-**noot**-sehn oom mīn "email" **nahkh**-tsoo-lay-zehn
Can we check our email?	Können wir unser E-Mail nachlesen?	**kurn**-nehn veer **oon**-ser **ee**-mayl **nahkh**-lay-zehn
Where is there access to the Internet?	Wo gibt es einen Internet zugang?	voh gipt ehs **ī**-nehn "internet" **tsoo**-gahng
Where is an Internet café?	Wo ist ein Internetcafé?	voh ist īn "internet café"
How much for... minutes?	Wie viel für... Minuten?	vee feel fewr... mee-**noo**-tehn
...10	...zehn	tsayn
...15	...fünfzehn	**fewnf**-tsayn
...30	...dreißig	**drī**-sig
...60	...sechzig	**zehkh**-tsig
Help me, please.	Hilfen Sie mir, bitte.	**hil**-fehn zee meer **bit**-teh

Key Phrases: Email and the Web

email	E-Mail	"email"
Internet	Internet	"internet"
Where is the nearest Internet café?	Wo ist das nächste Internetcafé?	voh ist dahs **naykh**-steh "internet café"
I'd like to check my email.	Ich möchte mein E-Mail nachlesen.	ikh **murkh**-teh mīn "email" **nahkh**-lay-zehn

How do I...	Wie...	vee
...start this?	...fange ich an?	**fahng**-eh ikh ahn
...send a file?	...sende ich einen Anhang?	**zehn**-deh ikh **ī**-nehn **ahn**-hahng
...print out a file?	...drucke ich einen Text?	**droo**-keh ikh **ī**-nehn tehkst
...make this symbol?	...mache ich dieses Symbol?	**mahkh**-eh ikh **dee**-zehs sewm-**bohl**
...type @?	...geht A-Affenschwanz?	gayt ah-**ah**-fehn-shvants
This isn't working.	Das funktioniert nicht.	dahs foonk-tsee-ohn-**eert** nikht

Web Words

email	E-Mail	"email"
email address	E-Mail-Adresse	"email" ah-**dreh**-seh
website	Internetseite	"internet" **zī**-teh
Internet	Internet	"internet"
surf the Web	im Internet schwimmen	im "internet" **shvim**-mehn
download	herunterladen	hehr-**oon**-ter-lah-dehn
@ sign	A-Affenschwanz ("A-monkey tail")	ah-**ah**-fehn-shvants
dot	Punkt	poonkt
hyphen (-)	Bindestrich	**bin**-deh-shtrikh
underscore (_)	Großstrich	**grohs**-shtrikh
Wi-Fi	WLAN	**vay**-lahn

On Screen

Ansicht	view	öffnen	open
bearbeiten	edit	Ordner	folder
drucken	print	Post	mail
löschen	delete	senden	send
Mitteilung	message	speichern	save

MAILING

Where is the post office?	*Wo ist die Post?*	voh ist dee pohst
Which window for...?	*An welchem Schalter ist...?*	ahn **vehlkh**-ehm **shahl**-ter ist
Is this the line for...?	*Ist das die Schlange für...?*	ist dahs dee **shlahng**-eh fewr
...stamps	*...Briefmarken*	**breef**-mar-kehn
...packages	*...Pakete*	pah-**kay**-teh
To the USA...	*In die USA...*	in dee oo ehs ah
...by air mail.	*...mit Luftpost.*	mit **looft**-pohst
...by surface mail.	*...per Schiff.*	pehr shif
...slow and cheap.	*...langsam und billig.*	**lahng**-zahm oont **bil**-lig
How much is it?	*Wie viel kostet das?*	vee feel **kohs**-teht dahs
How much to send a letter / postcard to ___?	*Wie viel ist ein Brief / Postkarte nach ___?*	vee feel ist īn breef / **pohst**-kar-teh nahk
I need stamps for ___ postcards to...	*Ich brauche Briefmarken für ___ Postkarten nach...*	ikh **browkh**-eh **breef**-mar-kehn fewr ___ **pohst**-kar-tehn nahk
...America / Canada.	*...Amerika / Kanada.*	ah-**mehr**-ee-kah / **kah**-nah-dah
Pretty stamps, please.	*Hübsche Briefmarken, bitte.*	**hewb**-sheh **breef**-mar-kehn **bit**-teh
I always choose the slowest line.	*Ich wähle immer die langsamste Schlange.*	ikh **vay**-leh **im**-mer dee **lahng**-zahm-steh **shlahng**-eh
How many days will it take?	*Wie viele Tage braucht das?*	vee **fee**-leh **tahg**-eh browkht dahs

In Germany, Austria, and Switzerland, you can often get stamps at a *Kiosk* (newsstand), stamp machine (yellow, marked *Briefmarken*), or *Tabak* (tobacco shop). As long as you know which stamps you need, this is a great convenience. At the post office, the window labeled *Alle Leistungen* handles everything.

Key Phrases: Mailing

post office	*Post(-amt)*	**pohst** (-ahmt)
stamp	*Briefmarke*	**breef**-mar-keh
postcard	*Postkarte*	**pohst**-kar-teh
letter	*Brief*	breef
airmail	*Luftpost*	**looft**-pohst
Where is the post office?	*Wo ist die Post?*	voh ist dee pohst
I need stamps for ___ postcards / letters to America.	*Ich brauche Briefmarken für ___ Postkarten / Briefe nach Amerika.*	ikh **browkh**-eh **breef**-mar-kehn few ___ **pohst**-kar-tehn / **breef**-eh nahkh ah-**mehr**-ee-kah

German mailboxes often come in pairs: the box for local mail is labeled with its range of zip codes, and the other box (labeled *Andere PLZ*) is for everything else.

Licking the Postal Code

German Postal Service	*Deutsche Bundespost*	**doy**-cheh **boon**-dehs-pohst
Austrian Postal Service	*Österreichische Post*	urs-ter-**rīkh**-is-she pohst
Swiss Postal Service	*Swiss Post*	"Swiss Post"
post office	*Post(-amt)*	**pohst** (-ahmt)
stamp	*Briefmarke*	**breef**-mar-keh
postcard	*Postkarte*	**pohst**-kar-teh
letter	*Brief*	breef
envelope	*Umschlag*	**oom**-shlahg
package	*Paket*	pah-**kayt**
box	*Karton / Schachtel*	kar-**tohn** / **shahkh**-tehl
string	*Schnur*	shnoor
tape	*Klebeband*	**klay**-beh-bahnd
mailbox	*Briefkasten*	**breef**-kahs-tehn
airmail	*Luftpost*	**looft**-pohst

express mail	*Eilpost*	**īl**-pohst
slow and cheap	*langsam und billig*	**lahng**-zahm oont **bil**-lig
book rate	*Büchersendung*	**bewkh**-er-zehn-doong
weight limit	*Gewichtsbe-grenzung*	geh-**vikhts**-beh-grehn-tsoong
registered	*Einschreiben*	**īn**-shrī-behn
insured	*versichert*	fehr-**zikh**-ert
fragile	*zerbrechlich*	tsehr-**brehkh**-likh
contents	*Inhalt*	**in**-hahlt
customs	*Zoll*	tsohl
to / from	*nach / von*	nahkh / fohn
address	*Adresse*	ah-**dreh**-seh
zip code	*Postleitzahl*	**pohst**-līt-sahl
general delivery	*postlagernd*	**pohst**-lahg-ernt

HELP!

Help!	*Hilfe!*	**hil**-feh
Help me!	*Helfen Sie mir!*	**hehl**-fehn zee meer
Call a doctor!	*Rufen Sie einen Arzt!*	**roo**-fehn zee **ī**-nehn artst
Call...	*Rufen Sie...*	**roo**-fehn zee
...the police.	*...die Polizei.*	dee poh-leet-**sī**
...an ambulance.	*...den Krankenwagen.*	dayn **krahnk**-ehn-vah-gehn
...the fire department.	*...die Feuerwehr.*	dee **foy**-er-vehr
I'm lost. (on foot)	*Ich habe mich verlaufen.*	ikh **hah**-beh mikh fehr-**lowf**-ehn
We're lost. (on foot)	*Wir haben uns verlaufen.*	veer **hah**-behn oons fehr-**lowf**-ehn
I'm lost. (by car)	*Ich habe mich verfahren.*	ikh **hah**-beh mikh fehr-**far**-ehn
We're lost. (by car)	*Wir haben uns verfahren.*	veer **hah**-behn oons fehr-**far**-ehn
Thank you for your help.	*Danke für Ihre Hilfe.*	**dahng**-keh fewr **ee**-reh **hil**-feh
You are very kind.	*Sie sind sehr freundlich.*	zee zint zehr **froynd**-likh

Theft and Loss

| Stop, thief! | *Halt, Dieb!* | hahlt deep |
| I've been robbed. | *Ich bin beraubt worden.* | ikh bin beh-**rowbt** **vor**-dehn |

Key Phrases: Help!

accident	*Unfall*	**oon**-fahl
emergency	*Notfall*	**noht**-fahl
police	*Polizei*	poh-leet-**sī**
Help!	*Hilfe!*	**hil**-feh
Call a doctor / the police!	*Rufen Sie einen Arzt / die Polizei!*	**roo**-fehn zee **ī**-nehn artst / dee poh-leet-**sī**
Stop, thief!	*Halt, Dieb!*	hahlt deep

We've been robbed.	*Wir sind beraubt worden.*	veer zint beh-**rowbt vor**-dehn
A thief took...	*Ein Dieb hat... genommen.*	īn deep haht... geh-**noh**-mehn
Thieves took...	*Die Diebe haben... genommen.*	dee **dee**-beh **hah**-behn... geh-**noh**-mehn
I've lost...	*Ich habe... verloren.*	ikh **hah**-beh... fehr-**lor**-ehn
...my money.	*...mein Geld*	mīn gehlt
...my passport.	*...meinen Paß*	**mī**-nehn pahs
...my train ticket / plane ticket.	*...meine Fahrkarte / Flugkarte*	**mī**-neh **far**-kar-teh / **floog**-kar-teh
...my baggage.	*...mein Gepäck*	mīn geh-**pehk**
...my purse.	*...meine Handtasche*	**mī**-neh **hahnt**-tahsh-eh
...my wallet.	*...meine Brieftasche*	**mī**-neh **breef**-tahsh-eh
...my faith in humankind.	*...meinen Glauben an die Menschheit*	**mī**-nehn **glow**-behn ahn dee **mehnsh**-hīt
We've lost our...	*Wir haben unsere... verloren.*	veer **hah**-behn **oon**-zer-eh... fehr-**lor**-ehn
...passports.	*...Pässe*	**peh**-seh
...train tickets / plane tickets.	*...Fahrkarten / Flugkarten*	**far**-kar-tehn / **floog**-kar-tehn
...baggage.	*...Gepäck*	geh-**pehk**
I want to contact my embassy.	*Ich möchte meine Botschaft kontaktieren.*	ikh **murkh**-teh **mī**-neh **boht**-shahft kohn-tahk-**tee**-rehn

HELP!

| I need to file a police report for my insurance. | Ich muß einen Polizeireport für meine Versicherung erstellen. | ikh mus **ī**-nehn poh-leet-**sī**-reh-port fewr **mī**-neh fehr-**zikh**-er-oong ehr-**shteh**-lehn |

See pages 261–262 in the appendix for information on US embassies in Germany, Austria, and Switzerland.

Helpful Words

ambulance	Krankenwagen	**krahnk**-ehn-vah-gehn
accident	Unfall	**oon**-fahl
injured	verletzt	fehr-**lehtst**
emergency	Notfall	**noht**-fahl
emergency room	Notfallaufnahme	noht-fahl-**owf**-nah-meh
fire	Feuer	**foy**-er
police	Polizei	poh-leet-**sī**
smoke	Rauch	rowkh
thief	Dieb	deep
pickpocket	Taschendieb	**tahsh**-ehn-deep

Help for Women

Leave me alone.	Lassen Sie mich in Ruhe.	**lah**-sehn zee mikh in **roo**-heh
I want to be alone.	Ich möchte alleine sein.	ikh **murkh**-teh ah-**lī**-neh zīn
I'm not interested.	Ich habe kein Interesse.	ikh **hah**-beh kīn in-tehr-**ehs**-seh
I'm married.	Ich bin verheiratet.	ikh bin fehr-**hī**-rah-teht
I'm a lesbian.	Ich bin lesbisch.	ikh bin **lehz**-bish
I have a contagious disease.	Ich habe eine ansteckende Krankheit.	ikh **hah**-beh **ī**-neh **ahn**-shtehk-ehn-deh **krahnk**-hīt
You are bothering me.	Sie sind mir lästig.	zee zint meer **lehs**-tig
He is bothering me.	Er belästigt mich.	ehr beh-**lehs**-tigt mikh
Don't touch me.	Fassen Sie mich nicht an.	**fah**-sehn zee mikh nikht ahn

You're disgusting.	Sie sind eklig.	zee zint **ehk**-lig
Stop following me.	Hör auf, mir nachzulaufen.	hur owf meer **nahkh**-tsoo-**lowf**-ehn
Stop it!	Hören Sie auf!	**hur**-ehn zee owf
Enough!	Das reicht!	dahs rīkht
Go away.	Gehen Sie weg.	**gay**-ehn zee vayg
Get lost!	Hau ab!	how ahp
Drop dead!	Verschwinde!	fehr-**shvin**-deh
I'll call the police.	Ich rufe die Polizei.	ikh **roo**-feh dee poh-leet-**sī**

SERVICES

Laundry

Is a... laundry nearby?	Ist ein Waschsalon... in der Nähe?	ist īn **vahsh**-zah-lohn... in dehr **nay**-heh
...self-service	...mit Selbstbedienung	mit zehlpst-beh-**dee**-noong
...full service	...mit Dienstleistung	mit **deenst**-līs-toong
Help me, please.	Hilfen Sie mir, bitte.	**hil**-fehn zee meer **bit**-teh
How does this work?	Wie funktioniert das?	vee foonk-tsee-ohn-**eert** dahs
Where is the soap?	Wo ist das Waschmittel?	voh ist dahs **vahsh**-mit-tehl
Are these yours?	Sind das Ihre?	zint dahs **ee**-reh
This stinks.	Das stinkt.	dahs shtinkt
Smells like...	Riecht wie...	rīkht vee
...spring time.	...Frühling.	**frew**-ling
...a locker room.	...eine Turnhalle.	**ī**-neh **toorn**-hah-leh
...cheese.	...Käse.	**kay**-zeh
I need change.	Ich brauche Kleingeld.	ikh **browkh**-eh **klīn**-gehlt
Same-day service?	Noch am selben Tag?	nohkh ahm **zehl**-behn tahg
By when do I need to drop off my clothes?	Bis wann kann ich meine Wäsche vorbeibringen?	bis vahn kahn ikh **mī**-neh **veh**-sheh for-**bī**-bring-ehn
When will my clothes be ready?	Wann wird meine Wäsche fertig sein?	vahn virt **mī**-neh **veh**-sheh **fehr**-tig zīn

160

Dried?	Getrocknet?	geh-**trohk**-neht
Folded?	Gefaltet?	geh-**fahl**-teht
Hey there, what's spinning?	Hey, worum dreht's sich?	hay **voh**-room drayts zikh

Clean Words

full-service laundry	Waschsalon mit Dienstleistung	**vahsh**-zah-lohn mit **deenst**-līs-toong
self-service laundry	Waschsalon mit Selbstbedienung	**vahsh**-zah-lohn mit zehlpst-beh-**dee**-noong
wash / dry	waschen / trocknen	**vahsh**-ehn / **trohk**-nehn
washer / dryer	Waschmaschine / Trockner	**vahsh**-mahs-shee-neh / **trohk**-ner
detergent	Waschmittel	**vahsh**-mit-tehl
token	Zahlmarke, Jeton	**tsahl**-mar-keh, **yeh**-tohn
whites	Helles	**hehl**-lehs
colors	Buntwäsche	**boont**-veh-sheh
delicates	Feinwäsche	**fīn**-veh-sheh
handwash	von Hand waschen	fohn hahnt **vah**-shehn

Haircuts

Where is a barber / hair salon?	Wo ist ein Herrenfrisör / Friseursalon?	voh ist īn heh-rehn-friz-**ur** / friz-**oor**-zah-lohn
I'd like...	Ich möchte...	ikh **murkh**-teh
...a haircut.	...meine Haare schneiden.	**mī**-neh **hah**-reh **shnī**-dehn
...a permanent.	...eine Dauerwelle.	**ī**-neh **dow**-er-veh-leh
...just a trim.	...nur stutzen.	noor **shtoot**-sehn
Cut about this much off.	Etwa so viel kürzen.	**eht**-vah zo feel **kewrt**-sehn
Cut my bangs here.	Meine Stirnhaare hier kürzen.	**mī**-neh **shteern**-hah-reh heer **kewrt**-sehn
Longer / shorter here.	Hier länger / kürzer.	heer **layng**-er / **kewrt**-ser

I'd like my hair...	Ich möchte meine Haare..	ikh **murkh**-teh **mī**-neh **hah**-reh
...short.	...kurz.	koorts
...colored.	...gefärbt.	geh-**fayrbt**
...shampooed.	...gewaschen.	geh-**vahsh**-ehn
...blow dried.	...getrocknet.	geh-**trohk**-neht
It looks good.	Es sieht gut aus.	ehs zeet goot ows

SERVICES

Repair

These handy lines can apply to any repair, whether it's a ripped rucksack, broken camera, or bad haircut.

This is broken.	Das hier ist kaputt.	dahs heer ist kah-**poot**
Can you fix it?	Können Sie das reparieren?	**kurn**-nehn zee dahs reh-pah-**reer**-ehn
Just do the essentials.	Machen Sie nur das Nötigste.	**mahkh**-ehn zee noor dahs **nur**-tig-steh
How much will it cost?	Wie viel kostet das?	vee feel **kohs**-teht-dahs
When will it be ready?	Wann ist es fertig?	vahn ist ehs **fehr**-tig
I need it by ___.	Ich brauche es bis ___.	ikh **browkh**-eh ehs bis
We need it by ___.	Wir brauchen es bis ___.	veer **browkh**-ehn ehs bis
Without it, I'm...	Ohne bin ich...	**oh**-neh bin ikh
...helpless.	...hilflos.	**hilf**-lohs
...a mess.	...aufgeschmissen. ("all thrown up in the air")	**owf**-geh-shmis-sehn
...done for.	...erledigt.	ehr-**lay**-digt

Filling Out Forms

Herr / Frau	Mr. / Ms.
Vorname	first name
Name (Familienname)	name (last name)
Adresse	address
Wohnort	address / city
Straße	street
Stadt	city
Staat	state
Land	country
Nationalität	nationality
Herkunft / Reiseziel	origin / destination
Alter	age
Geburtsdatum	date of birth
Geburtsort	place of birth
Geschlecht	sex
männlich / weiblich	male / female
verheiratet / ledig	married / single
geschieden / verwittwet	divorced / widowed
Beruf	profession
Erwachsener	adult
Kind / Junge / Mädchen	child / boy / girl
Kinder	children
Familie	family
Unterschrift	signature

When filling out dates, do it European-style: day/month/year.

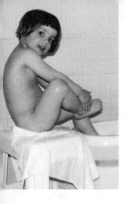

HEALTH

I am sick.	Ich bin krank.	ikh bin krahnk
I feel (very) sick.	Ich fühle mich (sehr) schlecht.	ikh **few**-leh mikh (zehr) shlehkht
My husband / My wife...	Mein Mann / Meine Frau...	mīn mahn / **mī**-neh frow
My son / My daughter...	Mein Sohn / Meine Tochter...	mīn zohn / **mī**-neh **tohkh**-ter
My male friend / My female friend...	Mein Freund / Meine Freundin...	mīn froynt / **mī**-neh **froyn**-din
...feels (very) sick.	...fühlt sich (sehr) schlecht.	fewlt zikh (zehr) shlehkht

---

Key Phrases: Health

doctor	Arzt	artst
hospital	Krankenhaus	**krahn**-kehn-hows
pharmacy	Apotheke	ah-poh-**tay**-keh
medicine	Medikament	meh-dee-kah-**mehnt**
I am sick.	Ich bin krank.	ikh bin krahnk
I need a doctor (who speaks English).	Ich brauche einen Arzt (der Englisch spricht).	ikh **browkh**-eh **ī**-nehn artst (dehr **ehng**-lish shprikht)
It hurts here.	Hier tut es weh.	heer toot ehs vay

164

It's urgent.	Es ist dringend.	ehs ist **dring**-ehnt
I need a doctor...	Ich brauche einen Arzt...	ikh **browkh**-eh **ī**-nehn artst
We need a doctor...	Wir brauchen einen Arzt...	veer **browkh**-ehn **ī**-nehn artst
...who speaks English.	...der Englisch spricht.	dehr **ehng**-lish shprikht
Please call a doctor.	Bitte rufen Sie einen Arzt.	**bit**-teh **roo**-fehn zee **ī**-nehn artst
Could a doctor come here?	Kann der Arzt hier kommen?	kahn dehr artst heer **koh**-mehn
I am...	Ich bin...	ikh bin
He / She is...	Er / Sie ist...	ehr / zee ist
...allergic to penicillin / sulfa.	...allergisch auf Penizillin / Sulfa.	ah-**lehr**-gish owf pehn-ee-tsee-**leen** / **zool**-fah
I am diabetic.	Ich bin Diabetiker.	ikh bin dee-ah-**beht**-ee-ker
I have cancer.	Ich habe Krebs.	ikh **hah**-beh krehbs
I had a heart attack ___ years ago.	Ich hatte einen Herzschlag vor ___ Jahren.	ikh **hah**-teh **ī**-nehn **hayrts**-shlahg for ___ **yah**-rehn
It hurts here.	Hier tut es weh.	heer toot ehs vay
I feel faint.	Ich fühle mich schwach.	ikh **few**-leh mikh shvahkh
It hurts to urinate.	Urinieren schmerzt.	oo-rin-**eer**-ehn shmehrtst
I have body odor.	Ich habe Körpergeruch.	ikh **hah**-beh **kur**-per-geh-rookh
I'm going bald.	Mir fallen die Haare aus.	meer **fah**-lehn dee **hah**-reh ows
Is it serious?	Ist es ernst?	ist ehs ehrnst
Is it contagious?	Ist es ansteckend?	ist ehs **ahn**-shtehk-ehnt
Aging sucks.	Altern stinkt.	**ahl**-tern shtinkt
Take one pill every ___ hours for ___ days.	Alle ___ Stunden eine Pille einnehmen während ___ Tagen.	**ah**-leh ___ **shtoon**-dehn **ī**-neh **pil**-leh **īn**-nay-mehn **vehr**-ehnt ___ **tah**-gehn

| I need a receipt for my insurance. | Ich brauche eine Quittung für meine Versicherung. | ikh **browkh**-eh **ī**-neh **kvit**-toong fewr **mī**-neh fehr-**zikh**-eh-roong |

Ailments

I have...	Ich habe...	ikh **hah**-beh
He / She has...	Er / Sie hat...	ehr / zee haht
I need / We need medication for...	Ich brauche / Wir brauchen Medikament für...	ikh **browkh**-eh / veer **browkh**-ehn meh-dee-kah-**mehnt** fewr
...arthritis.	...Gelenk-entzündung.	geh-**lehnk**-ehnt-tsewn-doong
...asthma.	...Asthma.	**ahst**-mah
...athlete's foot.	...Fußpilz.	**foos**-pilts
...bad breath.	...schlechten Atem.	**shlehkh**-tehn **ah**-tehm
...blisters.	...Blasen.	**blah**-zehn
...bug bites.	...Instektenstiche.	in-**zehk**-tehn-shtikh-eh
...a burn.	...eine Verbrennung.	**ī**-neh fehr-**breh**-noong
...chest pains.	...Schmerzen in der Brust.	**shmehrts**-ehn in dehr broost
...chills.	...Kälteschauer.	**kehl**-teh-show-ehr
...a cold.	...eine Erkältung.	**ī**-neh ehr-**kehl**-toong
...congestion.	...Nasenver-stopfung.	**nah**-zehn-fehr-**shtohp**-foong
...constipation.	...Verstopfung.	fehr-**shtohp**-foong
...a cough.	...einen Husten.	**ī**-nehn **hoo**-stehn
...cramps.	...Krämpfe.	**krehmp**-feh
...diabetes.	...Zuckerkrankheit.	**tsoo**-ker-krahnk-hīt
...diarrhea.	...Durchfall.	**doorkh**-fahl
...dizziness.	...Schwindel.	**shvin**-dehl
...earache.	...Ohrenschmerzen.	**or**-ehn-shmehrts-ehn
...epilepsy.	...Epilepsie.	eh-pil-ehp-**see**
...a fever.	...Fieber.	**fee**-ber
...the flu.	...die Grippe.	dee **grip**-peh
...food poisoning.	...Lebensmittel-vergiftung.	**lay**-behns-mit-tehl-fehr-**gift**-oong

HEALTH

...giggles.	...einen Lachanfall.	**ī**-nehn **lahkh**-ahn-fahl
...hay fever.	...Heuschnupfen.	**hoy**-shnoop-fehn
...a headache.	...Kopfschmerzen.	**kohpf**-shmehrts-ehn
...a heart condition.	...Herzbeschwerden.	**hayrts**-beh-shvehr-dehn
...hemorrhoids.	...Hämorrhoiden.	heh-mor-oh-**ee**-dehn
...high blood pressure.	...Bluthochdruck.	**bloot**-hohkh-drook
...indigestion.	...Verdauungs-störung.	fehr-**dow**-oongs-shtur-oong
...an infection.	...eine Infektion.	**ī**-neh in-fehk-tsee-**ohn**
...a migraine.	...Migräne.	mee-**gray**-neh
...nausea.	...Übelkeit.	**ew**-behl-kīt
...inflammation.	...eine Entzündung.	**ī**-neh ehnt-**tsewn**-doong
...pneumonia.	...Lungen-entzündung.	**loong**-ehn-ehnt-**tsewn**-doong
...a rash.	...einen Ausschlag.	**ī**-nehn **ows**-shlahg
...sinus problems.	...Schleimhaut-entzündung.	**shlīm**-howt-ehnt-**tsewn**-doong
...a sore throat.	...Halsschmerzen.	**hahls**-shmehrts-ehn
...a stomachache.	...Magenschmerzen.	**mah**-gehn-shmehrts-ehn
...sunburn.	...Sonnenbrand.	**zoh**-nehn-brahnt
...a swelling.	...eine Schwellung.	**ī**-neh **shvehl**-loong
...a toothache.	...Zahnschmerzen.	**tsahn**-shmehrts-ehn
...urinary infection.	...Harnröhren-entzündung.	**harn**-rur-rehn-ehnt-**tsewn**-doong
...a venereal disease.	...eine Geschlechts-krankheit.	**ī**-neh geh-**shlehkhts**-krahnk-hīt
...vicious sunburn.	...üblen Sonnenbrand.	**ew**-blehn **zoh**-nehn-brahnt
...vomiting.	...Übergeben.	ew-ber-**gay**-behn
...worms.	...Würmer.	**vewr**-mer

Women's Health

menstruation	Menstruation	mehn-stroo-ah-see-**ohn**
menstrual cramps	Monatskrämpfe	**moh**-nahts-krehmp-feh
period	Periode	pehr-ee-**oh**-deh
pregnancy (test)	Schwanger-schaft(-stest)	**shvahng**-er-shahft(-stehst)

HEALTH

miscarriage	*Fehlgeburt*	**fayl**-geh-boort
abortion	*Abtreibung*	**ahp**-trī-boong
birth control pills	*Verhütungspille*	fehr-**hewt**-oongs-pil-leh
diaphragm	*Spirale*	shpee-**rah**-leh
I'd like to see	*Ich möchte gern*	ikh **murkh**-teh gehrn
a female...	*zu einer...*	tsoo **ī**-ner
...doctor.	*...Ärztin.*	**ayrts**-tin
...gynecologist.	*...Gynäkologin.*	gewn-eh-koh-**loh**-gin
I've missed	*Ich habe meine*	ikh **hah**-beh **mī**-neh
a period.	*Tage nicht*	**tahg**-eh nikht
	bekommen.	beh-**kohm**-mehn
My last period	*Meine letzte*	**mī**-neh **lehts**-teh
started on ___.	*Periode fing*	pehr-ee-**oh**-deh fing
	am ___ an.	ahm ___ ahn
I am / She is...	*Ich bin / Sie ist...*	ikh bin / zee ist...
pregnant.	*schwanger.*	**shvahng**-er
...___ months	*...im ___ Monat*	im ___ **moh**-naht

Parts of the Body

ankle	*Fußgelenk*	**foos**-geh-lehnk
arm	*Arm*	arm
back	*Rücken*	**rew**-kehn
bladder	*Blase*	**blah**-zeh
breast	*Busen*	**boo**-sehn
buttocks	*Hinterbacken*	**hin**-ter-bahk-ehn
chest	*Brust*	broost
ear	*Ohr*	or
elbow	*Ellbogen*	**ehl**-boh-gehn
eye	*Auge*	**ow**-geh
face	*Gesicht*	geh-**zikht**
finger	*Finger*	**fing**-er
foot	*Fuß*	foos
hair	*Haare*	har-reh
hand	*Hand*	hahnt
head	*Kopf*	kohpf
heart	*Herz*	hayrts

HEALTH

hip	*Hüfte*	**hewf**-teh
intestines	*Därme*	**dayr**-meh
knee	*Knie*	kuh-**nee**
leg	*Bein*	bīn
lung	*Lunge*	**loong**-eh
mouth	*Mund*	moont
neck	*Nacken*	**nahk**-ehn
nose	*Nase*	**nah**-zeh
penis	*Penis*	**peh**-nees
rectum	*Anus*	**ah**-noos
shoulder	*Schulter*	**shool**-ter
stomach	*Magen*	**mah**-gehn
teeth	*Zähne*	**tsay**-neh
testicles	*Hoden*	**hoh**-dehn
throat	*Hals*	hahls
toe	*Zehe*	**tsay**-heh
urethra	*Harnröhre*	**harn**-rur-eh
uterus	*Gebärmutter*	geh-**bayr**-moo-ter
vagina	*Vagina*	vah-**gee**-nah
waist	*Bund*	boont
wrist	*Handgelenk*	**hahnt**-geh-lehnk

Healthy Words

24-hour pharmacy	*Vierundzwanzig- Stunden- Apotheke*	**feer**-oont-tsvahn-tsig- **shtoon**-dehn- ah-poh-**tay**-keh
bleeding	*bluten*	**bloot**-ehn
blood	*Blut*	bloot
contraceptives	*Verhütungsmittel*	fehr-**hewt**-oongs-mit-tehl
dentist	*Zahnarzt*	**tsahn**-artst
doctor	*Arzt*	artst
health insurance	*Kranken versicherung*	**krahn**-kehn fehr-**zikh**-eh-roong
hospital	*Krankenhaus*	**krahn**-kehn-hows
medical clinic	*Klinik*	**klee**-nik
medicine	*Medikament*	meh-dee-kah-**mehnt**

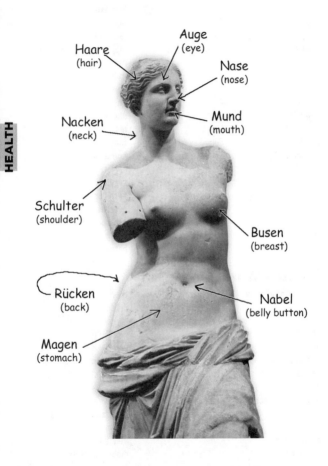

Haare
(hair)

Auge
(eye)

Nase
(nose)

Mund
(mouth)

Nacken
(neck)

Schulter
(shoulder)

Busen
(breast)

Rücken
(back)

Nabel
(belly button)

Magen
(stomach)

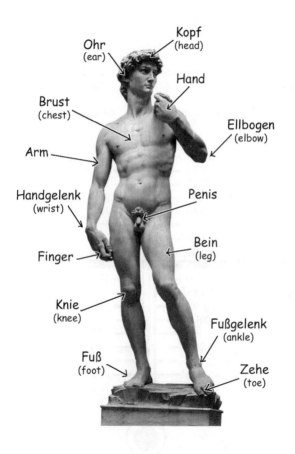

Kopf
(head)

Ohr
(ear)

Hand

Brust
(chest)

Ellbogen
(elbow)

Arm

Handgelenk
(wrist)

Penis

Finger

Bein
(leg)

Knie
(knee)

Fußgelenk
(ankle)

Fuß
(foot)

Zehe
(toe)

nurse	*Krankenschwester*	**krahn**-kehn-shvehs-ter
pain	*Schmerz*	shmehrts
pharmacy	*Apotheke*	ah-poh-**tay**-keh
pill	*Pille*	**pil**-leh
prescription	*Rezept,*	reh-**tsehpt**,
	Verschreibung	fehr-**shrī**-boong
refill	*Erneuerung*	ehr-**noy**-er-oong
unconscious	*bewußtlos*	beh-**voost**-lohs
X-ray	*Röntgenbild*	**rurnt**-gehn-bilt

HEALTH

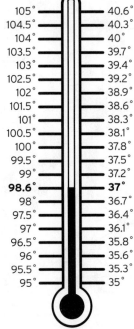

First-Aid Kit

antacid	*Mittel gegen Magenbrennen*	**mit**-tehl **gay**-gehn **mah**-gehn-breh-nehn
antibiotic	*Antibiotika*	ahn-tee-bee-**oh**-tee-kah
aspirin	*Aspirin*	ah-spir-**een**
non-aspirin substitute	*Ben-u-ron*	**behn**-oo-rohn
bandage	*Verband*	fehr-**bahnt**
Band-Aids	*Pflaster*	**pflahs**-ter
cold medicine	*Grippemittel*	**grip**-eh-mit-tehl
cough drops	*Hustenbonbons*	**hoo**-stehn-bohn-bohns
disinfectant	*Desinfektions-mittel*	dehs-in-fehk-tsee-**ohns**-mit-tehl
first-aid cream	*Erste-Hilfe-Salbe*	**ehrst**-eh-**hil**-feh-**zahl**-beh
gauze / tape	*Verband*	fehr-**bahnt**
laxative	*Laxativ*	lahks-ah-**teef**
medicine for diarrhea	*Durchfall-medikament*	**doorkh**-fahl-meh-dee-kah-**mehnt**
moleskin	*Pflaster gegen Blasen*	**pflahs**-ter **gay**-gehn **blah**-zehn
painkiller	*Schmerzmittel*	**shmehrts**-mit-tehl
Preparation H	*Hämorrhoiden Salbe*	heh-mor-oh-**ee**-dehn **zahl**-beh
support bandage	*Stützverband*	**shtewts**-fehr-bahnt
thermometer	*Thermometer*	tehr-moh-**may**-ter
Vaseline	*Vaseline, Mineralsalbe*	vah-zeh-**lee**-neh, min-eh-**rahl**-zahl-beh
vitamins	*Vitamine*	vee-tah-**mee**-neh

Contacts and Glasses

glasses	*Brille*	**bril**-leh
sunglasses	*Sonnenbrille*	**zoh**-nehn-bril-leh
prescription	*Rezept, Verschreibung*	reh-**tsehpt**, fehr-**shrī**-boong
soft...	*weiche...*	**vīkh**-eh

hard...	harte...	**har**-teh
...contact lenses	...Linsen	**lin**-zehn
cleaning solution	Reinigungslösung	**rī**-nee-goongs-lur-zoong
soaking solution	Kontaktlinsenbad	kon-**tahkt**-lin-zehn-baht
all-purpose solution	Salzlösung	**zahlts**-lur-zoong
20/20 vision	perfekte	pehr-**fehk**-teh
	Dioptrie	dee-ohp-**tree**
I've... a	Ich habe meine	ikh **hah**-beh **mī**-neh
contact lens.	Kontaktlinse...	kohn-**tahkt**-lin-zeh
...lost	...verloren.	fehr-**lor**-ehn
...swallowed	...verschluckt.	fehr-**shlookt**

Toiletries

comb	Kamm	kahm
conditioner for hair	Haarfestiger	**har**-fehs-tig-er
condoms	Kondome	kohn-**doh**-meh
dental floss	Zahnseide	**tsahn**-zī-deh
deodorant	Deodorant	deh-oh-doh-**rahnt**
facial tissue	Papiertuch	pah-**peer**-tookh
hairbrush	Haarbürste	**har**-bewr-steh
hand lotion	Handlotion	**hahnt**-loh-tsee-ohn
lip salve	Lippenbalsam	**lip**-pehn-bahl-zahm
mirror	Spiegel	**shpee**-gehl
nail clipper	Nagelschere	**nah**-gehl-sheh-reh
razor	Rasierapparat	rah-**zeer**-ahp-ar-aht
sanitary napkins	Damenbinden	**dah**-mehn-bin-dehn
scissors	Schere	**sheh**-reh
shampoo	Shampoo	**shahm**-poo
shaving cream	Rasierschaum	rah-**zeer**-showm
soap	Seife	**zī**-feh
sunscreen	Sonnenschutz	**zoh**-nehn-shoots
suntan lotion	Sonnenöl	**zoh**-nehn-url
tampons	Tampons	**tahm**-pohns
tissues	Taschentücher	**tah**-shehn-tewkh-er
toilet paper	Klopapier	kloh-pah-**peer**
toothbrush	Zahnbürste	**tsahn**-bewr-steh

| toothpaste | *Zahnpasta* | **tsahn**-pah-stah |
| tweezers | *Pinzette* | pin-**tseh**-teh |

Makeup

blush	*Wangenröte*	**vahng**-ehn-rur-teh
eye shadow	*Augenschatten*	**ow**-gehn-shah-tehn
eyeliner	*Augenkontour*	**ow**-gehn-kohn-toor
face cleanser	*Gesichtsseife*	geh-**zikhts**-zī-feh
face powder	*Gesichtspulver*	geh-**zikhts**-pool-ver
foundation	*Grundlage*	**groont**-lah-geh
lipstick	*Lippenstift*	**lip**-pehn-shtift
makeup	*Makeup*	"makeup"
mascara	*Maskara*	mahs-**kah**-rah
moisturizer...	*Feuchtigkeitscreme...*	**foykh**-tig-kīts-**kreh**-meh
...with sunblock	*...mit Sonnenschutz*	mit **zoh**-nehn-shoots
nail polish	*Nagellack*	**nah**-gehl-lahk
nail polish remover	*Nagellack-entferner*	**nah**-gehl-lahk-ehnt-**fehr**-ner
perfume	*Parfum*	par-**foom**

For Babies

baby	*Baby*	**bay**-bee
baby food	*Babynahrung*	**bay**-bee-nah-roong
bib	*Latz*	lahts
bottle	*Flasche*	**flah**-sheh
diapers	*Windeln*	**vin**-dehln
diaper wipes	*Feuchtigkeitstücher*	**foykh**-tig-kīts-tewkh-er
diaper ointment	*Babysalbe*	**bay**-bee-zahl-beh
formula...	*Babynahrung...*	**bay**-bee-nah-roong
...powdered	*...in Pulver*	in **pool**-ver
...liquid	*...flüssig*	**flew**-sig
...soy	*...mit Soya*	mit **zoh**-yah
medication for...	*Medikament für...*	meh-dee-kah-**mehnt** fewr
...diaper rash	*...Windeldermatitis*	vin-del-dehr-ma-**tee**-tis
...teething	*...Zahnen*	**tsahn**-ehn

HEALTH

nipple	Nippel	**nip**-pehl
pacifier	Nuggel	**noog**-gehl
Will you refrigerate this?	Können Sie das kühl stellen?	**kurn**-nehn zee dahs kewl **shteh**-lehn
Will you warm... for a baby?	Können Sie... fürs Baby wärmen?	**kurn**-nehn zee... fewrs **bay**-bee **vayrm**-ehn
...this	...das	dahs
...some water	...etwas Wasser	**eht**-vahs **vah**-ser
...some milk	...etwas Milch	**eht**-vahs milkh
Not too hot, please.	Nicht zu heiß, bitte.	nikht tsoo hīs **bit**-teh

More Baby Things

backpack to carry baby	Rucksack- Babyträger	**rook**-zahk- **bay**-bee-**tray**-ger
booster seat	Kindersitz	**kin**-der-zits
car seat	Sicherheitssitz	**zikh**-er-hīts-zits
high chair	Kinderstuhl	**kin**-der-shtool
playpen	Babygitter	**bay**-bee-git-ter
stroller	Kinderwagen	**kin**-der-**vah**-gehn

CHATTING

My name is ___.	Ich heiße ___.	ikh **hī**-seh
What's your name?	Wie heißen Sie?	vee **hī**-sehn zee
Pleased to meet you.	Freut mich.	froyt mikh
This is ___.	Das ist ___.	dahs ist
How are you?	Wie geht's?	vee gayts
Very well, thanks.	Sehr gut, danke.	zehr goot **dahng**-keh
Where are you from?	Woher kommen Sie?	**voh**-hehr **koh**-mehn zee
What...?	Von welcher...?	fohn **vehlkh**-er
...city	...Stadt	shtaht
...country	...Land	lahnt
...planet	...Planet	plahn-**ayt**
I'm from...	Ich bin aus...	ikh bin ows
...America.	...Amerika.	ah-**mehr**-ee-kah
...Canada.	...Kanada.	**kah**-nah-dah
Where are you going?	Wo hin gehen Sie?	voh hin **gay**-hehn zee
I'm going to ___.	Ich gehe nach ___.	ikh **gay**-heh nahkh
We're going to ___.	Wir gehen nach ___.	veer **gay**-hehn nahkh
Will you take my / our photo?	Machen Sie ein Foto von mir / uns?	**mahkh**-ehn zee īn **foh**-toh fohn meer / oons
Can I take a photo of you?	Kann ich ein Foto von Ihnen machen?	kahn ikh īn **foh**-toh fohn **ee**-nehn **mahkh**-ehn
Smile!	Lächeln!	**laykh**-ehln

177

CHATTING

Key Phrases: Chatting

My name is ___.	*Ich heiße ___.*	ikh **hī**-seh
What's your name?	*Wie heißen Sie?*	vee **hī**-sehn zee
Pleased to meet you.	*Freut mich.*	froyt mikh
Where are you from?	*Woher kommen Sie?*	**voh**-hehr **koh**-mehn zee
I'm from ___.	*Ich bin aus ___.*	ikh bin ows
Where are you going?	*Wohin gehen Sie?*	voh-hin **gay**-hehn zee
I'm going to ___.	*Ich gehe nach ___.*	ikh **gay**-heh nahkh
I like...	*Ich mag...*	ikh mahg
Do you like...?	*Mögen Sie...?*	**mur**-gehn zee
Thank you very much.	*Vielen Dank.*	**fee**-lehn dahngk
Have a good trip!	*Gute Reise!*	**goo**-teh **rī**-zeh

Nothing More Than Feelings...

I am / You are...	*Ich bin / Sie sind...*	ikh bin / zee zint
He / She is...	*Er / Sie ist...*	ehr / zee ist
...happy.	*...glücklich.*	**glewk**-likh
...sad.	*...traurig.*	**trow**-rig
...tired.	*...müde.*	**mew**-deh
...hungry.	*...hungrig.*	**hoon**-grig
...thirsty.	*...durstig.*	**door**-stig
I'm hot.	*Mir ist zu warm.*	meer ist tsoo varm
I'm cold.	*Mir ist kalt.*	meer ist kahlt
I'm homesick.	*Ich habe Heimweh.*	ikh **hah**-beh **hīm**-vay
I'm lucky.	*Ich habe Glück.*	ikh **hah**-beh glewk

Who's Who

This is...of mine.	*Das ist... von mir.*	dahs ist... fohn meer
...a male friend	*...ein Freund*	īn froynt
...a female friend	*...eine Freundin*	**ī**-neh **froyn**-din

This is my... (male / female)	*Das ist mein / meine...*	dahs ist mīn / **mī**-neh
...boyfriend / girlfriend.	*...Freund / Freundin.*	froynt / **froyn**-din
...husband / wife.	*...Mann / Frau.*	mahn / frow
...son / daughter.	*...Sohn / Tochter.*	zohn / **tohkh**-ter
...brother / sister.	*...Bruder / Schwester.*	**broo**-der / **shvehs**-ter
...father / mother.	*...Vater / Mutter.*	**fah**-ter / **moo**-ter
...uncle / aunt.	*...Onkel / Tante.*	**ohn**-kehl / **tahn**-teh
...nephew / niece.	*...Neffe / Nichte.*	**nehf**-feh / **neekh**-teh
...male / female cousin.	*...Vetter / Base.*	**feh**-ter / **bah**-zeh
...grandfather / grandmother.	*...Großvater / Großmutter.*	**grohs**-fah-ter / **grohs**-moo-ter
...grandson / granddaughter.	*...Enkel / Enkelin.*	**ehn**-kehl / **ehn**-kehl-in

Family

Are you married?	*Sind Sie verheiratet?*	zint zee fehr-**hī**-rah-teht
Do you have children?	*Haben Sie Kinder?*	**hah**-behn zee **kin**-der
How many boys / girls?	*Wie viele Jungen / Mädchen?*	vee **fee**-leh **yoong**-ehn / **mayd**-khehn
Do you have photos?	*Haben Sie Fotos?*	**hah**-behn zee **foh**-tohs
How old is your child?	*Wie alt ist Ihr Kind?*	vee ahlt ist eer kint
Beautiful child!	*Schönes Kind!*	**shur**-nehs kint
Beautiful children!	*Schöne Kinder!*	**shur**-neh **kin**-der

Work

What is your occupation?	*Was machen Sie beruflich?*	vahs **mahkh**-ehn zee beh-**roof**-likh
Do you like your work?	*Gefällt Ihnen Ihre Arbeit?*	geh-**fehlt ee**-nehn **eer**-eh **ar**-bīt
I'm a student (male / female).	*Ich bin Student / Studentin.*	ikh bin shtoo-**dehnt** / shtoo-**dehnt**-in

CHATTING

CHATTING

I'm studying	*Ich studiere, um*	ikh shtoo-**deer**-eh oom
to work in...	*in... zu arbeiten.*	in... tsoo **ar**-bīt-ehn
I work in...	*Ich arbeite in...*	ikh **ar**-bīt-eh in
I used to work in...	*Ich habe in...*	ikh **hah**-beh in...
	gearbeitet.	geh-**ar**-bīt-eht
I want a job in...	*Ich möchte eine*	ikh **murkh**-teh ī-neh
	Stelle in...	**shteh**-leh in
...accounting.	*...Buchhaltung*	**bookh**-hahl-toong
...the medical field.	*...Medizin*	meh-deh-**tseen**
...social services.	*...Sozialwesen*	zoh-tsee-**ahl**-vay-zehn
...the legal	*...Rechtswesen*	**rehkhts**-vay-zehn
profession.		
...banking.	*...Finanz*	fee-**nahnts**
...business.	*...Management*	"management"
...government.	*...Verwaltung*	fehr-**vahl**-toong
...engineering.	*...Technik*	tehkh-**neek**
...public relations.	*...Öffentlichkeits-*	**urf**-ehnt-likh-kīts-
	arbeit	**ar**-bīt
...science.	*...Wissenschaft*	**vis**-sehn-shahft
...teaching.	*...Schulwesen*	**shool**-vay-zehn
...the computer	*...Informatik*	in-for-**mah**-teek
field.		
...the travel industry.	*...Reiseindustrie*	**rī**-zeh-in-doos-**tree**
...the arts.	*...Kunstgewerbe*	**koonst**-geh-vehr-beh
...journalism.	*...Journalismus*	yorn-ahl-**ees**-moos
...a restaurant.	*...einem*	**ī**-nehm
	Restaurant	rehs-tow-**rahnt**
...a store.	*...einem Laden*	**ī**-nehm **lah**-dehn
...a factory.	*...einer Fabrik*	**ī**-ner fah-**breek**
I am...	*Ich bin...*	ikh bin
...unemployed.	*...arbeitslos.*	**ar**-bīts-lohs
...retired.	*...pensioniert.*	pehn-zee-ohn-**eert**
...a professional	*...professioneller*	proh-fehs-see-ohn-**neh**-ler
traveler.	*Reisender.*	**rī**-zehn-der
Do you have a...?	*Haben Sie eine...?*	**hah**-behn zee **ī**-neh

Here is my / our...	*Hier ist meine / unsere...*	heer ist **mī**-neh / **oon**-zer-eh
...business card.	*...Visitenkarte.*	vi-**zee**-tehn-kar-teh
...email address.	*...Email-Adresse.*	**ee**-mayl ah-**dreh**-seh

Chatting with Children

What's your name?	*Wie heißt du?*	vee hīst doo
My name is ___.	*Ich heiße ___.*	ikh **hī**-seh
How old are you?	*Wie alt bist du?*	vee ahlt bist doo
How old am I?	*Wie alt bin ich?*	vee ahlt bin ikh
I'm ___ years old.	*Ich bin ___ Jahre alt.*	ikh bin ___ **yah**-reh ahlt
Do you have siblings?	*Hast du Geschwister?*	hahst doo geh-**shvis**-ter
Do you like school?	*Magst du die Schule?*	mahgst doo dee **shoo**-leh
What are you studying?	*Was studierst du?*	vahs shtoo-**deerst** doo
What's your favorite subject?	*Was ist dein Lieblingsfach?*	vahs ist dīn **lee**-blings-fahkh
What is this?	*Was ist das?*	vahs ist dahs
Will you teach me / us some German words?	*Bringst du mir / uns einige deutsche Wörter bei?*	bringst doo meer / oons **ī**-nig-eh **doy**-cheh **vur**-ter bī
Will you teach me / us a simple German song?	*Kannst du mir / uns ein einfaches deutsches Lied beibringen?*	kahnst doo meer / oons īn **in**-fahkh-ehs **doy**-chehs leet **bī**-bring-ehn
Guess which country I live / we live in.	*Rate mal, in welchem Land ich wohne / wir wohnen.*	**rah**-teh mahl in **vehlkh**-ehm lahnt ikh **voh**-neh / veer **voh**-nehn
Do you have pets?	*Hast du Haustiere?*	hahst doo **hows**-teer-eh
I have...	*Ich habe...*	ikh **hah**-beh
We have...	*Wir haben...*	veer **hah**-behn
...a cat / a dog / a fish / a bird	*...eine Katze / einen Hund / einen Fisch / einen Vogel*	**ī**-neh **kaht**-seh / **ī**-nehn hoont / **ī**-nehn fish / **ī**-nehn **voh**-gehl

CHATTING

Want to hear me burp?	Willst du meinen Rülpser hören?	vilst doo **mī**-nehn **rewlp**-zer **hur**-ehn
Teach me a fun game.	Bringe mir ein lustiges Spiel bei.	**bring**-eh meer īn **loo**-shtig-ehs shpeel bī
Got any candy?	Hast du Süßigkeiten?	hahst doo **zew**-sig-kī-tehn
Want to thumb-wrestle?	Willst du Daumenziehen?	vilst doo **dow**-mehn-tsee-hehn
Give me a handshake.	Handschlag.	**hahnt**-shlahg

If you do break into song, you'll find the words for "Happy Birthday" on page 23, and words to more songs beginning on page 257.

German kids usually shake hands instead of doing a "high five," but teaching them can be a fun icebreaker. Just say "*So machen wir das in Amerika*" ("This is how we do it in America") and give 'em five!

Travel Talk

I am / Are you...?	Ich bin / Sind Sie...?	ikh bin / zint zee
...on vacation	...auf Urlaub	owf **oor**-lowp
...on business	...auf Geschäftsreise	owf geh-**shehfts**-rī-zeh
How long have you been traveling?	Wie lange sind Sie schon unterwegs?	vee **lahng**-eh zint zee shohn oont-er-**vehgs**
day / week	Tag / Woche	tahg / **vohkh**-eh
month / year	Monat / Jahr	**moh**-naht / yar
When are you going home?	Wann fahren Sie zurück?	vahn **far**-ehn zee tsoo-**rewk**
This is my first time in ___.	Ich bin zum ersten Mal in ___.	ikh bin tsoom **ehr**-stehn mahl in
This is our first time in ___.	Wir sind zum ersten Mal in ___.	veer zint tsoom **ehr**-stehn mahl in
It's (not) a tourist trap.	Es ist (nicht) nur für Touristen.	ehs ist (nikht) noor fewr too-**ris**-tehn
This is paradise.	Das ist das Paradies.	dahs ist dahs **pah**-rah-dees

CHATTING

This is a wonderful country.	Dies ist ein wunderbares Land.	deez ist īn **voon**-dehr-bah-rehs lahnt
The Germans / Austrians / Swiss...	Die Deutschen / Österreicher / Schweizer...	dee **doy**-chehn / **urs**-teh-rīkh-er / **shvīt**-ser
...are friendly / boring / rude.	...sind freundlich / langweilig / unhöflich.	zint **froynd**-likh / **lahng**-vī-lig / oon-**hurf**-likh
So far...	Bis jetzt...	bis yehtst
Today...	Heute...	**hoy**-teh
...I have seen ___ and ___.	...habe ich ___ und ___ gesehen.	**hah**-beh ikh ___ oont ___ geh-**zay**-hehn
...we have seen ___.	...haben wir ___ gesehen.	**hah**-behn veer ___ geh-**zay**-hehn
Next...	Nächste...	**nehkh**-steh
Tomorrow...	Morgen...	**mor**-gehn
...I will see ___.	...werde ich ___ sehen.	**vehr**-deh ikh ___ **zay**-hehn
...we will see ___.	...werden wir ___ sehen.	**vehr**-dehn veer ___ **zay**-hehn
Yesterday...	Gestern...	**geh**-stern
...I saw ___.	...habe ich ___ gesehen.	**hah**-beh ikh ___ geh-**zay**-hehn
...we saw ___.	...haben wir ___ gesehen.	**hah**-behn veer ___ geh-**zay**-hehn
My / Our vacation is ___ days long, starting in ___ and ending in ___.	Meine / Unsere Ferien dauern ___ Tage, fangen in ___ an und enden in ___.	**mī**-neh / **oon**-zer-eh **fay**-ree-ehn **dow**-ern ___ **tah**-geh, **fahng**-ehn in ___ ahn oont **ehn**-dehn in ___
Travel is enlightening.	Reisen ist aufschlußreich.	**rī**-zehn ist **owf**-schloos-rīkh
I wish all (American) politicians traveled.	Ich wünschte alle (amerikanischen) Politiker würden reisen.	ikh **vewnsh**-teh **ah**-leh (ah-mehr-i-**kahn**-ish-ehn) poh-**lee**-tik-er vewr-dehn **rī**-zehn
Have a good trip!	Gute Reise!	**goo**-teh **rī**-zeh
To travel is to live.	Reisen heißt leben.	**rī**-zehn hīst **lay**-behn

Map Musings

These phrases and maps will help you delve into family history and explore travel dreams.

I live here.	*Ich wohne hier.*	ikh **voh**-neh heer
We live here.	*Wir wohnen hier.*	veer **voh**-nehn heer
I was born here.	*Ich bin hier geboren.*	ikh bin heer geh-**boh**-rehn
My ancestors came from ___.	*Meine Vorfahren kamen aus ___.*	**mī**-neh **for**-far-ehn **kah**-mehn ows
I'd like/We'd like to go to ___.	*Ich möchte / Wir möchten nach ___ gehen.*	ich **murkh**-teh / veer **murkh**-tehn nahkh ___ **gay**-hehn
I've / We've traveled to ___.	*Ich bin / Wir sind in ___ gewesen.*	ikh bin / veer zint in ___ geh-**vay**-zehn
Next I'll go to ___.	*Als Nächstes gehe ich nach ___.*	als **nehkh**-stehs **gay**-heh ikh nahkh
Next we'll go to ___.	*Als Nächstes gehen wir nach ___.*	als **nehkh**-stehs **gay**-hehn veer nahkh
Where do you live?	*Wo wohnen Sie?*	voh **voh**-nehn zee
Where were you born?	*Wo sind Sie geboren?*	voh zint zee geh-**boh**-rehn
Where did your ancestors come from?	*Woher kommen Ihre Vorfahren?*	voh-hehr **koh**-mehn **ee**-reh **for**-far-ehn
Where have you traveled?	*Wo sind Sie schon gewesen?*	voh zint zee shohn geh-**vay**-zehn
Where are you going?	*Wohin gehen Sie?*	voh-hin **gay**-hehn zee
Where would you like to go?	*Wohin möchten Sie?*	voh-hin **murkh**-tehn zee

Favorite Things

What is your favorite...?	*Was ist Ihr Lieblings...?*	vahs ist eer **lee**-bleengs
What kind of... do you like?	*Welche Art... mögen Sie?*	**wehlkh**-eh art... **mur**-gehn zee

Germany

Austria

Switzerland

Europe

CHATTING

The United States

The World

...art	...Kunst	koonst
...book	...Buch	bookh
...hobby	...Hobby	"hobby"
...ice cream	...Eis	īs
...food	...Essen	**eh**-sehn
...movie	...Film	"film"
...music	...Musik	moo-**zeek**
...sport	...Sport	shport
...vice	...Sünde	**zewn**-deh
Who is your favorite...?	Wer ist Ihr Lieblings...?	vayr ist eer **lee**-bleengs
...movie star	...Filmstar	"filmstar"
...male singer	...Sänger	**zehng**-er
...male artist	...Künstler	**kewnst**-ler
...male author	...Schriftsteller	**shrift**-shteh-ler
...female singer	...Sängerin	**zehng**-er-in
...female artist	...Künstlerin	**kewnst**-ler-in
...female author	...Schriftstellerin	**shrift**-shteh-ler-in
Can you recommend a good German CD?	Können Sie eine gute deutsche CD empfehlen?	**kurn**-nehn zee **ī**-neh **goo**-teh **doy**-cheh say-day ehmp-**fay**-lehn
Can you recommend a good German book translated in English?	Können Sie ein gutes deutsches Buch, in Englisch übersetzt empfehlen?	**kurn**-nehn zee īn **goo**-tehs **doy**-chehs bookh in **ehng**-lish ew-ber-**zehtst** ehmp-**fay**-lehn

Weather

What's the weather tomorrow?	Wie wird das Wetter morgen?	vee virt dahs **veh**-ter **mor**-gehn
sunny / cloudy	sonnig / bewölkt	**zoh**-nig / beh-**vurlkt**
hot / cold	heiß / kalt	hīs / kahlt
muggy / windy	schwül / windig	shvewl / **vin**-dig
rain / snow	Regen / Schnee	**ray**-gehn / shnay
Should I bring a jacket?	Soll ich eine Jacke mitbringen?	zohl ikh **ī**-neh **yah**-keh **mit**-bring-ehn

CHATTING

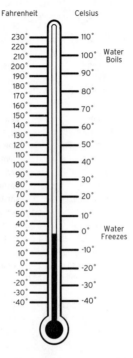

Fahrenheit   Celsius

230° — — 110°
220° —
210° — — 100°   Water
200° —   Boils
190° — — 90°
180° —
170° — — 80°
160° —
150° — — 70°
140° —
130° — — 60°
120° —
110° — — 50°
100° —
90° — — 40°
80° —
70° — — 30°
60° —
50° — — 20°
40° —
30° — — 10°
20° —
10° — — 0°   Water
0° —   Freezes
-10° — — -10°
-20° —
-30° — — -20°
-40° —
            — -30°
            — -40°

It's raining buckets.	Es regnet wie aus Kübeln.	ehs **rayg**-neht vee ows **kew**-behln
The fog is like milk soup.	Das ist eine Milchsuppe.	dahs ist **ī**-neh **milkh**-zoo-peh
It's so hot you can boil an egg on the sidewalk.	Es ist so heiß, daß man Eier auf dem Gehsteig braten kann.	es ist zo hīs dahs mahn **ī**-er owf daym **geh**-shtīg **brah**-tehn kahn
The wind could blow your ears off.	Der Wind könnte mir die Ohren wegblasen.	dehr vint **kurn**-teh meer dee **or**-ehn **vehg**-blah-zehn

Thanks a Million

Thank you very much.	*Vielen Dank.*	**fee**-lehn dahngk
This is great fun.	*Das ist ein Riesenspaß.*	dahs ist īn **ree**-zehn-shpahs
You are...	*Sie sind...*	zee zint
...helpful.	*...hilfreich.*	**hilf**-rīkh
...wonderful.	*...wunderbar.*	**voon**-der-bar
...generous.	*...großzügig.*	**grohs**-tsew-gig
You spoil me / us.	*Sie verwöhnen mich / uns.*	zee fehr-**vur**-nehn mikh / oons
You've been a great help.	*Sie waren sehr hilfreich.*	zee **vah**-rehn zehr **hilf**-rīkh
You are an angel from God.	*Sie sind ein Engel, von Gott gesandt.*	zee zint īn **ehng**-ehl fohn goht geh-**zahndt**
I will remember you...	*Ich werde Sie... in Erinnerung behalten.*	ikh **vehr**-deh zee... in eh-**rin**-er-oong beh-**hahl**-tehn
We will remember you...	*Wir werden Sie... in Erinnerung behalten.*	veer **vehr**-dehn zee... in eh-**rin**-er-oong beh-**hahl**-tehn
...always.	*...immer*	**im**-mer
...till Tuesday.	*...bis Dienstag*	bis **deen**-stahg

Smoking

Do you smoke?	*Rauchen Sie?*	**rowkh**-ehn zee
Do you smoke pot?	*Rauchen Sie Haschisch?*	**rowkh**-ehn zee hah-**sheesh**
I (don't) smoke.	*Ich rauche (nicht).*	ikh **rowkh**-eh (nikht)
We (don't) smoke.	*Wir rauchen (nicht).*	veer **rowkh**-ehn (nikht)
I haven't any.	*Ich habe keine.*	ikh **hah**-beh **kī**-neh
lighter	*Feuerzeug*	**foy**-er-tsoyg
cigarettes	*Zigaretten*	tsig-ah-**reh**-tehn
marijuana	*Marihuana*	mah-ri-**wah**-nah
hash	*Haschisch*	hah-**sheesh**

joint	*Joint, Kiffe*	"joint," **ki**-feh
stoned	*benebelt*	beh-**nay**-behlt
Wow!	*Woah!*	woh-**ah**

Responses for All Occasions

I like that.	*Das gefällt mir.*	dahs geh-**fehlt** meer
We like that.	*Das gefällt uns.*	dahs geh-**fehlt** oons
I like you.	*Sie gefallen mir.*	zee geh-**fah**-lehn meer
We like you.	*Sie gefallen uns.*	zee geh-**fah**-lehn oons
That's cool!	*Hey, cool! Toll!*	"hey, cool," tohl
Excellent!	*Ausgezeichnet!*	ows-geh-**tsikh**-neht
What a nice place.	*Was für ein herrlicher Ort.*	vahs fewr īn **hehr**-likh-er ort
Perfect.	*Perfekt.*	pehr-**fehkt**
Funny.	*Komisch.*	**koh**-mish
Interesting.	*Interessant.*	in-tehr-eh-**sahnt**
Really?	*Wirklich?*	**virk**-likh
Wow!	*Woah!*	woh-**ah**
Congratulations!	*Herzlichen Glückwunsch!*	**hehrts**-likh-ehn **glewk**-voonsh
Well done!	*Gut gemacht!*	goot geh-**mahkht**
You're welcome.	*Bitte schön.*	**bit**-teh shurn
Bless you! (after sneeze)	*Gesundheit!*	geh-**zoond**-hīt
What a pity.	*Wie schade.*	vee **shah**-deh
That's life.	*So geht's eben.*	zoh gayts **ay**-behn
No problem.	*Kein Problem.*	kīn proh-**blaym**
O.K.	*O.K.*	"O.K."
This is the good life!	*So läßt es sich leben!*	zoh lehst ehs zikh **lay**-ben
Have a good day!	*Schönen Tag!*	**shurn**-ehn tahg
Good luck!	*Viel Glück!*	feel glewk
Let's go!	*Auf geht's!*	owf gayts

CHATTING

Conversing with Animals

rooster / cock-a-doodle-doo	Hahn / kikeriki	hahn / kee-keh-ree-**kee**
bird / tweet tweet	Vogel / piep piep	**foh**-gehl / peep peep
cat / meow	Katze / miau	**kaht**-seh / mee-**ow**
dog / woof woof	Hund / wuff wuff	hoont / vuff vuff
duck / quack quack	Ente / quak quak	**ehn**-teh / kvahk kvahk
cow / moo	Kuh / muh	koo / moo
pig / oink oink	Schwein / nöff nöff	shvīn / nurf nurf

Profanity

People make animal noises too. These words will help you understand what the more colorful locals are saying...

Go to hell!	Geh zur Hölle!	gay tsur **hurl**-leh
Damn it.	Verdammt.	fehr-**dahmt**
bastard (pig-dog)	Schweinehund	**shvī**-neh-hoont
bitch (goat)	Ziege	**tsee**-geh
breasts (colloq.)	Titten	**tit**-ehn
penis (colloq.)	Schwanz	shvahnts
butthole	Arschloch	**arsh**-lohkh
drunk	besoffen	beh-**zohf**-fehn
idiot	Idiot	id-ee-**oht**
imbecile	Trottel	**troh**-tehl
jerk	Blödmann	**blurd**-mahn
stupid (dumb head)	Dummkopf	**doom**-kohpf
Did someone fart?	Hat jemand gefurzt?	haht **yay**-mahnt geh-**foortst**
I burped.	Ich habe gerülpst.	ikh **hah**-beh geh-**rewlpst**
This sucks.	Das ödet an.	dahs **ur**-deht ahn
Shit.	Scheiße.	**shī**-seh
Bullshit.	Blödsinn.	**blurd**-zin
Sit on it.	Am Arsch.	ahm arsh
Shit on it.	Scheiß drauf.	shīs drowf
You are...	Du bist...	doo bist

Don't be...	Sei kein...	zī kīn
...a "shit guy."	...Scheißkerl.	**shīs**-kehrl
...an asshole.	...Arschloch.	**arsh**-lohkh
...an idiot.	...Idiot.	id-ee-**oht**
...a creep.	...Psychopath.	**psew**-koh-paht
...a cretin.	...Blödmann.	**blurd**-mahn
...a pig.	...Schwein.	shvīn

Sweet Curses

My goodness.	Meine Güte.	**mī**-neh **gew**-teh
Goodness gracious.	Ach du liebe Zeit.	ahkh doo **lee**-beh tsīt
Oh, my gosh.	Oh, Jemine.	oh **yeh**-mee-neh
Shoot.	Scheibenkleister.	**shī**-behn-klī-ster
Darn it!	Verflixt!	fehr-**flikst**

CREATE YOUR OWN CONVERSATION

You can mix and match these words into a conversation. Make it as deep or silly as you want.

Who

I / you	ich / Sie	ikh / zee
he / she	er / sie	ehr / zee
we / they	wir / sie	veer / zee
my / your...	mein / Ihr...	mīn / eer
...parents / children	...Eltern / Kinder	**ehl**-tern / **kin**-der
men / women	Männer / Frauen	**mehn**-ner / **frow**-ehn
rich / poor people	Reichen / Armen	**rīkh**-ehn / **ar**-mehn
young / old people	Junge / Alte	**yoong**-eh /**ahl**-teh
middle-aged people	Mittelalterliche	**mit**-ehl-ahl-ter-likh-eh
Germans	Deutschen	**doy**-chehn
Austrians	Österreicher	**urs**-teh-rīkh-er
Swiss	Schweizer	**shvīt**-ser
Czechs	Tschechen	**chehkh**-ehn
French	Franzosen	frahn-**tsoh**-zehn
Italians	Italiener	i-tah-lee-**ehn**-er

CHATTING

Europeans	Europäer	oy-roh-**pay**-er
EU (European Union)	EU	ay oo
Americans	Amerikaner	ah-mehr-ee-**kahn**-er
liberals	Liberale	lib-eh-**rah**-leh
conservatives	Konservative	kohn-zehr-vah-**teev**-eh
radicals	Radikale	rah-di-**kah**-leh
terrorists	Terroristen	tehr-or-**ist**-ehn
politicians	Politiker	poh-**lee**-tik-er
big business	Großkapital	**grohs**-kahp-i-**tahl**
multinational corporations	Multis	**mool**-tees
military	Militär	mil-ee-**tehr**
mafia	Mafia	"mafia"
Neo-Nazis	Neonazis	"Neo-Nazis"
eastern Germany	Ostdeutschland	**ohst**-doych-lahnt
western Germany	Westen von Deutschland	**vehs**-tehn fohn **doych**-lahnt
eastern / western Germans	Ostdeutscher/ Westdeutscher	**ohst**-doy-cher/ **vehst**-doy-cher
refugees	Flüchtlinge	**flewkht**-ling-eh
travelers	Reisende	**rī**-zehn-deh
God	Gott	goht
Christians	Christen	**kris**-tehn
Catholics	Katholiken	kah-**toh**-li-kehn
Protestants	Protestanten	proh-tehs-**tahn**-tehn
Jews	Juden	**yoo**-dehn
Muslims	Moslems	**mohz**-lehms
everyone	alle Leute	**ah**-leh **loy**-teh

What

buy / sell	kaufen / verkaufen	**kow**-fehn / fehr-**kow**-fehn
have / lack	haben / haben nicht	**hah**-behn / **hah**-behn nikht
help / abuse	helfen / mißbrauchen	**hehl**-fehn / mis-**browkh**-ehn

learn / fear	lernen / fürchten	**lehrn**-ehn / **fewrkh**-tehn
love / hate	lieben / hassen	**lee**-behn / **hah**-sehn
prosper / suffer	florieren / leiden	floh-**ree**-rehn / **lī**-dehn
take / give	nehmen / geben	**nay**-mehn / **gay**-behn
want / need	wollen / brauchen	**vol**-lehn / **browkh**-ehn
work / play	arbeiten / spielen	**ar**-bīt-ehn / **shpeel**-ehn

Why

(anti-)	(Anti-)	(**ahn**-tee-)
globalization	Globalisierung	gloh-bahl-is-**eer**-oong
class warfare	Klassenkampf	**klahs**-ehn-kahmpf
corruption	Korruption	kor-rupt-see-**ohn**
democracy	Demokratie	day-moh-krah-**tee**
education	Ausbildung	**ows**-bil-doong
family	Familie	fah-**mee**-lee-eh
food	Essen	**eh**-sehn
guns	Waffen	**vah**-fehn
happiness	Glück	glewk
health	Gesundheit	geh-**zoond**-hīt
hope	Hoffnung	**hohf**-noong
imperialism	Kolonisation	koh-loh-nee-saht-see-**ohn**
lies	Lügen	**lew**-gehn
love / sex	Liebe / Sex	**lee**-beh / zehx
marijuana	Marihuana	mah-ri-**wah**-nah
money / power	Geld / Macht	gehlt / mahkht
pollution	Umweltverschmutzung	**oom**-vehlt-fehr-**shmut**-tsoong
racism	Rassismus	rah-**sis**-moos
regime change	Regimewechsel	reh-**zheem**-vehkh-sehl
relaxation	Entspannung	ehnt-**shpah**-noong
religion	Religion	reh-leeg-ee-**ohn**
respect	Respekt	rehs-**pehkt**
reunification	Wiedervereinigung	**vee**-dehr-fehr-**īn**-i-goong

taxes	*Steuern*	**shtoy**-ern
television	*Fernsehen*	**fehrn**-zay-hehn
violence	*Gewalt*	geh-**vahlt**
war / peace	*Krieg / Frieden*	kreeg / **free**-dehn
work	*Arbeit*	**ar**-bīt
global perspective	*Gesamt- perspektive*	geh-**zahmt**- per-spehk-**tee**-veh

You Be the Judge

(no) problem	*(kein) Problem*	(kīn) proh-**blaym**
(not) good	*(nicht) gut*	(nikht) goot
(not) dangerous	*(nicht) gefährlich*	(nikht) geh-**fehr**-likh
(not) fair	*(nicht) fair*	(nikht) "fair"
(not) guilty	*(nicht) schuldig*	(nikht) **shool**-dig
(not) powerful	*(nicht) mächtig*	(nikht) **mehkh**-tig
(not) stupid	*(nicht) dumm*	(nikht) doom
(not) happy	*(nicht) glücklich*	(nikht) **glewk**-likh
because / for	*weil / wegen*	vīl / **vay**-gehn
and / or / from	*und / oder / von*	oont / **oh**-dehr / fohn
too much	*zu viel*	tsoo feel
(never) enough	*nie) genug*	(nee) geh-**noog**
same	*gleich*	glīkh
better / worse	*besser / schlechter*	**behs**-ser / **shlehkh**-ter
here / everywhere	*hier / überall*	heer / ew-ber-**ahl**

Beginnings and Endings

I like...	*Ich mag...*	ikh mahg
We like...	*Wir mögen...*	veer **mur**-gehn
I don't like...	*Ich mag... nicht.*	ikh mahg... nikht
We don't like...	*Wir mögen... nicht.*	veer **mur**-gehn... nikht
Do you like...?	*Mögen Sie...?*	**mur**-gehn zee
In the past...	*Früher...*	**frew**-her
When I was younger, I thought...	*Als ich jünger war, dachte ich...*	ahls ikh **yewng**-er var, **dahkh**-teh ikh
Now, I think...	*Jetzt denke ich...*	yetst **dehnk**-eh ikh

I am / Are you...?	Ich bin / Sind Sie...?	ikh bin / zint zee
...an optimist / pessimist	...ein Optimist / Pessimist	īn **ohp**-ti-meest / **pehs**-i-meest
I believe in...	Ich glaube an...	ikh **glow**-beh ahn
I don't believe in...	Ich glaube nicht an...	ikh **glow**-beh nikht ahn
Do you believe in...?	Glauben Sie an...?	**glow**-behn zee ahn
...God	...Gott	goht
...life after death	...Leben nach dem Tod	**lay**-behn nahkh daym tohd
...extraterrestrial life	...Leben im Weltall	**lay**-behn im **vehlt**-ahl
...Santa Claus	...Weihnachtsmann	**vī**-nahkhts-mahn
Yes. / No.	Ja. / Nein.	yah / nīn
Maybe. / I don't know.	Vielleicht. / Ich weiß nicht.	fee-**līkht** / ikh vīs nikht
What is most important in life?	Was ist das Wichtigste im Leben?	vahs ist dahs **vikh**-tig-steh im **lay**-behn
The problem is...	Das Problem ist...	dahs proh-**blaym** ist
The answer is...	Die Antwort ist...	dee **ahnt**-vort ist
We have solved the world's problems.	Wir haben die Probleme der Welt gelöst.	veer **hah**-behn dee proh-**blay**-meh dehr vehlt geh-**lurst**

A GERMAN ROMANCE

Words of Love

I / me / you / we	ich / mich / dich / wir	ikh / mikh / dikh / veer
flirt	flirten	**flir**-tehn
kiss	Kuß	kus
hug	Umarmung	oom-**arm**-oong
love	Liebe	**lee**-beh
make love (sleep together)	miteinander schlafen	mit-īn-**ahn**-dehr **shlah**-fehn
condom	Kondom, Präservativ	**kon**-dohm, pray-zehr-fah-**tif**
contraceptive	Verhütungs-mittel	fehr-**hew**-toongs-**mit**-tehl

safe sex	safe sex	"safe sex"
sexy	sexy	"sexy"
cozy	gemütlich	geh-**mewt**-likh
romantic	romantisch	roh-**mahn**-tish
cupcake	Schnuckel	**shnook**-ehl
little rabbit	Häschen	**hay**-shyehn
little sugar mouse	Zuckermäuschen	**tsoo**-ker-**moy**-shyehn
pussy cat	Miezekatze	**meets**-eh-**kaht**-seh
baby	Baby	"baby"

Ah, Liebe

What's the matter?	Was ist los?	vahs ist lohs
Nothing.	Nichts.	nikhts
I am / Are you...?	Ich bin / Sind Sie...?	ikh bin / zint zee
...straight	...hetero	**hay**-ter-oh
...gay	...schwul	shvul
...bisexual	...bisexual	bee-zeks-oo-**ahl**
...undecided	...mir nicht sicher	meer nikht **zikh**-er
...prudish	...verklemmt	fehr-**klehmt**
...horny	...geil	gīl
We are on our honeymoon.	Wir sind auf unserer Hochzeitsreise.	veer zint owf **oon**-zer-er **hohkh**-tsīts-rī-zeh
I have...	Ich habe...	ikh **hah**-beh
...a boyfriend.	...einen Freund.	**ī**-nehn froynt
...a girlfriend.	...eine Freundin.	**ī**-neh **froyn**-din
I'm married, but...	Ich bin verheiratet, aber...	ikh bin fehr-**hī**-rah-teht **ah**-ber
I'm not married.	Ich bin nicht verheiratet.	ikh bin nikht fehr-**hī**-rah-teht
Do you have a boyfriend / a girlfriend?	Haben Sie einen Freund / eine Freundin?	**hah**-behn zee **ī**-nehn froynt / **ī**-neh **froyn**-din
I'm adventurous.	Ich bin auf Abenteuer aus.	ikh bin owf **ah**-behn-toy-er ows
I'm lonely (tonight).	Ich bin einsam (heut' Nacht).	ikh bin **īn**-zahm (hoyt nahkht)

CHATTING

I'm rich and single.	Ich bin reich und zu haben.	ikh bin rīkh oont tsoo **hah**-behn
Do you mind if I sit here?	Stört es Sie, wenn ich hier sitze?	shturt ehs zee vehn ikh heer **zit**-seh
Would you like a drink?	Möchten Sie einen Drink?	**murkh**-tehn zee **ī**-nehn drink
Will you go out with me?	Gehen Sie mit mir aus?	**gay**-hehn zee mit meer ows
Would you like to go out tonight for...?	Möchten Sie heute ausgehen für...?	**murkh**-tehn zee **hoy**-teh **ows**-gay-hehn fewr
...a walk	...einen Spaziergang	**ī**-nehn shpaht-**seer**-gahng
...dinner	...ein Abendessen	īn **ah**-behnt-eh-sehn
...a drink	...einen Drink	īn drink
Where's the best place to dance nearby?	Wo geht man hier am besten Tanzen?	voh gayt mahn heer ahm **beh**-stehn **tahn**-tsehn
Do you want to dance?	Möchten Sie tanzen?	**murkh**-tehn zee **tahn**-tsehn
Again?	Noch einmal?	nokh **ī**-mahl
Let's party!	Feiern wir!	**fī**-ern veer
Let's have fun like idiots!	Feiern wir wie blöd!	**fī**-ern veer vee blurd
Let's have a wild and crazy night!	Machen wir einen 'drauf!	**mahkh**-ehn veer **ī**-nehn drowf
I have no diseases.	Ich habe keine Krankheiten.	ikh **hah**-behh **kī**-neh **krahnk**-hī-tehn
I have many diseases.	Ich habe viele Krankheiten.	ikh **hah**-beh **fee**-leh **krahnk**-hī-tehn
I have only safe sex.	Mit mir nur safe sex.	mit meer noor "safe sex"
Can I take you home?	Kann ich Sie nach Hause bringen?	kahn ikh zee nahkh **how**-zeh **bring**-ehn
Why not?	Warum nicht?	vah-**room** nikht
How can I change your mind?	Wie kann ich Sie umstimmen?	vee kahn ikh zee **oom**-shtim-mehn

Kiss me.	Küß mich.	kews mikh
May I kiss you?	Darf ich dich küssen?	darf ikh dikh **kews**-ehn
Can I see you again?	Können wir uns wiedersehen?	**kurn**-nehn veer oons **vee**-der-zayn
Your place or mine?	Bei dir oder bei mir?	bī deer **oh**-der bī meer
How does this feel?	Wie fühlt sich das an?	vee fewlt zikh dahs ahn
Is this an aphrodisiac?	Ist dies ein Aphrodisiakum?	ist deez īn ah-froh-dee-zee-**ahk**-oom
This is (not) my first time.	Dies ist für mich (nicht) das erste Mal.	deez ist fewr mikh (nikht) dahs **ehr**-steh mahl
You are my most beautiful souvenir.	Du bist mein schönstes Andenken.	doo bist mīn **shurn**-stehs **ahn**-dehnk-ehn
Do you do this often?	Machst du das oft?	mahkhst doo dahs oft
Do I have bad breath?	Habe ich Mundgeruch?	**hah**-beh ikh **moont**-geh-rookh
Let's just be friends.	Wir können doch einfach Freunde sein.	veer **kurn**-nehn dohkh **īn**-fahkh **froyn**-deh zīn
I'll pay for my share.	Ich bezahle meinen Anteil.	ikh beht-**sah**-leh **mī**-nehn **ahn**-tīl
Would you like a... massage?	Darf ich dir den... massieren?	darf ikh deer dayn... mah-**see**-rehn
...back	...Rücken	**rew**-kehn
...foot	...Fuß	foos
Why not?	Warum nicht?	vah-**room** nikht
Try it.	Versuch's doch mal.	fehr-**zookhs** dokh mahl
That tickles.	Das kitzelt.	dahs **kit**-sehlt
Oh my God!	Oh mein Gott!	oh mīn goht
I love you.	Ich liebe dich.	ikh **lee**-beh dikh
Darling, marry me!	Liebling, heirate mich!	**lee**-bleeng **hī**-rah-teh mikh

CHATTING

DICTIONARY

GERMAN/ENGLISH

A

A-Affenschwanz	"at" sign (@)
Abend	evening
Abendessen	dinner
aber	but
abfahren	depart
Abfahrten	departures
Abflußstöpsel	sink stopper
Abführmittel	decongestant
Abschleppwagen	tow truck
abschließen	lock (v)
abstempeln	validate
abstrakt	abstract
Abtreibung	abortion
Adresse	address
Afrika	Africa
aggressiv	aggressive
agnostisch	agnostic
ähnlich	similar
AIDS	AIDS
Alkohol	alcohol
allein	alone
Allergien	allergies
allergisch	allergic
alles	everything
alt	old
Altar	altar
Alter	age
altertümlich	ancient
am besten	best
Ampel	stoplight
anderes	other
ändern	change (v)
anfangen	begin
ängstlich	shy, afraid
Anhalter fahren	hitchhike
ankommen	arrive
Ankunften	arrivals
annullieren	cancel
Anschluß	connection
anstatt	instead
ansteckend	contagious
Antibiotika	antibiotic
Antiquitäten	antiques
Antiquitäten-laden	antiques shop

Antwort	answer
Anus	rectum
Anwalt	lawyer
Apfel	apple
Apfelsine	orange (fruit)
Apotheke	pharmacy
April	April
Arbeit	work (n)
arbeiten	work (v)
arbeitslos	unemployed
Arm	arm
arm	poor
Armband	bracelet
Ärmel	sleeves
Arzt	doctor
Aschenbecher	ashtray
Atem	breath
atheistisch	atheist
attraktiv	attractive
auf	on
auf dem Land	countryside
auf Wiedersehen	goodbye
aufwachen	wake up
aufwarmen	heat (v)
Auge	eye
Augenkontour	eyeliner
Augenschatten	eye shadow
August	August
Ausbildung	education
Ausblick	view
Ausfahrt	exit (road)
Ausgang	exit (door)
ausgeben	spend
ausgezeichnet	excellent
Ausschlag	rash
außer	except
Aussprache	pronunciation

Ausverkauf	clearance sale
Auto	car

B

BH (Büstenhalter)	bra
Baby	baby
Babygitter	playpen
Babynahrung	baby formula
Babypuder	talcum powder
Babysitter	babysitter
Bäckerei	bakery
Bad	bath; bathroom
Badeanzug	swimsuit
Badehose	swim trunks
Badelatschen	thongs
Bademantel	bathrobe
Badetuch	bath towel
Badewanne	bathtub
Bahnsteig	platform (train)
bald	soon
Balkon	balcony
Ball	ball
Banane	banana
Bank	bank
Bankomat	cash machine
Bargeld	cash
Bart	beard
Batterie	battery
Bauer	farmer
Bauernhof	farm
Baum	tree
Baumwolle	cotton
Baustelle	construction site
bearbeiten	edit
Bedienung	service
beeilen (sich)	hurry (v)

beenden	finish (v)
beendet	over (finished)
Beerdigung	funeral
behalten	keep
behindert	handicapped
bei	at
Bein	leg
Beispiel	example
Beleg	receipt
belegt	no vacancy
belegtes Brot	sandwich
Belgien	Belgium
benebelt	stoned
Ben-u-ron	non-aspirin substitute
Benzin	gas
beobachten	watch (v)
beraubt	robbed
bereit	ready
Berg	mountain
Beruf	job, profession
berühmt	famous
beschweren (sich)	complain
besetzt	occupied
besitzen	own (v)
Besitzer	owner
besonders	especially
besser	better
bestätigen	confirm
besten, am	best
Besuch	visit (n)
besuchen	visit (v)
betrunken	drunk
Bett	bed
Bettwäsche	sheets
bewölkt	cloudy
bewußtlos	unconscious
bezahlen	pay

bezaubernd	charming
Bier	beer
Bildhauer	sculptor
billig	cheap
Bindestrich	hyphen (-)
Birne	pear, bulb
bitte	please
Blase	bladder
Blasen	blisters
Blasen, Pflaster gegen	moleskin
blau	blue
Bleistift	pencil
Blick	view
Blinker	turn signal
Blitz	flash (camera)
Blume	flower
Blumenmarkt	flower market
Bluse	blouse
Blut	blood
bluten	bleeding
Bluthochdruck	high blood pressure
Boden	bottom
Bombe	bomb
Bonbons	candy
Botschaft	embassy
brauchen	need
braun	brown
Bremsen	brakes
Brief	letter
Briefmarke	stamp
Brieftasche	wallet
Briefumschlag	envelope
Brille	glasses (eye)
Brosche	brooch
Brot	bread

German	English
Brücke	bridge
Bruder	brother
Brunnen	well; fountain
Brust	chest
Brust, Schmerzen in der	chest pains
Buch	book
Buchhalter	accountant
Buchladen	book shop
Bund	waist
Burg	castle
Burggraben	moat
Burgmauer	wall, fortified
Büro	office
Bürobedarf	office supplies store
Büroklammer	paper clip
Busbahnhof	bus station
Busen	breast
Bushaltestelle	bus stop
Büstenhalter	bra

C

German	English
Chef	boss, manager
chinesisch	Chinese
Chor	choir
christlich	Christian (adj)

D

German	English
Dach	roof
Damen	women, ladies
Damenbinden	sanitary napkins
danke	thanks
Därme	intestines
Decke	blanket
Deckel	cap
deklarieren	declare (customs)

German	English
Demokratie	democracy
denken	think
Denkmal	monument
Desinfektionsmittel	disinfectant
Deutschland	Germany
Dezember	December
diabetisch	diabetic
Diamant	diamond
dick	thick; fat
Dieb	thief
Dienstag	Tuesday
Dienstleistung, mit	full-service
Ding	thing
direkt	direct
Dom	cathedral
Donau	Danube
Donnerstag	Thursday
doppel	double
Dorf	village
Dose	can (n)
Dosenöffner	can opener
dringend	urgent
drucken	print
drücken	push
du	you (informal)
dumm	stupid
dunkel	dark
dünn	thin, skinny
durch	through
Durchfall	diarrhea
Durchfall-medikament	diarrhea medicine
durchgehen	go through
durstig	thirsty
Dusche	shower
Dutzend	dozen

E

echt	genuine
Ecke	corner
Ehefrau	wife
Ehemann	husband
ehrlich	honest
Eimer	bucket
ein, noch	another
Einbahnstraße	one-way street
einfach	simple; easy; plain; one way (street)
Einfahrt	entrance (road)
Eingang	entrance (door)
eingeschlossen	included
einige	some
einkaufen	shopping
Einkaufszentrum	shopping mall
Einladung	invitation
einmal	once
einmal, noch	again; repeat
Eintrittskarte	ticket (show)
einverstanden	agree
Eis	ice; ice cream
Eisenbahn	railway
Eisenwaren- geschäft	hardware store
Eislaufen	ice skating
Ellbogen	elbow
Eltern	parents
E-mail-Adresse	email address
Empfangsperson	receptionist
empfehlen	recommend
eng	tight
Englisch	English
Enkel	grandson
Enkelin	granddaughter
Entschuldigung	excuse me; sorry
Entspannung	relaxation
Entzündung	infection, inflammation
Epilepsie	epilepsy
er	he
Erde	earth
erhalten	receive
erholen (sich)	relax (v)
erinnern (sich)	remember
Erkältung	cold (n)
erklären	explain
Ermäßigung	discount
Erneuerung	refill (n)
ernsthaft	serious
erschöpft	exhausted
erst	first
Erste Hilfe	first aid
erste Klasse	first class
Erste-Hilfe-Salbe	first-aid cream
Erwachsener	adult
Esel	donkey
essen	eat
Essen	food
etwas	something
Europa	Europe
evangelisch	Protestant

F

Fabrik	factory
Faden	thread
Fahne	flag
Fähre	ferry
fahren	drive (v)
fahren per Anhalter	hitchhike
Fahrer	driver
Fahrkarte	ticket (train or bus)

DICTIONARY

Fahrplan	timetable	**Flasche**	bottle
Fahrrad	bicycle	**Fleisch**	meat
Fahrstuhl	elevator	**fliegen**	fly
Fahrt	trip	**Floh**	flea
fair	fair (just)	**Flohmarkt**	flea market
fallen	fall (v)	**florieren**	prosper
falsch	false	**Floß**	raft
Familie	family	**Flüchtlinge**	refugees
fangen	catch (v)	**Flug**	flight
Farbe	color	**Flügel**	wing
farbenfest	color-fast	**Fluggesellschaft**	airline
faul	lazy	**Flughafen**	airport
Februar	February	**Flugkarte**	ticket (plane)
Fehler	mistake	**Flugzeug**	plane
Fehlgeburt	miscarriage	**Flur**	corridor
Feiertag	holiday	**Fluß**	river; stream (n)
Feinkostgeschäft	delicatessen	**Football**	American football
Feld	field	**Fotokopie**	photocopy
Fels	rock (n)	**Frage**	question (n)
Fenster	window	**fragen**	ask
Fernbus	long-distance bus	**Frankreich**	France
Fernseher	television	**Frau**	Mrs.
Festival	festival	**Fräulein**	Miss
festsitzen	stuck	**frei**	vacant
fett	fat (adj)	**Freitag**	Friday
Fett	fat (n)	**fremd**	foreign
fettig	greasy	**Fremden-**	bed & breakfast
Feuchtigkeits-	moisturizer	**zimmer**	
creme		**Freund**	friend
Feuer	fire	**freundlich**	kind
Feuerwerk	fireworks	**Freundschaft**	friendship
Feuerzeug	lighter (n)	**Frieden**	peace
Fieber	fever	**frisch**	fresh
Film	movie	**Friseursalon**	beauty salon
Finger	finger	**Frisör**	barber
Fisch	fish (n)	**Frisur**	haircut
fischen	fish (v)	**früh**	early

German / English

Frühling	spring
Frühstück	breakfast
Führer	guide
Führung	guided tour
für	for
fürchten	fear (v)
Fuß	foot
Fußball	soccer
Fußgänger	pedestrian
Fußgelenk	ankle
Fußpilz	athlete's foot

G

Gabel	fork
Galerie	gallery
Gang	aisle
Garage	garage
Garantie	guarantee
Garten	garden
Gärtnern	gardening
Gast	guest
Gästezimmer	bed & breakfast
Gasthaus	country inn
Gasthof	country inn
Gebärmutter	uterus
Gebäude	building
geben	give
Gebühr	toll
gebührenfrei	toll-free
Geburtstag	birthday
Gefahr	danger
gefährlich	dangerous
Gefrierbeutel	zip-lock bag
Geheimnis	secret (n)
Geheimnummer	PIN code
gehen	go; walk (v)

gekocht	boiled
gelb	yellow
Geld	money
Gelenkentzündung	arthritis
Gemälde	painting
gemütlich	cozy
genau	exactly
genießen	enjoy
genug	enough
geöffnet	open (adj)
Gepäck	baggage
Gepäckaufgabe	baggage check
Gepäckausgabe	baggage claim
geradeaus	straight ahead
Geruch	smell (n)
Geschäft	business; store
Geschäftsführer	manager
Geschenk	gift
Geschichte	history
geschieden	divorced
Geschlechts-krankeit	venereal disease
geschlossen	closed
Geschmack	taste (v), flavor (n)
Geschwindigkeit	speed
Gesicht	face
Gesichtspulver	face powder
Gesichtsseife	face cleanser
gestern	yesterday
gesund	healthy
Gesundheit	health
Getränk	drink (n)
getrennt	separate (adj)
Getriebeöl	transmission fluid
Gewalt	violence
Gewehr	gun
Gewicht	weight

Gitarre	guitar
Glas	glass
glatt	smooth; slippery
gleiche	same
Gleis	train track
Glocken	bells
Glück	happiness; luck
glücklich	happy
Glückwünsche	congratulations
Glühbirne	lightbulb
Gold	gold
gothisch	Gothic
Gott	God
Gottesdienst	church service
Grammatik	grammar
grau	gray
Grenze	border
Griechenland	Greece
Griff	handle (n)
Grippe	flu
Grippemittel	cold medicine
groß	big
Großbritannien	Great Britain
Größe	size
Großmutter	grandmother
Großstrich	underscore (_)
Großvater	grandfather
großzügig	generous
grün	green
Grundlage	foundation
gucken	look
gültig	valid
Gürtel	belt
gut	good
gutaussehend	handsome
guten Tag	good day
Gymnastik	gymnastics
Gynäkologin	gynecologist

H

Haarbürste	hairbrush
Haare	hair
Haarfestiger	conditioner (hair)
Haarsalon	beauty salon
haben	have
Hafen	harbor
Hähnchen	chicken
hallo	hello
Hals	throat
Halsband	necklace
Halsbonbon	lozenges
Halsschmerzen	sore throat
Halt	stop (n)
haltbar	sturdy
halten	stop (v)
Hämorrhoiden Salbe	Preparation H
Hämorrhoiden	hemorrhoids
Hand	hand
Handarbeiten	handicrafts
Handgelenk	wrist
Handgepäck	carry-on luggage
Handlotion	hand lotion
Handschuhe	gloves
Handtasche	purse
Handtuch	towel
Handy	cell phone
Harnröhre	urethra
Harnröhren-entzündung	urinary infection
hart	hard
Haschisch	hash
Hase	rabbit

hassen	hate (v)
häßlich	ugly
Haupt	main
Hauptbahnhof	main train station
Haus	house
Häuserblock	block (street)
hausgemacht	homemade
Haustier	pet (n)
Haut	skin
Heiliger	saint
Heimweh	homesickness
heiß	hot
Helm	helmet
Hemd	shirt
Herbst	autumn
Herr	gentleman; Mr.
Herren	men
Herrenfrisör	barber shop
herunterladen	download
Herz	heart
Herzbesch- werden	heart condition
Heuschnupfen	hay fever
heute	today
heute abend	tonight
hier	here
Hilfe	help (n)
Hilfe, Erste	first aid
hilfen	help (v)
hilfreich	helpful
Himmel	heaven; sky
Hinfahrkarte	one way (ticket)
hinter	behind
Hinterbacken	buttocks
Hitze	heat (n)
hoch	high; tall; up

Hochzeit	wedding
Hochzeitsreise	honeymoon
Hoden	testicles
Hoffnung	hope
Höhle	cave
Holz	wood
hören	hear
Hosen	pants
hübsch	pretty
Hüfte	hip
Hügel	hill
Hund	dog
hungrig	hungry
Husten	cough (n)
husten	cough (v)
Hustenbonbons	cough drops
Hut	hat

I

ich	I
ihr	her; their
Ihr	your (formal)
im Freien	outdoors
Imbiß	snack
immer	always
importiert	imported
impressionistisch	Impressionist
in	in
Industrie	industry
Infektion	infection
Information	information
Ingenieur	engineer
inklusive	included
innen	inside
Insekt	insect
Insel	island

interessant	interesting
Internet	Internet
Internet-	Internet access
anschluß	
Internetcafé	Internet café
Internetseite	website
Irland	Ireland
ist	is
Italien	Italy

J

ja	yes
Jacke	jacket
Jahr	year
Jahrhundert	century
Januar	January
jede	each; every
Jeton	token
jetzt	now
Jod	iodine
Joint	joint (marijuana)
jüdisch	Jewish
Jugendherberge	youth hostel
Jugendliche	youths
Jugendlicher	teenager
Jugendstil	Art Nouveau
Juli	July
jung	young
Junge	boy
Juni	June

K

Kaffee	coffee
Kaffeeladen	coffee shop
Kaiser	emperor
Kaiserin	empress

Kakerlake	cockroach
Kalender	calendar
Kalorie	calorie
kalt	cold (adj)
Kälteschauer	chills
Kamm	comb (n)
Kanada	Canada
Kanal	canal
Kanu	canoe
Kanzel	pulpit
Kapelle	chapel
Kapitän	captain
kaputt	broken
Karaffe	carafe
Karte	card; map
Karten	cards (deck)
Karton	box
Käse	cheese
Käserei	cheese shop
Kassette	cassette (tape)
Kassierer	cashier
Kathedrale	cathedral
katholisch	Catholic (adj)
Katze	cat
kaufen	buy
Kaufhaus	department store
Kaugummi	gum
Kaution	deposit
Keilriemen	fan belt
kein	no
Keller	basement
Kellner	waiter
Kellnerin	waitress
Keramik	ceramic
Kerze	candle
Kessel	kettle
Kiefer	jaw

Kiffe	joint (marijuana)
Kinder	children
Kinderaufsicht	babysitting service
Kinderbett	crib
Kindereinteiler	sleeper (for baby)
Kindersitz	booster seat
Kinderstuhl	highchair
Kinderwagen	stroller
Kino	cinema
Kiosk	newsstand
Kirche	church
Kirchenkonzert	church concert
Kissen	pillow
klar	clear
Klasse	class
Klasse, erste	first class
Klasse, zweite	second class
klassisch	classical (music)
klassizistisch	classical (period)
Klebeband	tape (adhesive)
Kleid	dress (n)
Kleider	clothes
Kleiderbügel	coat hanger
Kleiderladen	clothing boutique
klein	small
Kleinküche	kitchenette
Kliff	cliff
Klimaanlage	air conditioning
Klinik	medical clinic
Klopapier	toilet paper
Kloster	cloister, monastery
klug	clever
Knie	knee
Knopf	button
kochen	cook (v)

Koffer	suitcase
Kohlensäure	carbon dioxide
Kojen	bunk beds
komisch	funny
kommen	come
kompliziert	complicated
Komputer	computer
Konditorei	pastry shop
Kondom	condom
König	king
Königin	queen
können	can (v)
Konzert	concert
Kopf	head
Kopfschmerzen	headache
Kopie	copy
Kopierladen	photocopy shop
Korb	basket
Korbballspiel	basketball
Korken	cork
Korkenzieher	corkscrew
Körper	body
Korruption	corruption
kosten	cost (v)
kostenlos	free (no cost)
kostet, wie viel	how much ($)
Krämpfe	cramps
krank	sick
Krankenhaus	hospital
Krankenschwester	nurse
Kranken-versicherung	health insurance
Krankenwagen	ambulance
Krankheit	disease
Kreditkarte	credit card
Kreisel	roundabout
Kreuz	cross

DICTIONARY

German / English

Kreuzung	intersection
Krieg	war
Krypte	crypt
Küche	kitchen
Kugelschreiber	ballpoint pen
Kuh	cow
kühl	cool
Kühler	radiator
Kunst	art
Kunstgalerie	art gallery
Kunstgewerbe	crafts
Künstler	artist
künstlich	artificial
Kupfer	copper
Kuppel	dome
kurz	short
kurze Hosen	shorts
Küß	kiss
Küste	coast

L

Lächeln	smile (n)
lachen	laugh (v)
Laden	store
Laken	bedsheet
Lamm	lamb
Lampe	lamp
Land	country; countryside
Landstraße	highway
langsam	slow
Latz	bib
Lätzchen	bib
lau	lukewarm
laufen	run (v)
laut	loud
Laxativ	laxative

Leben	life
leben	live
Lebensmittel	food
Lebensmittel-geschäft	grocery store
Lebensmittel-vergiftung	food poisoning
lecker	delicious
Leder	leather
ledig	single
leer	empty
Lehrer	teacher
leiden	suffer
Leihbücherei	library
leihen	borrow; lend
Leine	string
Leinen	linen
Leiter	ladder
Leitungswasser	tap water
lernen	learn
letzte	last
Leute	people
Licht	light (n)
Liebe	love (n)
lieben	love (v)
Liebhaber	lover
Lied	song
Liege	cot
Liegewagen	sleeper car (train)
Liegewagenplatz	berth (train)
Linienbus	city bus
links	left
Linsen	contact lenses
Lippe	lip
Lippenbalsam	lip salve
Lippenstift	lipstick

Liste	list
Liter	liter
Loch	hole
Löffel	spoon
löschen	delete
Luft	air
Luftpost	air mail
Lügen	lies
Lungen	lungs
Lungenentzündung	pneumonia

M

machen	make (v)
macho	macho
Macht	power
mächtig	powerful
Mädchen	girl
Magen	stomach
Magenbrennen, Mittel gegen	antacid
Magen- schmerzen	stomachache
Mai	May
Mann	man
männlich	male
Marihuana	marijuana
Markt	market
Marmor	marble (material)
März	March
Maskara	mascara
Maximum	maximum
Mechaniker	mechanic
Medikament	medicine
Meer	ocean, sea
Meeresfrüchte	seafood
mehr	more

mein	my
mein Herr	sir
Meisterschaft	championship
Menge	crowd (n); amount
Menstruation	menstruation
merkwürdig	strange
Messer	knife
Messing	brass
Metall	metal
mieten	rent (v)
Migräne	migraine
Militär	military
Mineralsalbe	Vaseline
Mineralwasser	mineral water
Minuten	minutes
Mischung	mix (n)
mißbrauchen	abuse (v)
Mißver- ständnis	misunderstanding
mit	with
mitnehmen	take out (food)
Mittag	noon
Mitteilung	message (email)
mittel	medium
Mittel gegen Magenbrennen	antacid
mittelalterlich	medieval
Mitternacht	midnight
Mittwoch	Wednesday
Möbel	furniture
möchte	want
Mode	fashion
mögen	like (v)
möglich	possible
Monat	month
Monats krämpfe	menstrual cramps
Mond	moon

Montag	Monday
Moped	motor scooter
Morgen	morning
morgen	tomorrow
Moschee	mosque
Motorrad	motorcycle
Mücke	mosquito
Mückenspray	insect repellant
müde	tired
Mund	mouth
Münzen	coins
muselmanisch	Muslim
Musik	music
Muskel	muscle
Mutter	mother

N

nabel	navel
nach	after; to
nachher	afterwards
Nachmittag	afternoon
Nachricht	message
nachschenken	refill (v)
nächste	next
Nacht	night
Nachthemd	nightgown
Nachtisch	dessert
Nacken	neck
nackt	naked
Nadel	needle, pin
Nagel	fingernail
Nagellack	nail polish
Nagellackentferner	nail polish remover
Nagelschere	nail clipper
nahe	near

Name	name
Nase	nose
Nasenverstopfung	congestion (sinus)
naß	wet
Natel	cell phone (Switz.)
Nationalität	nationality
Natur	nature
natürlich	natural
Nebel	fog
Neffe	nephew
nehmen	take
nein	no
neoklassizistisch	Neoclassical
nervös	nervous
nett	nice
neu	new
nicht	not
Nichte	niece
Nichtraucher	non-smoking
nichts	nothing
nie	never
Niederlande	Netherlands
niedrig	low
Niesen	sneeze (n)
noch ein	another
noch einmal	again; repeat
Norden	north
normal	normal
Notausgang	emergency exit
Notfall	emergency
Notfallaufnahme	emergency room
Notizbuch	notebook
notwendig	necessary
November	November
Nuggel	pacifier

null	zero
nur	only
nutzen	use
Nylon	nylon (material)

O

ob	if
oben	upstairs
Obst	fruit
oder	or
Ofen	oven
offen	open (adj)
öffentlich	public
öffnen	open (v)
Öffnungszeiten	opening hours
ohne	without
Ohr	ear
Ohrenschmerzen	earache
Ohrenschützer	earplugs
Ohrringe	earrings
Ökonomie	economy
Oktober	October
Öl	oil
Olympiade	Olympics
Onkel	uncle
Oper	opera
Optiker	optician
orange	orange (color)
Orange	orange (fruit)
Ordner	folder (computer)
Orgel	organ
örtlich	local
Ostdeutschland	eastern Germany
Osten	east
Ostern	Easter
Österreich	Austria

P

Paket	package
Pantoffeln	slippers
Papa	dad
Papier	paper
Papiertuch	facial tissue
Parfum	perfume
Park	park (garden)
parken	park (v)
Parkplatz	parking lot
Paß	passport
peinlich	embarrassing
Pension	small hotel
pensioniert	retired
per Anhalter fahren	hitchhike
perfekt	perfect
Periode	period (woman's)
Pferd	horse
Pflanze	plant
Pflaster	Band-Aid
Pflaster gegen Blasen	moleskin
phantastisch	fantastic
Photoapparat	camera
Photoladen	camera shop
Picknick	picnic
Pille	pill
Pinzette	tweezers
Plastik	plastic
Plastiktüte	plastic bag
Platz	square (town); seat
plötzlich	suddenly
Politiker	politicians
Polizei	police
Porzellan	porcelain
Post	mail (n)
Poster	poster
Postkarte	postcard

Postleitzahl	zip code
praktisch	practical
Präservativ	condom
Preis	price
Priester	priest
privat	private
probieren	try; taste (v)
Prost!	Cheers!
Prozent	percent
Pullover	sweater
Puls	pulse
Pumpe	pump (n)
Punkt	dot
pünktlich	on time
Puppe	doll

Q

Qualität	quality

R

Rad	wheel
Radiergummi	eraser
Rasierapparat	razor
Rasiercreme	shaving cream
Rasierwasser	aftershave
Rassimus	racism
Rauch	smoke
Rauchen	smoking
Rechnung	bill (payment)
rechts	right
reden	talk
Regen	rain (n)
Regenbogen	rainbow
Regenmantel	raincoat
Regenschirm	umbrella
Regionalbus	long-distance bus

reich	rich
reif	ripe
Reifen	tire
Reise	trip, journey
Reisebüro	travel agency
Reiseführer	guidebook
reisen	travel
Reisende	passenger, traveler
Reisescheck	traveler's check
Reißverschluß	zipper
reiten	horse riding
Religion	religion
Reliquie	relic
Renaissance	Renaissance
reparieren	repair (v)
reservieren	reserve
Reservierung	reservation
Respekt	respect
Rezept	prescription; recipe
Richtung	direction
Rindfleisch	beef
Ring	ring (n)
Ringstraße	ring road
Ritter	knight
Rock	skirt
roh	raw
Rollschuhe	roller skates
rollstuhlgängig	wheelchair-accessible
romanisch	Romanesque
Romantik	Romantic (art)
romantisch	romantic
Röntgenbild	X-ray
rosa	pink
rot	red
Rücken	back
Rückfahrt	round-trip

German / English

Rückgabe	refund (n)
Rücklichtern	tail lights
Rucksack	backpack
Ruderboot	rowboat
Ruhe	silence
ruhig	quiet
Ruine	ruins
runter	down
Rußland	Russia

S

Saal	hall
Saft	juice
Sahne	cream
Samstag	Saturday
Samt	velvet
Sandalen	sandals
Sänger	singer
sauber	clean (adj)
sauer	sour
schade, wie	It's a pity
Schaffner	conductor
Schal	scarf
Schale	bowl; shell
Schatzkammer	treasury
Scheck	check
Scheibe	slice
Scheiben-	windshield wipers
wischern	
Scheinwerfern	headlights
Schenkel	thigh
Schere	scissors
schicken	send; ship (v)
Schiff	boat
Schild	sign
schlafen	sleep (v)

DICTIONARY

schläfrig	sleepy
Schlafsaal	dormitory
Schlafsack	sleeping bag
Schlafwagen-	sleeper (train)
platz	
Schlagsahne	whipped cream
schlecht	bad
schlechter	worse
schlechteste	worst
Schleim-	sinus problems
hautentzündung	
Schließfächer	lockers
Schloß	palace; lock (n)
schlucken	swallow (v)
Schlüssel	key
Schlussverkauf	sale
schmal	narrow
Schmerz	pain
Schmerzen in	chest pains
der Brust	
Schmerzmittel	painkiller
Schmuck	jewelry
Schmuckladen	jewelry shop
schmutzig	dirty
schnarchen	snore
Schnee	snow
Schnorchel	snorkel
Schnuller	pacifier
Schnur	string
Schnurrbart	moustache
Schnürsenkel	shoelaces
Schokolade	chocolate
schon	already
schön	beautiful
Schraubenzieher	screwdriver
schrecklich	terrible
schreiben	write

Schuhe	shoes
schuldig	guilty
Schule	school
Schulter	shoulder
schwanger	pregnant
Schwangerschaft	pregnancy
Schwanger-schaftstest	pregnancy test
Schwanz	tail
schwarz	black
Schwein	pig
Schweinefleisch	pork
Schweiz	Switzerland
Schwellung	swelling (n)
schwer	heavy
Schwester	sister
Schwiegermutter	mother-in-law
Schwiegervater	father-in-law
schwierig	difficult
Schwierigkeiten	troubles
Schwimmbad	swimming pool
schwimmen	swim
Schwindel	dizziness
schwitzen	sweat (v)
schwul	gay
schwül	muggy
See	lake
Segelboot	sailboat
segeln	sailing
sehen	see
sehr	very
Seide	silk
Seife	soap
Seil	rope
Seite	page
Selbstbedienung	self-service
senden	send

Senioren	seniors
September	September
Serviette	napkin
Shampoo	shampoo
sich beeilen	hurry (v)
sich beschweren	complain
sich erholen	relax (v)
sich erinnern	remember
sich sonnen	sunbathe
sich übergeben	vomit (v)
sicher	safe
Sicherheitsnadel	safety pin
Sicherheitssitz	car seat (baby)
Sicherungen	fuses
sie	she; they
Sie	you (formal)
Silber	silver
singen	sing
Skandinavien	Scandinavia
Skifahren	skiing
Skulptur	sculpture
Slip	men's briefs
Socken	socks
sofort	immediately
sofortig	instant
Sohn	son
Sommer	summer
Sonnabend	Saturday
Sonne	sun
sonnen (sich)	sunbathe
Sonnenaufgang	sunrise
Sonnenbrand	sunburn
Sonnenbräune	suntan (n)
Sonnenbrille	sunglasses
Sonnenöl	suntan lotion
Sonnenschein	sunshine
Sonnenschutz	sunscreen

German	English
Sonnenstich	sunstroke
Sonnenuntergang	sunset
sonnig	sunny
Sonntag	Sunday
Souvenirladen	souvenir shop
Spanien	Spain
Spaß	fun
spät	late
später	later
speichern	save (computer)
Speisekarte	menu
Speisewagen	dining car (train)
Spezialität	specialty
Spiegel	mirror
Spiel	game
spielen	play (v)
Spielplatz	playground
Spielzeug	toy
Spielzeugladen	toy store
Spinne	spider
Spirale	diaphragm (birth control)
Spitze	lace
Spitzname	nickname
Sportler	athlete
Sprache	language
sprechen	speak
springen	jump (v)
sprudelnd	fizzy
Staat	state
Stadt	city, town
Stadtmitte	downtown
stark	strong
Station	station
Stativ	tripod
sterben	die
Stern	star (in sky)
Steuer	tax

German	English
Stiefel	boots
Stil	style
Stimme	voice
Stock	story (floor)
Stoff	cloth
stören	disturb
Strand	beach
Strandsandalen	flip-flops
Straße	street
Streichhölzer	matches
Streik	strike (no work)
Streit	fight (n)
streiten	fight (v)
Strom- wandler	electrical adapter
Strümpfe	stockings
Stück	piece
Stuhl	chair
Stunde	hour
Sturm	storm
Stützverband	bandage, support
Süden	south
sündig	scandalous
super	great
Supermarkt	supermarket
süß	sweet
Süßwaren- geschäft	sweets shop
Synagoge	synagogue
synthetisch	synthetic

T

German	English
Tacker	stapler
Tag	day
Tag, guten	good day
Tal	valley

Tankstelle	gas station
Tante	aunt
tanzen	dance (v)
Tasche	pocket
Taschendieb	pick-pocket
Taschenlampe	flashlight
Taschentuch	tissues
Taschentücher	facial tissue
Tasse	cup
Telefon	telephone
Telefonkabine	phone booth
Telefonkarte	telephone card
Teller	plate
Temperatur	temperature
Tennisschuhe	tennis shoes
Teppich	carpet, rug
Terroristen	terrorists
Tesafilm	scotch tape
teuer	expensive
Theater	theater
Theaterstück	play (n)
Tier	animal
Tipp-Ex	white-out
Tisch	table
Tochter	daughter
Toilette	toilet
Tonbandführer	audioguide
tot	dead
töten	kill
Tour	tour
traditionell	traditional
tragen	carry
Tragflächenboot	hydrofoil
Traum	dream (n)
träumen	dream (v)
traurig	sad
Treppe	stairs

trinken	drink (v)
Trinkwasser	drinkable water
trocken	dry (adj)
trocknen	dry (v)
Trockner	dryer
Tschechien	Czech Republic
Tür	door
Türkei	Turkey
Turm	tower
Tüte	bag

U

U-Bahn	subway
U-Bahn-Ausgang	subway exit
U-Bahn-Eingang	subway entrance
U-Bahn-Haltestelle	subway stop
U-Bahn-Station	subway station
U-Bahn-Streckenplan	subway map
Übelkeit	nausea
über	above
übergeben (sich)	vomit (v)
übermorgen	day after tomorrow
Überraschung	surprise (n)
übersetzen	translate
Uhr	clock, watch (n)
Umleitung	detour
umsonst	free (no cost)
umsteigen	transfer (v)
Umweltverschmutzung	pollution
umwickeln	wrap
unabhängig	independent
und	and
Unfall	accident

German / English

DICTIONARY

ungefähr	approximately
unglaublich	incredible
unglücklicher-weise	unfortunately
Universität	university
unmöglich	impossible
uns	us
unschuldig	innocent
unter	under
Unterhose	underpants
Unterrock	slip
Unterschrift	signature
Unterwäsche	underwear
Urlaub	vacation

V

Vater	father
Vegetarier	vegetarian (n)
Verabredung	appointment
Verband	bandage, gauze
verboten	prohibited
Verbrennung	burn (n)
Verdauungsstörung	indigestion
verdorben	rotten
Vereinigte Staaten	United States
Vergangenheit	past
vergessen	forget
Vergewaltigung	rape (n)
verheiratet	married
Verhütungsmittel	contraceptives
Verhütungspille	birth-control pills
verkaufen	sell
Verkehr	traffic

verletzt	injured
Verlies	dungeon
verloren	lost
vermieten	rent out
Vermittlung	operator
versichert	insured
Versicherung	insurance
Verspätung	delay
verstehen	understand
Verstopfung	constipation
Versuchen	try (attempt)
Vetter	cousin
Videogerät	video recorder
Videokamera	video camera
viel	much
viele	many
vielleicht	maybe
Viertel	quarter (¼)
violett	purple
Virus	virus
Visitenkarte	business card
Vitamine	vitamins
Vogel	bird
Völlig	total
von	from; of
vor	before
Vorfahre	ancestor
Vorführung	show (n)
vorsichtig	careful
Vorspeise	appetizer

W

Waffe	gun
Wagen	train car
wandern	hike
Wangenröte	blush (makeup)

German	English
wann	when
Wanzen	bedbugs
warm	warm (adj)
warten	wait
Wartesaal	waiting room
warum	why
was	what
Waschbecken	sink
Wäscheklammern	clothespins
Wäscheleine	clothesline
waschen	wash (v)
Waschmaschine	washer
Waschmittel	laundry detergent
Waschsalon	launderette
Wasser	water
Wasserfahrrad	paddleboat
Wasserfall	waterfall
Wasserhahn	faucet
Wasserskifahren	waterskiing
Wechsel	exchange (n)
wechseln	change (v, money)
Wecker	alarm clock
weiblich	female
Weihnachten	Christmas
Weihnachtsmann	Santa Claus
weil	because
Wein	wine
Weinberg	vineyard
weinen	cry (v)
Weinhandlung	wine shop
weiß	white
weit	far
Wellenreiter	surfer
Welt	world
wenig	few
wer	who
werfen	throw
Weste	vest
Westen	west
Westen von Deutschland	western Germany
Wetter	weather
Wettervor- hersage	weather forecast
wichtig	important
wie	how
wie schade	it's a pity
wie viel kostet	how much ($)
wie viele	how many
Wiedersehen, auf	goodbye
Wiedervereinigung	reunification
wild	wild
willkommen	welcome
Wind	wind
Windel	diaper
Windelscheuern	diaper rash
windig	windy
Windsurfen	windsurfing
Winter	winter
wir	we
Wirtschaft	inn, restaurant; economy
Wischtücher	handiwipes
wissen	know
Wissenschaft	science
Wissenschaftler	scientist
Witwe	widow
Witwer	widower
Witz	joke (n)
WLAN	Wi-Fi
wo	where
Woche	week
Wohnung	apartment
Wohnwagen	R.V.

German / English

DICTIONARY

Wolle	wool
Wort	word
Wörterbuch	dictionary
wünschen	wish (v)
wütend	angry

Z

Zähler	taxi meter
Zahlmarke	token
Zahn	tooth
Zahnarzt	dentist
Zahnbürste	toothbrush
Zähne	teeth
Zahnen	teething (baby)
Zahnpasta	toothpaste
Zahnschmerzen	toothache
Zahnseide	dental floss
Zahnstocher	toothpick
Zange	pliers
zart	tender
Zehe	toe
zeigen	show (v); point (v)
Zeitabschnitt	period (of time)
Zeitschrift	magazine
Zeitung	newspaper
Zeitungsstand	newsstand

Zelt	tent
Zelthäringe	tent pegs
Zeltstelle	campsite
Zentrum	center; downtown
zerbrechlich	fragile
ziehen	pull
Zigarette	cigarette
Zimmer	room
Zimmer frei	vacancy (sign)
Zinn	pewter
Zoll	customs
zollfrei	duty free
zu	too
Zuckerbäcker	pastry shop
Zuckerkrankheit	diabetes
Zug	train
zuhören	listen
Zukunft	future
Zündkerzen	sparkplugs
zurück	back (return)
zurückgeben	return
zusammen	together
Zuschlag	supplement
zweite	second
zweite Klasse	second class
Zwillinge	twins

ENGLISH/GERMAN

A

English	German
abortion	Abtreibung
above	über
abstract	abstrakt
abuse (v)	mißbrauchen
accident	Unfall
accountant	Buchhalter
adapter, electrical	Stromwandler
address	Adresse
address, email	E-mail-Adresse
adult	Erwachsener
afraid	ängstlich
Africa	Afrika
after	nach
afternoon	Nachmittag
aftershave	Rasierwasser
afterwards	nachher
again	noch einmal
age	Alter
aggressive	aggressiv
agnostic	agnostisch
agree	einverstanden
AIDS	AIDS
air	Luft
air conditioning	Klimaanlage
air mail	Luftpost
airline	Fluggesellschaft
airport	Flughafen
aisle	Gang
alarm clock	Wecker
alcohol	Alkohol
allergic	allergisch
allergies	Allergien
alone	allein
already	schon
altar	Altar
always	immer
ambulance	Krankenwagen
ancestor	Vorfahre
ancient	altertümlich
and	und
angry	wütend
animal	Tier
ankle	Fußgelenk
another	noch ein
answer	Antwort
antacid	Mittel gegen Magenbrennen
antibiotic	Antibiotika
antiques shop	Antiquitätenladen
antiques	Antiquitäten
apartment	Wohnung
apology	Entschuldigung
appetizer	Vorspeise
apple	Apfel
appointment	Verabredung
approximately	ungefähr
April	April
arm	Arm
arrivals	Ankunften
arrive	ankommen
art	Kunst
art gallery	Kunstgalerie
Art Nouveau	Jugendstil
arthritis	Gelenkentzündung
artificial	künstlich
artist	Künstler

ashtray	Aschenbecher
ask	fragen
aspirin	Aspirin
asthma	Asthma
at	bei
"at" sign (@)	A-Affenschwanz
atheist	atheistisch
athlete	Sportler
athlete's foot	Fußpilz
attractive	attraktiv
audioguide	Tonbandführer
August	August
aunt	Tante
Austria	Österreich
autumn	Herbst

B

baby	Baby
baby booster seat	Kindersitz
baby car seat	Sicherheitssitz
baby food	Babynahrung
baby formula	Babynahrung
babysitter	Babysitter
babysitting service	Kinderaufsicht
back	Rücken
backpack	Rucksack
bad	schlecht
bag	Tüte
bag, plastic	Plastiktüte
bag, zip-lock	Gefrierbeutel
baggage	Gepäck
baggage check	Gepäckaufgabe
baggage claim	Gepäckausgabe
bakery	Bäckerei
balcony	Balkon

ball	Ball
banana	Banane
bandage	Verband
bandage, support	Stützverband
Band-Aid	Pflaster
bank	Bank
barber	Frisör
barber shop	Herrenfrisör
baseball	Baseball
basement	Keller
basket	Korb
basketball	Basketball, Korbballspiel
bath	Bad
bathrobe	Bademantel
bathroom	Bad
bathtub	Badewanne
battery	Batterie
beach	Strand
beard	Bart
beautiful	schön
beauty salon	Friseursalon, Haarsalon
because	weil
bed	Bett
bedbugs	Wanzen
bedroom	Zimmer
bedsheet	Laken
beef	Rindfleisch
beer	Bier
before	vor
begin	anfangen
behind	hinter
Belgium	Belgien
bells	Glocken
below	unter

English	German	English	German
belt	Gürtel	bottom	Boden
berth (train)	Liegewagenplatz	boutique, clothing	Kleiderladen
best	am besten	bowl	Schale
better	besser	box	Karton
bib	Latz, Lätzchen	boy	Junge
bicycle	Fahrrad	bra	BH (Büstenhalter)
big	groß	bracelet	Armband
bill (payment)	Rechnung	brakes	Bremsen
bird	Vogel	brass	Messing
birth control pills	Verhütungspille	bread	Brot
birthday	Geburtstag	breakfast	Frühstück
black	schwarz	breast	Busen
bladder	Blase	breath	Atem
blanket	Decke	bridge	Brücke
bleeding	bluten	briefs	Unterhose, Slip
blisters	Blasen	broken	kaputt
block (street)	Häuserblock	bronze	Bronze
blond	blond	brooch	Brosche
blood	Blut	brother	Bruder
blood pressure, high	Bluthochdruck	brown	braun
		bucket	Eimer
blouse	Bluse	building	Gebäude
blue	blau	bulb	Birne
blush (makeup)	Wangenröte	bunk beds	Kojen
boat	Schiff	burn (n)	Verbrennung
body	Körper	bus	Bus
boiled	gekocht	bus station	Busbahnhof
bomb	Bombe	bus stop	Bushaltestelle
book	Buch	bus, city	Linienbus
book shop	Buchladen	bus, long-distance	Regionalbus, Fernbus
booster seat	Kindersitz		
boots	Stiefel	business	Geschäft
border	Grenze	business card	Visitenkarte
borrow	leihen	but	aber
boss	Chef, Boss	buttocks	Hinterbacken
bottle	Flasche	button	Knopf

C

buy	kaufen
by (train, car, etc.)	mit
calendar	Kalender
calorie	Kalorie
camera	Photoapparat
camera shop	Photoladen
camping	Camping
campsite	Zeltstelle
can (n)	Dose
can (v)	können
can opener	Dosenöffner
Canada	Kanada
canal	Kanal
cancel	annullieren
candle	Kerze
candy	Bonbons
canoe	Kanu
cap	Deckel
captain	Kapitän
car	Auto
car (train)	Wagen
car seat (baby)	Sicherheitssitz
car, dining (train)	Speisewagen
car, sleeper (train)	Liegewagen
carafe	Karaffe
carbon dioxide	Kohlensäure
card	Karte
card, telephone	Telefonkarte
cards (deck)	Karten
careful	vorsichtig
carpet	Teppich
carry	tragen
carry-on luggage	Handgepäck
cash	Bargeld
cash machine	Bankomat
cashier	Kassierer
cassette	Kassette
castle	Burg
cat	Katze
catch (v)	fangen
cathedral	Dom, Kathedrale
Catholic (adj)	katholisch
cave	Höhle
cell phone	Handy
cell phone shop	Natelladen
cellar	Keller
center	Zentrum
century	Jahrhundert
ceramic	Keramik
chair	Stuhl
championship	Meisterschaft
change (n)	Wechsel
change (v)	ändern, wechseln (money)
chapel	Kapelle
charming	bezaubernd
cheap	billig
check	Scheck
Cheers!	Prost!
cheese	Käse
cheese shop	Käserei
chest	Brust
chest pains	Schmerzen in der Brust
chicken	Hähnchen
children	Kinder
chills	Kälteschauer
Chinese	chinesisch
chocolate	Schokolade
choir	Chor
Christian (adj)	christlich

Christmas	Weihnachten
church	Kirche
church concert	Kirchenkonzert
church service	Gottesdienst
cigarette	Zigarette
cinema	Kino
city	Stadt
class	Klasse
classical (music)	klassisch
classical (period)	klassizistisch
clean (adj)	sauber
clear	klar
clever	klug
cliff	Kliff
clinic, medical	Klinik
clock	Uhr
clock, alarm	Wecker
cloister	Kloster
closed	geschlossen
cloth	Stoff
clothes	Kleider
clothespins	Wäscheklammern
clothesline	Wäscheleine
clothing boutique	Kleiderladen
cloudy	bewölkt
coast	Küste
coat	Jacke
coat hanger	Kleiderbügel
cockroach	Kakerlake
coffee	Kaffee
coffee shop	Kaffeeladen
coins	Münzen
cold (adj)	kalt
cold (n)	Erkältung
cold medicine	Grippemittel
color	Farbe
color-fast	farbenfest

comb (n)	Kamm
come	kommen
comfortable	bequem
compact disc	C.D.
complain	sich beschweren
complicated	kompliziert
computer	Komputer
concert	Konzert
concert, church	Kirchenkonzert
conditioner (hair)	Haarfestiger
condom	Präservativ, Kondom
conductor	Schaffner
confirm	bestätigen
congestion (sinus)	Nasenverstopfung
congratulations	Glückwünsche
connection	Anschluß
constipation	Verstopfung
construction site	Baustelle
contact lenses	Linsen
contagious	ansteckend
contraceptives	Verhütungsmittel
convenient	praktish
cook (v)	kochen
cool	kühl
copper	Kupfer
copy	Kopie
copy shop	Kopierladen
cork	Korken
corkscrew	Korkenzieher
corner	Ecke
corridor	Flur
corruption	Korruption
cost (v)	kosten
cot	Liege
cotton	Baumwolle
cough (n)	Husten

cough (v)	husten
cough drops	Hustenbonbons
country	Land
countryside	(auf dem) Land
cousin	Vetter
cow	Kuh
cozy	gemütlich
crafts	Kunstgewerbe
cramps	Krämpfe
cramps, menstrual	Monatskrämpfe
cream	Sahne
cream, first-aid	Erste-Hilfe-Salbe
credit card	Kreditkarte
crib	Kinderbett
cross	Kreuz
crowd (n)	Menge
cry (v)	weinen
crypt	Krypte
cup	Tasse
customs	Zoll
Czech Republic	Tschechien

D

dad	Papa
dance (v)	tanzen
danger	Gefahr
dangerous	gefährlich
Danube	Donau
dark	dunkel
dash (-)	Bindestrich
daughter	Tochter
day	Tag
day after tomorrow	übermorgen

dead	tot
December	Dezember
declare (customs)	deklarieren
decongestant	Abführmittel
delay	Verspätung
delete	löschen
delicatessen	Feinkostgeschäft
delicious	lecker
democracy	Demokratie
dental floss	Zahnseide
dentist	Zahnarzt
deodorant	Deodorant
depart	abfahren
department store	Kaufhaus
departures	Abfahrten
deposit	Kaution
dessert	Nachtisch
detergent	Waschmittel
detour	Umleitung
diabetes	Zuckerkrankheit
diabetic	diabetisch
diamond	Diamant
diaper	Windel
diaper rash	Windelscheuern
diaphragm (birth control)	Spirale
diarrhea	Durchfall
diarrhea medicine	Durchfallmedikament
dictionary	Wörterbuch
die	sterben
difficult	schwierig
dining car (train)	Speisewagen
dinner	Abendessen
direct	direkt
direction	Richtung
dirty	schmutzig

discount	Ermäßigung
disease	Krankheit
disease, venereal	Geschlechtskrankheit
disinfectant	Desinfektionsmittel
disturb	stören
divorced	geschieden
dizziness	Schwindel
doctor	Arzt
dog	Hund
doll	Puppe
dome	Kuppel
donkey	Esel
door	Tür
dormitory	Schlafsaal
dot	Punkt
double	doppel
down	runter
download	herunterladen
downtown	Stadtmitte, Zentrum
dozen	Dutzend
dream (n)	Traum
dream (v)	träumen
dress (n)	Kleid
drink (n)	Getränk
drink (v)	trinken
drive (v)	fahren
driver	Fahrer
drunk	betrunken
dry (adj)	trocken
dry (v)	trocknen
dryer	Trockner
dungeon	Verlies
duty free	zollfrei

E

each	jede
ear	Ohr
earache	Ohrenschmerzen
early	früh
earplugs	Ohrenschützer
earrings	Ohrringe
earth	Erde
east	Osten
Easter	Ostern
eastern Germany	Ostdeutschland
easy	einfach
eat	essen
economy	Ökonomie, Wirtschaft
edit	bearbeiten
education	Ausbildung
elbow	Ellbogen
electrical adapter	Stromwandler
elevator	Fahrstuhl
email	Email
email address	E-mail-Adresse
embarrassing	peinlich
embassy	Botschaft
emergency	Notfall
emergency exit	Notausgang
emergency room	Notfallaufnahme
emperor	Kaiser
empress	Kaiserin
empty	leer
engineer	Ingenieur
English	Englisch
enjoy	genießen
enough	genug
entrance (door)	Eingang

English / German

DICTIONARY

entrance (road)	Einfahrt
entry	Eingang
envelope	Briefumschlag
epilepsy	Epilepsie
eraser	Radiergummi
especially	besonders
Europe	Europa
evening	Abend
every	jede
everything	alles
exactly	genau
example	Beispiel
excellent	ausgezeichnet
except	außer
exchange (n)	Wechsel
excuse me	Entschuldigung
exhausted	erschöpft
exit (door)	Ausgang
exit (road)	Ausfahrt
exit, emergency	Notausgang
expensive	teuer
explain	erklären
eye	Auge
eye shadow	Augenschatten
eyeliner	Augenkontour

F

face	Gesicht
face cleanser	Gesichtsseife
face powder	Gesichtspulver
facial tissue	Papiertuch, Taschentücher
factory	Fabrik
fair (just)	fair
fall (v)	fallen
false	falsch
family	Familie

famous	berühmt
fan belt	Keilriemen
fantastic	phantastisch
far	weit
farm	Bauernhof
farmer	Bauer
fashion	Mode
fat (adj)	fett
fat (n)	Fett
father	Vater
father-in-law	Schwiegervater
faucet	Wasserhahn
fear (v)	fürchten
February	Februar
female	weiblich
ferry	Fähre
festival	Festival
fever	Fieber
few	wenig
field	Feld
fight (n)	Streit
fight (v)	streiten
fine (good)	gut
finger	Finger
fingernail	Nagel
finish (v)	beenden
fire	Feuer
fireworks	Feuerwerk
first	erst
first aid	Erste Hilfe
first class	erste Klasse
first-aid cream	Erste-Hilfe-Salbe
fish (n)	Fisch
fish (v)	fischen
fix (v)	reparieren
fizzy	sprudelnd, mit Kohlensäure

flag	Fahne
flash (camera)	Blitz
flashlight	Taschenlampe
flavor (n)	Geschmack
flea	Floh
flea market	Flohmarkt
flight	Flug
flip-flops	Strandsandalen
floss, dental	Zahnseide
flower	Blume
flower market	Blumenmarkt
flu	Grippe
fly	fliegen
fog	Nebel
folder (computer)	Ordner
food	Essen, Lebensmittel
food poisoning	Lebensmittelvergiftung
foot	Fuß
football	Fußball
football, American	Football
for	für
forbidden	verboten
foreign	fremd
forget	vergessen
fork	Gabel
formula (for baby)	Babynahrung
foundation	Grundlage
fountain	Brunnen
fragile	zerbrechlich
France	Frankreich
free (no cost)	umsonst, kostenlos
fresh	frisch
Friday	Freitag
friend	Freund
friendship	Freundschaft
Frisbee	Frisbee
from	von
fruit	Obst
full-service	mit Dienstleistung
fun	Spaß
funeral	Beerdigung
funny	komisch
furniture	Möbel
fuses	Sicherungen
future	Zukunft

G

gallery	Galerie
game	Spiel
garage	Garage
garden	Garten
gardening	Gärtnern
gas	Benzin
gas station	Tankstelle
gauze	Verband
gay	schwul
generous	großzügig
gentleman	Herr
genuine	echt
Germany	Deutschland
gift	Geschenk
girl	Mädchen
give	geben
glass	Glas
glasses (eye)	Brille
gloves	Handschuhe
go	gehen
go through	durchgehen
God	Gott
gold	Gold

golf	Golf
good	gut
good day	guten Tag
goodbye	auf Wiedersehen
Gothic	gothisch
grammar	Grammatik
granddaughter	Enkelin
grandfather	Großvater
grandmother	Großmutter
grandson	Enkel
gray	grau
greasy	fettig
great	super
Great Britain	Großbritannien
Greece	Griechenland
green	grün
grocery store	Lebensmittelgeschäft
guarantee	Garantie
guest	Gast
guide	Führer
guidebook	Reiseführer
guided tour	Führung
guilty	schuldig
guitar	Gitarre
gum	Kaugummi
gun	Waffe, Gewehr
gymnastics	Gymnastik
gynecologist	Gynäkologin

H

hair	Haare
hairbrush	Haarbürste
haircut	Frisur
hall	Saal
hand	Hand
hand lotion	Handlotion
handicapped	behindert
handicrafts	Handarbeiten
handiwipes	Wischtücher
handle (n)	Griff
handsome	gutaussehend
happiness	Glück
happy	glücklich
harbor	Hafen
hard	hart
hardware store	Eisenwarengeschäft
hash	Haschisch
hat	Hut
hate (v)	hassen
have	haben
hay fever	Heuschnupfen
he	er
head	Kopf
headache	Kopfschmerzen
headlights	Scheinwerfern
health	Gesundheit
health insurance	Krankenversicherung
healthy	gesund
hear	hören
heart	Herz
heart condition	Herzbeschwerden
heat (n)	Hitze
heat (v)	aufwarmen
heaven	Himmel
heavy	schwer
hello	hallo
helmet	Helm
help (n)	Hilfe
help (v)	hilfen

helpful	hilfreich
hemorrhoids	Hämorrholden
her	ihr
here	hier
hi	hallo
high	hoch
high blood pressure	Bluthochdruck
highchair	Kinderstuhl
highway	Landstraße
hike	wandern
hill	Hügel
hip	Hüfte
history	Geschichte
hitchhike	per Anhalter fahren
hobby	Hobby
hockey	Hockey
hole	Loch
holiday	Feiertag
homemade	hausgemacht
homesickness	Heimweh
honest	ehrlich
honeymoon	Hochzeitsreise
hope	Hoffnung
horrible	schrecklich
horse	Pferd
horse riding	reiten
hospital	Krankenhaus
hot	heiß
hotel	Hotel
hotel, bed & breakfast	Gästezimmer, Fremdenzimmer
hotel, country inn	Gasthaus, Gasthof
hotel, small	Pension
hour	Stunde
house	Haus

how	wie
how many	wie viele
how much ($)	wie viel kostet
hungry	hungrig
hurry (v)	sich beeilen
husband	Ehemann
hydrofoil	Tragflächenboot
hyphen (-)	Bindestrich

I

I	ich
ice	Eis
ice cream	Eis
if	ob
ill	krank
immediately	sofort
important	wichtig
imported	importiert
impossible	unmöglich
Impressionist	impressionistisch
in	in
included	inklusive, eingeschlossen
incredible	unglaublich
independent	unabhängig
indigestion	Verdauungsstörung
industry	Industrie
infection	Infektion, Entzündung
infection, urinary	Harnröhrenentzündung
inflammation	Entzündung
information	Information
injured	verletzt
innocent	unschuldig
insect	Insekt

insect repellant	Mückenspray
inside	innen
instant	sofortig
instead	anstatt
insurance	Versicherung
insurance, health	Kranken-versicherung
insured	versichert
intelligent	intelligent
interesting	interessant
Internet	Internet
Internet access	Internetanschluß
Internet café	Internetcafé
intersection	Kreuzung
intestines	Därme
invitation	Einladung
iodine	Jod
Ireland	Irland
is	ist
island	Insel
Italy	Italien

J

jacket	Jacke
January	Januar
jaw	Kiefer
jeans	Jeans
jewelry	Schmuck
jewelry shop	Schmuckladen
Jewish	jüdisch
job	Beruf
jogging	Jogging
joint (marijuana)	Joint, Kiffe
joke (n)	Witz
journey	Reise

juice	Saft
July	Juli
jump (v)	springen
June	Juni

K

keep	behalten
kettle	Kessel
key	Schlüssel
kill	töten
kind	freundlich
king	König
kiss	Küß
kitchen	Küche
kitchenette	Kleinküche
knee	Knie
knife	Messer
knight	Ritter
know	wissen

L

lace	Spitze
ladder	Leiter
ladies	Damen
lake	See
lamb	Lamm
lamp	Lampe
language	Sprache
large	groß
last	letzte
late	spät
later	später
laugh (v)	lachen
launderette	Waschsalon
laundry soap	Waschmittel
lawyer	Anwalt

laxative	Laxativ
lazy	faul
learn	lernen
leather	Leder
leave	gehen
left	links
leg	Bein
lend	leihen
lenses, contact	Linsen
letter	Brief
library	Leihbücherei
lies	Lügen
life	Leben
light (n)	Licht
light bulb	Glühbirne
lighter (n)	Feuerzeug
like (v)	mögen
linen	Leinen
lip	Lippe
lip salve	Lippenbalsam
lipstick	Lippenstift
list	Liste
listen	zuhören
liter	Liter
little (adj)	klein
live	leben
local	örtlich
locally made	heimisch, einheimisch
lock (n)	Schloß
lock (v)	abschließen
lockers	Schließfächer
look	gucken
lost	verloren
lotion, hand	Handlotion
loud	laut
love (n)	Liebe
love (v)	lieben

lover	Liebhaber
low	niedrig
lozenges	Halsbonbon
luck	Glück
luggage	Gepäck
luggage, carry-on	Handgepäck
lukewarm	lau
lungs	Lungen

M

macho	macho
mad	wütend
magazine	Zeitschrift
mail (n)	Post
main	Haupt
make (v)	machen
makeup	Makeup
male	männlich
man	Mann
manager	Chef, Geschäftsführer
many	viele
map	Karte
marble (material)	Marmor
March	März
marijuana	Marihuana
market	Markt
market, flea	Flohmarkt
market, flower	Blumenmarkt
market, open-air	Markt
married	verheiratet
mascara	Maskara
matches	Streichhölzer
maximum	Maximum
May	Mai
maybe	vielleicht
meat	Fleisch

mechanic	Mechaniker
medicine	Medikament
medicine for a cold	Grippemittel
medicine, non-aspirin substitute	Ben-u-ron
medieval	mittelalterlich
medium	mittel
men	Herren
menstrual cramps	Monatskrämpfe
menstruation	Menstruation
menu	Speisekarte
message	Nachricht, Mitteilung (email)
metal	Metall
meter, taxi	Zähler
midnight	Mitternacht
migraine	Migräne
military	Militär
mineral water	Mineralwasser
minimum	Minimum
minutes	Minuten
mirror	Spiegel
miscarriage	Fehlgeburt
Miss	Fräulein
mistake	Fehler
misunderstanding	Mißverständnis
mix (n)	Mischung
moat	Burggraben
modern	modern
moisturizer	Feuchtigkeitscreme
moleskin	Pflaster gegen Blasen
moment	Moment

monastery	Kloster
Monday	Montag
money	Geld
month	Monat
monument	Denkmal
moon	Mond
more	mehr
morning	Morgen
mosque	Moschee
mosquito	Mücke
mother	Mutter
mother-in-law	Schwiegermutter
motor scooter	Moped
motorcycle	Motorrad
mountain	Berg
moustache	Schnurrbart
mouth	Mund
movie	Film
Mr.	Herr
Mrs.	Frau
much	viel
muggy	schwül
muscle	Muskel
museum	Museum
music	Musik
Muslim	muselmanisch
my	mein

N

nail clipper	Nagelschere
nail polish	Nagellack
nail polish remover	Nagellackentferner
nail, finger	Nagel
naked	nackt

name	Name
napkin	Serviette
narrow	schmal
nationality	Nationalität
natural	natürlich
nature	Natur
nausea	Übelkeit
near	nahe
necessary	notwendig
neck	Nacken
necklace	Halsband
need	brauchen
needle	Nadel
Neoclassical	neoklassizistisch
Neo-Nazis	Neonazis
nephew	Neffe
nervous	nervös
Netherlands	Niederlande
never	nie
new	neu
newspaper	Zeitung
newsstand	Kiosk, Zeitungsstand
next	nächste
nice	nett
nickname	Spitzname
niece	Nichte
night	Nacht
nightgown	Nachthemd
no	nein, kein
no vacancy	belegt
noisy	laut
non-aspirin substitute	Ben-u-ron
non-smoking	Nichtraucher
noon	Mittag
normal	normal

north	Norden
nose	Nase
not	nicht
notebook	Notizbuch
nothing	nichts
November	November
now	jetzt
nurse	Krankenschwester
nylon (material)	Nylon
nylons (panty hose)	Strümpfe

O

O.K.	O.K.
occupation	Beruf
occupied	besetzt
ocean	Meer
October	Oktober
of	von
office	Büro
office supplies store	Bürobedarf
oil	Öl
old	alt
Olympics	Olympiade
on	auf
on time	pünktlich
once	einmal
one way (street)	einfach
one way (ticket)	Hinfahrkarte
one-way street	Einbahnstraße
only	nur
open (adj)	offen, geöffnet
open (v)	öffnen
open-air market	Markt
opening hours	Öffnungszeiten
opera	Oper

operator	Vermittlung
optician	Optiker
or	oder
orange (color)	orange
orange (fruit)	Orange, Apfelsine
organ	Orgel
original	Original
other	anderes
outdoors	im Freien
oven	Ofen
over (finished)	beendet
own (v)	besitzen
owner	Besitzer

P

pacifier	Nuggel, Schnuller
package	Paket
paddleboat	Wasserfahrrad
page	Seite
pail	Eimer
pain	Schmerz
painkiller	Schmerzmittel
pains, chest	Schmerzen in der Brust
painting	Gemälde
pajamas	Pyjama
palace	Schloß
panties	Unterhosen
pants	Hose
paper	Papier
paper clip	Büroklammer
parents	Eltern
park (garden)	Park
park (v)	parken
parking lot	Parkplatz
party	Party

passenger	Reisende
passport	Paß
past	Vergangenheit
pastry shop	Konditorei, Zuckerbäcker
pay	bezahlen
peace	Frieden
pear	Birne
pedestrian	Fußgänger
pen, ballpoint	Kugelschreiber
pencil	Bleistift
penis	Penis
people	Leute
percent	Prozent
perfect	perfekt
perfume	Parfum
period (of time)	Zeitabschnitt
period (woman's)	Periode
person	Person
pet (n)	Haustier
pewter	Zinn
pharmacy	Apotheke
phone booth	Telefonkabine
phone, mobile	Handy
photo	Photo
photocopy	Fotokopie
photocopy shop	Kopierladen
pick-pocket	Taschendieb
picnic	Picknick
piece	Stück
pig	Schwein
pill	Pille
pillow	Kissen
pills, birth control	Verhütungspille
pin	Nadel
PIN code	Geheimnummer

pink	rosa
pity, it's a	wie schade
pizza	Pizza
plain	einfach
plane	Flugzeug
plant	Pflanze
plastic	Plastik
plastic bag	Plastiktüte
plate	Teller
platform (train)	Bahnsteig
play (n)	Theaterstück
play (v)	spielen
playground	Spielplatz
playpen	Babygitter
please	bitte
pliers	Zange
pneumonia	Lungenentzündung
pocket	Tasche
point (v)	zeigen
police	Polizei
politicians	Politiker
pollution	Umwelt- verschmutzung
polyester	Polyester
poor	arm
porcelain	Porzellan
pork	Schweinefleisch
Portugal	Portugal
possible	möglich
postcard	Postkarte
poster	Poster
power	Macht
powerful	mächtig
practical	praktisch
pregnancy	Schwangerschaft
pregnancy test	Schwanger- schaftstest

pregnant	schwanger
Preparation H	Hämorrhoiden Salbe
prescription	Rezept
present (gift)	Geschenk
pretty	hübsch
price	Preis
priest	Priester
print	drucken
private	privat
problem	Problem
profession	Beruf
prohibited	verboten
pronunciation	Aussprache
prosper	florieren
Protestant	evangelisch
public	öffentlich
pull	ziehen
pulpit	Kanzel
pulse	Puls
pump (n)	Pumpe
punctual	pünktlich
purple	violett
purse	Handtasche
push	drücken

Q

quality	Qualität
quarter (¼)	Viertel
queen	Königin
question (n)	Frage
quiet	ruhig

R

R.V.	Wohnwagen
rabbit	Hase

racism	Rassimus
radiator	Kühler
radio	Radio
raft	Floß
railway	Eisenbahn
rain (n)	Regen
rainbow	Regenbogen
raincoat	Regenmantel
rape (n)	Vergewaltigung
rash	Ausschlag
rash, diaper	Windelscheuern
raw	roh
razor	Rasierapparat
ready	bereit
receipt	Beleg
receive	erhalten
receptionist	Empfangsperson
recipe	Rezept
recommend	empfehlen
rectum	Anus
red	rot
refill (n)	Erneuerung
refill (v)	nachschenken
refugees	Flüchtlinge
refund (n)	Rückgabe
relax (v)	sich erholen
relaxation	Entspannung
relic	Reliquie
religion	Religion
remember	sich erinnern
Renaissance	Renaissance
rent (out)	vermieten
rent (v)	mieten
repair (v)	reparieren
repeat	noch einmal
reservation	Reservierung
reserve	reservieren

respect	Respekt
retired	pensioniert
return	zurückgeben
reunification	Wieder-vereinigung
rich	reich
right	rechts
ring (n)	Ring
ring road	Ringstraße
ripe	reif
river	Fluß
robbed	beraubt
rock (n)	Fels
roller skates	Rollschuhe
Romanesque	romanisch
Romantic (art)	romantisch
romantic	romantisch
roof	Dach
room	Zimmer
rope	Seil
rotten	verdorben
roundabout	Kreisel
round-trip	Rückfahrt
rowboat	Ruderboot
rucksack	Rucksack
rug	Teppich
ruins	Ruine
run (v)	laufen
Russia	Rußland

S

sad	traurig
safe	sicher
safety pin	Sicherheitsnadel
sailboat	Segelboot
sailing	segeln

saint	Heiliger	service, church	Gottesdienst
sale	Schlussverkauf	sex	Sex
same	gleiche	sexy	sexy
sandals	Sandalen	shampoo	Shampoo
sandwich	belegtes Brot	shaving cream	Rasiercreme
sanitary napkins	Damenbinden	she	sie
		sheet	Laken
Santa Claus	Weihnachtsmann	shell	Schale
Saturday	Samstag, Sonnabend	ship (n)	Schiff
		ship (v)	schicken
save (computer)	speichern	shirt	Hemd
scandalous	sündig	shoelaces	Schnürsenkel
Scandinavia	Skandinavien	shoes	Schuhe
scarf	Schal	shoes, tennis	Tennisschuhe
school	Schule	shop (n)	Laden, Geschäft
science	Wissenschaft	shop, antique	Antiquitäten-laden
scientist	Wissenschaftler		
scissors	Schere	shop, barber	Herrenfrisör
scotch tape	Tesafilm	shop, camera	Photoladen
screwdriver	Schraubenzieher	shop, cell phone	Natelladen
sculptor	Bildhauer	shop, cheese	Käserei
sculpture	Skulptur	shop, coffee	Kaffeeladen
sea	Meer	shop, jewelry	Schmuckladen
seafood	Meeresfrüchte	shop, pastry	Zuckerbäcker / Konditorei
seat	Platz		
second	zweite	shop, photocopy	Kopierladen
second class	zweite Klasse	shop, souvenir	Souvenirladen
secret	Geheimnis	shop, sweets	Süßwarengeschäft
see	sehen		
self-service	Selbstbedienung	shop, wine	Weinhandlung
sell	verkaufen	shopping	einkaufen
send	senden	shopping mall	Einkaufszentrum
seniors	Senioren		
separate (adj)	getrennt	short	kurz
September	September	shorts	kurze Hosen
serious	ernsthaft	shoulder	Schulter
service	Bedienung	show (n)	Vorführung

show (v)	zeigen	slice	Scheibe
shower	Dusche	slip	Unterrock
shy	ängstlich	slippers	Pantoffeln
sick	krank	slippery	glatt
sign	Schild	slow	langsam
signature	Unterschrift	small	klein
silence	Ruhe	smell (n)	Geruch
silk	Seide	smile (n)	Lächeln
silver	Silber	smoke	Rauch
similar	ähnlich	smoking	Rauchen
simple	einfach	snack	Imbiß
sing	singen	sneeze (n)	Niesen
singer	Sänger	snore	schnarchen
single	ledig	snorkel	Schnorchel
sink	Waschbecken	snow	Schnee
sink stopper	Abflußstöpsel	soap	Seife
sinus problems	Schleimhautentzündung	soap, laundry	Waschmittel
		soccer	Fußball
sir	mein Herr	socks	Socken
sister	Schwester	some	einige
size	Größe	something	etwas
skating (ice)	Eislaufen	son	Sohn
ski (v)	ski fahren	song	Lied
skiing	Skifahren	soon	bald
skin	Haut	sore throat	Halsschmerzen
skinny	dünn	sorry	Entschuldigung
skirt	Rock	sour	sauer
sky	Himmel	south	Süden
sleep (v)	schlafen	souvenir shop	Souvenirladen
sleeper (for baby)	Kindereinteiler	Spain	Spanien
		sparkplugs	Zündkerzen
sleeper (train)	Schlafwagenplatz	speak	sprechen
		specialty	Spezialität
sleeper car (train)	Liegewagen	speed	Geschwindigkeit
sleeping bag	Schlafsack	spend	ausgeben
sleepy	schläfrig	spider	Spinne
sleeves	Ärmel	spoon	Löffel

sport	Sport
spring	Frühling
square (town)	Platz
stairs	Treppe
stamp	Briefmarke
stapler	Tacker
star (in sky)	Stern
state	Staat
station	Station
stomach	Magen
stomach-ache	Magenschmerzen
stoned	benebelt
stop (n)	Halt
stop (v)	halten
stoplight	Ampel
stopper, sink	Abflußstöpsel
store	Laden, Geschäft
store, department	Kaufhaus
store, hardware	Eisenwarengeschäft
store, office supplies	Bürobedarf
store, toy	Spielzeugladen
storm	Sturm
story (floor)	Stock
straight ahead	geradeaus
strange	merkwürdig
stream (n)	Fluß
street	Straße
strike (no work)	Streik
string	Schnur
string	Leine
stroller	Kinderwagen
strong	stark
stuck	festsitzen
student	Student
stupid	dumm
sturdy	haltbar
style	Stil
subway	U-Bahn
subway entrance	U-Bahn-Eingang
subway exit	U-Bahn-Ausgang
subway map	U-Bahn-Streckenplan
subway station	U-Bahn-Station
subway stop	U-Bahn-Haltestelle
suddenly	plötzlich
suffer	leiden
suitcase	Koffer
summer	Sommer
sun	Sonne
sunbathe	sich sonnen
sunburn	Sonnenbrand
Sunday	Sonntag
sunglasses	Sonnenbrille
sunny	sonnig
sunrise	Sonnenaufgang
sunscreen	Sonnenschutz
sunset	Sonnenuntergang
sunshine	Sonnenschein
sunstroke	Sonnenstich
suntan (n)	Sonnenbräune
suntan lotion	Sonnenbräune
supermarket	Supermarkt
supplement	Zuschlag
surfboard	Surfboard
surfer	Wellenreiter
surprise (n)	Überraschung
swallow (v)	schlucken
sweat (v)	schwitzen
sweater	Pullover

sweet	süß
sweets shop	Süßwarengeschäft
swelling (n)	Schwellung
swim	schwimmen
swim trunks	Badehose
swimming pool	Schwimmbad
swimsuit	Badeanzug
Switzerland	Schweiz
synagogue	Synagoge
synthetic	synthetisch

T

table	Tisch
tail	Schwanz
tail lights	Rücklichtern
take	nehmen
take out (food)	mitnehmen
talcum powder	Babypuder
talk	reden
tall	hoch
tampons	Tampons
tape (adhesive)	Klebeband
tape (cassette)	Kassette
taste (n)	Geschmack
taste (v)	probieren
tax	Steuer
taxes	Steuern
taxi meter	Zähler
teacher	Lehrer
team	Team
teenager	Jugendlicher
teeth	Zähne
teething (baby)	Zahnen
telephone	Telefon
telephone card	Telefonkarte
television	Fernseher
temperature	Temperatur

tender	zart
tennis	Tennis
tennis shoes	Tennisschuhe
tent	Zelt
tent pegs	Zelthäringe
terrible	schrecklich
terrorists	Terroristen
testicles	Hoden
thanks	danke
theater	Theater
thermometer	Thermometer
they	sie
thick	dick
thief	Dieb
thigh	Schenkel
thin	dünn
thing	Ding
think	denken
thirsty	durstig
thongs	Badelatschen
thread	Faden
throat	Hals
through	durch
throw	werfen
Thursday	Donnerstag
ticket (plane)	Flugkarte
ticket (show)	Eintrittskarte
ticket (train or bus)	Fahrkarte
tight	eng
tights	Strümpfe
time, on	pünktlich
timetable	Fahrplan
tire	Reifen
tired	müde
tires	Reifen
tissue, facial	Papiertuch, Taschentuch

DICTIONARY

English / German

tissues	Taschentücher	travel	reisen
to	nach, zu	travel agency	Reisebüro
today	heute	travelers	Reisende
toe	Zehe	traveler's check	Reisescheck
together	zusammen	treasury	Schatzkammer
toilet	Toilette	tree	Baum
toilet paper	Klopapier	trip	Reise, Fahrt
token	Zahlmarke, Jeton	tripod	Stativ
toll	Gebühr	troubles	Schwierigkeiten
toll-free	gebührenfrei	try (attempt)	versuchen
tomorrow	morgen	try (try out)	probieren
tonight	heute abend	T-shirt	T-Shirt
too	zu	Tuesday	Dienstag
tooth	Zahn	tunnel	Tunnel
toothache	Zahnschmerzen	Turkey	Türkei
toothbrush	Zahnbürste	turn signal	Blinker
toothpaste	Zahnpasta	tweezers	Pinzette
toothpick	Zahnstocher	twins	Zwillinge
total	Völlig		
tour	Tour	**U**	
tour, guided	Führung	ugly	häßlich
tourist	Tourist	umbrella	Regenschirm
tow truck	Abschleppwagen	uncle	Onkel
towel	Handtuch	unconscious	bewußtlos
towel, bath	Badetuch	under	unter
tower	Turm	underpants	Unterhose
town	Stadt	underscore (_)	Großstrich
toy	Spielzeug	understand	verstehen
toy store	Spielzeugladen	underwear	Unterwäsche,
track (train)	Gleis		Unterhose
traditional	traditionell	unemployed	arbeitslos
traffic	Verkehr	unfortunately	unglückliche-
train	Zug		weise
train car	Wagen	United States	Vereinigte
transfer (v)	umsteigen		Staaten
translate	übersetzen	university	Universität
transmission fluid	Getriebeöl		

up	hoch
upstairs	oben
urethra	Harnröhre
urgent	dringend
urinary infection	Harnröhrenentzündung
us	uns
use	nutzen
uterus	Gebärmutter

V

vacancy (sign)	Zimmer frei
vacant	frei
vacation	Urlaub
vagina	Vagina
valid	gültig
validate	abstempeln
valley	Tal
Vaseline	Vaseline, Mineralsalbe
vegetarian (n)	Vegetarier
velvet	Samt
venereal disease	Geschlechtskrankeit
very	sehr
vest	Weste
video	Video
video camera	Videokamera
video recorder	Videogerät
view	(Aus-)Blick
village	Dorf
vineyard	Weinberg
violence	Gewalt
virus	Virus
visit (n)	Besuch
visit (v)	besuchen

vitamins	Vitamine
voice	Stimme
vomit (v)	sich übergeben

W

waist	Bund
wait	warten
waiter	Kellner
waiting room	Wartesaal
waitress	Kellnerin
wake up	aufwachen
walk (v)	gehen
wall, fortified	Burgmauer
wallet	Brieftasche
want	möchte
war	Krieg
warm (adj)	warm
wash (v)	waschen
washer	Waschmaschine
watch (n)	Uhr
watch (v)	beobachten
water	Wasser
water, drinkable	Trinkwasser
water, tap	Leitungswasser
waterfall	Wasserfall
waterskiing	Wasserski fahren
we	wir
weather	Wetter
weather forecast	Wettervorhersage
website	Internetseite
wedding	Hochzeit
Wednesday	Mittwoch
week	Woche
weight	Gewicht
welcome	willkommen

west	west	women	Damen
western	Westen von	wood	Holz
Germany	Deutschland	wool	Wolle
wet	naß	word	Wort
what	was	work (n)	Arbeit
wheel	Rad	work (v)	arbeiten
wheelchair-	rollstuhlgängig	world	Welt
accessible		worse	schlechter
when	wann	worst	schlechteste
where	wo	wrap	umwickeln
whipped cream	Schlagsahne	wrist	Handgelenk
white	weiß	write	schreiben
white-out	Tipp-Ex		
who	wer	**X**	
why	warum	X-ray	Röntgenbild
widow	Witwe		
widower	Witwer	**Y**	
wife	Ehefrau		
Wi-Fi	WLAN	year	Jahr
wild	wild	yellow	gelb
wind	Wind	yes	ja
window	Fenster	yesterday	gestern
windshield	Scheibenwischern	you (formal)	Sie
wipers		you (informal)	du
windsurfing	Windsurfen	young	jung
windy	windig	youth hostel	Jugendherberge
wine	Wein	youths	Jugendliche
wine shop	Weinhandlung		
wing	Flügel	**Z**	
winter	Winter	zero	null
wipers,	Scheibenwischern	zip code	Postleitzahl
windshield		zip-lock bag	Gefrierbeutel
wish (v)	wünschen	zipper	Reißverschluß
with	mit	zoo	Zoo
without	ohne		

TIPS FOR HURDLING THE LANGUAGE BARRIER

Don't Be Afraid to Communicate

Even the best phrase book won't satisfy your needs in every situation. To really hurdle the language barrier, you need to leap beyond the printed page, and dive into contact with the locals. Never allow your lack of foreign language skills to isolate you from the people and cultures you traveled halfway around the world to experience. Remember that in every country you visit, you're surrounded by expert, native-speaking tutors. Spend bus and train rides letting them teach you.

Start conversations by asking politely in the local language, "Do you speak English?" When you speak English with someone from another country, talk slowly, clearly, and with carefully chosen words. Use what the Voice of America calls "simple English." You're talking to people who are wishing it was written down, hoping to see each letter as it tumbles out of your mouth. Pronounce each letter, avoiding all contractions and slang. For bad examples, listen to other tourists.

Keep things caveman-simple. Make single nouns work as entire sentences ("Photo?"). Use internationally-understood words ("auto kaput" works in Bordeaux). Butcher the language if you must. The important thing is to make the effort. To get air mail stamps, you can flap your wings and say "tweet, tweet." If you want milk, moo and pull two imaginary udders. Risk looking like a fool.

If you're short on words, make your picnic a potluck. Pull out a map and point out your journey. Draw what you mean. Bring photos from home and introduce your family. Play cards or toss a Frisbee. Fold an origami bird for kids or dazzle 'em with sleight-of-hand magic.

Go ahead and make educated guesses. Many situations are easy-to-fake multiple choice questions. Practice. Read timetables, concert posters, and newspaper headlines. Listen to each language on a multilingual tour. Be melodramatic. Exaggerate the local accent. Self-consciousness is the deadliest communication-killer.

Choose multilingual people to communicate with, such as students, business people, urbanites, young well-dressed people, or anyone in the tourist trade. Use a small note pad to jot down handy phrases and to help you communicate more clearly with the locals by scribbling down numbers, maps, and so on. Some travelers carry important messages written on a small card: allergic to nuts, strict vegetarian, your finest ice cream.

International Words

As our world shrinks, more and more words hop across their linguistic boundaries and become international. Savvy travelers develop a knack for choosing words most likely to be universally understood ("auto" instead of "car," "kaput" instead of "broken," "photo" instead of "picture"). Internationalize your pronunciation. "University," if you play around with its sound (oo-nee-vehr-see-tay), will be understood anywhere. Practice speaking English with a heavy German accent. Wave your arms a lot. Be creative.

Here are a few internationally understood words. Remember, cut out the Yankee accent and give each word a pan-European sound.

Amigo	Bank	Casanova	Coke, Coca-Cola
Attila	Beer	(romantic)	Communist
(mean, crude)	Bill Gates	Central	Computer
Auto	Bon voyage	Chocolate	Disco
Autobus	Bye-bye	Ciao	Disneyland
("booos")	Camping	Coffee	(wonderland)

Elephant (big clod)	Mama mia	Passport	Stop
	Mañana	Photo	Super
English ("Engleesh")	McDonald's	Photocopy	Taxi
	Michelangelo (artistic)	Picnic	Tea
Europa		Police	Telephone
Fascist	Moment	Post	Toilet
Hello	No	Rambo	Tourist
Hercules (strong)	No problem	Restaurant	US profanity
Hotel	Nuclear	Rock 'n' roll	University
Information	OK	Self-service	Vino
Internet	Oo la la	Sex / Sexy	Yankee, Americano
Kaput	Pardon	Sport	

German Verbs

These conjugated verbs will help you assemble a caveman sentence in a pinch.

Many Americans are confused and dismayed by German sentence structure, which sometimes tacks verbs onto the end of a sentence. Mark Twain joked that German newspaper writers, under deadline, often didn't even get around to writing the verb before they had to go to press. Actually, this verb placement usually occurs only when the sentence has two verbs–most often when you're saying that you want or like to do something, or when you're saying that something will or would happen. In these sentences, the main verb is exactly where we'd expect it to be in English, and only the secondary verb is sent to the end. To keep things simple, you can say *"Ich gehe nach Deutschland"* ("I'm going to Germany")–and the verb (*gehe*) is right there where English-speakers like it, after the pronoun. But if you say, *"Ich möchte nach Deutschland gehen"* ("I would like to go to Germany"), then the two verbs split up. The main verb (*möchte*, or "would like") stays where it is in English–right after the pronoun. But the secondary verb (*gehen*, or "go") moves to the end. So the German sentence order is literally, "I would like to Germany go."

There are also a handful of prepositions such as *weil* (because) or *wenn* (if) that push the verb to the end of the sentence: "I'm going to Germany because it is so beautiful" is translated as "*Ich gehe nach Deutschland weil es so schön ist,*" which is literally "I'm going to Germany because it so beautiful is."

My favorite German teacher insisted, "*Deutsch ist leicht und logisch*"–German is easy and logical. And it is, if you know the rules.

TO GO	*GEHEN*	**gay**-hehn
I go	*ich gehe*	ikh **gay**-heh
you go	*Sie gehen*	zee **gay**-hehn
(formal, singular or plural)		
you go	*du gehst*	doo gayst
(informal, singular)		
he / she goes	*er / sie geht*	ehr / zee gayt
we go	*wir gehen*	veer **gay**-hehn
they go	*sie gehen*	zee **gay**-hehn

TO BE	*SEIN*	zīn
I am	*ich bin*	ikh bin
you are	*Sie sind*	zee zint
(formal, singular or plural)		
you are	*du bist*	doo bist
(informal, singular)		
he / she is	*er / sie ist*	ehr / zee ist
we are	*wir sind*	veer zint
they are	*sie sind*	zee zint

TO DO, TO MAKE	*MACHEN*	**mahkh**-ehn
I do	*ich mache*	ikh **mahkh**-eh
you do	*Sie machen*	zee **mahkh**-ehn
(formal, singular or plural)		
you do	*du machst*	doo mahkhst
(informal, singular)		
he / she does	*er / sie macht*	ehr / zee mahkht
we do	*wir machen*	veer **mahkh**-ehn
they do	*sie machen*	zee **mahkh**-ehn

TO HAVE	*HABEN*	**hah**-behn
I have	*ich habe*	ikh **hah**-beh
you have	*Sie haben*	zee **hah**-behn
(formal, singular or plural)		
you have	*du hast*	doo hahst
(informal, singular)		
he / she has	*er / sie hat*	ehr / zee haht
we have	*wir haben*	veer **hah**-behn
they have	*sie haben*	zee **hah**-behn

TO SEE	*SEHEN*	**zay**-hehn
I see	*ich sehe*	ikh **zay**-heh
you see	*Sie sehen*	zee **zay**-hehn
(formal, singular or plural)		
you see	*du siehst*	doo zeest
(informal, singular)		
he / she sees	*er / sie sieht*	ehr / zee zeet
we see	*wir sehen*	veer **zay**-hehn
they see	*sie sehen*	zee **zay**-hehn

TO SPEAK	*SPRECHEN*	**shprehkh**-ehn
I speak	*ich spreche*	ikh **shprehkh**-eh
you speak	*Sie sprechen*	zee **shprehkh**-ehn
(formal, singular or plural)		
you speak	*du sprichst*	doo shprikhst
(informal, singular)		
he / she speaks	*er / sie spricht*	ehr / zee shprikht
we speak	*wir sprechen*	veer **shprehkh**-ehn
they speak	*sie sprechen*	zee **shprehkh**-ehn

TO LIKE	*MÖGEN*	**mur**-gehn
I like	*ich mag*	ikh mahg
you like	*Sie mögen*	zee **mur**-gehn
(formal, singular or plural)		
you like	*du magst*	doo mahgst
(informal, singular)		
he / she likes	*er / sie mag*	ehr / zee mahg
we like	*wir mögen*	veer **mur**-gehn
they like	*sie mögen*	zee **mur**-gehn

TO WANT	*MÖCHTEN*	**murkh**-tehn
(literally "would like")		
I would like	*ich möchte*	ikh **murkh**-teh
you would like	*Sie möchten*	zee **murkh**-tehn
(formal, singular or plural)		
you would like	*du möchtest*	doo **murkh**-tehst
(informal, singular)		
he / she would like	*er / sie möchtet*	ehr / zee **murkh**-teht
we would like	*wir möchten*	veer **murkh**-tehn
they would like	*sie möchten*	zee **murkh**-tehn

TO NEED	*BRAUCHEN*	**browkh**-ehn
I need	*ich brauche*	ikh **browkh**-eh
you need	*Sie brauchen*	zee **browkh**-ehn
(formal, singular or plural)		
you need	*du brauchst*	doo browkhst
(informal, singular)		
he / she needs	*er / sie braucht*	ehr / zee browkht
we need	*wir brauchen*	veer **browkh**-ehn
they need	*sie brauchen*	zee **browkh**-ehn

German Tongue Twisters

Tongue twisters are a great way to practice a language and break the ice with the locals. Here are a few *Zungenbrecher* that are sure to challenge you, and amuse your hosts:

Zehn zame Ziegen zogen Zucker zum Zoo.	Ten domesticated goats pulled sugar to the zoo.
Blaukraut bleibt Blaukraut und Brautkleid bleibt Brautkleid.	Bluegrass remains bluegrass and a wedding dress remains a wedding dress.
Fischers Fritze fischt frische Fische, frische Fische fischt Fischers Fritze.	Fritz Fischer catches fresh fish, fresh fish Fritz Fisher catches.

Die Katze trapst die Treppe rauf.	The cat is walking up the stairs.
Ich komme über Oberammergau, oder komme ich über Unterammergau?	I am coming via Oberammergau, or am I coming via Unterammergau?

English Tongue Twisters

After your German friends have laughed at you, let them try these tongue twisters in English:

If neither he sells seashells, nor she sells seashells, who shall sell seashells? Shall seashells be sold?	Wenn er keine Muscheln verkauft, und sie verkauft keine Muscheln, wer verkauft dann Muscheln? Werden Muscheln verkauft?
Peter Piper picked a peck of pickled peppers.	Peter Pfeiffer erntete einen Korb voll eingemachter Pfefferschoten.
Rugged rubber baby buggy bumpers.	Starke Gummistoßdämpfer am Kinderwagen.
The sixth sick sheik's sixth sheep's sick.	Das sechste Schaf vom sechsten Scheich ist krank.
Red bug's blood and black bug's blood.	Blut vom roten Käfer und Blut vom schwarzen Käfer.
Soldiers' shoulders.	Soldatenschultern.
Thieves seize skis.	Diebe klauen Schi.
I'm a pleasant mother pheasant plucker. I pluck mother pheasants. I'm the most pleasant mother pheasant plucker that ever	Ich bin ein freundlicher Federrupfer von Fasanenhennen. Ich rupfe Federn von Fasanenhennen. Ich bin der freundlichste Federrupfer von

plucked a mother pheasant. Fasanenhennen, der je die Federn
einer Fasanenhenne gerupft hat.

German Songs

Another way to connect with locals is to sing a song together.
Most folks are familiar with "*Stille Nacht, Heilige Nacht*" ("Silent
Night, Holy Night") and "*O Tannenbaum*" ("O Christmas Tree").
Here are the words to a few more German songs. Get a local to
teach you the tunes.

First, a favorite folksong:

Du, Du Liegst Mir Im Herzen You Are in My Heart
–Anonymous

Du, du liegst mir im Herzen,	You are in my heart,
Du, du liegst mir in Sinn.	You are in my mind.
Du, du machst mir viel Schmertzen,	You cause me much pain,
Weißt nicht wie gut ich dir bin.	You do not know how good I am for you.
Ja, ja, ja, ja, weißt nicht wie gut ich dir bin.	Yes, you do not know how good I am for you.
So, so, wie ich dich liebe,	Just as I love you,
So, so, liebe auch mich.	So love me too.
Die, die zärtlichsten Triebe,	The most affectionate instincts,
Fühl' ich allein ewig für dich.	I feel lonesome always for you.
Doch, doch, darf ich dir trauen,	But yes, I may trust you,
Dir, dir, mit leichtem Sinn.	You, with light thoughts.
Du, du kannst auf mich bauen,	You can count on me,
Weißt ja, wie gut ich dir bin.	You do know how good I am for you.
Ja, ja, ja, ja, weißt ja, wie gut ich dir bin.	Yes, you do know how good I am for you.
Und, und, wenn in der Ferne,	And if in the distance,
Mir, mir, dein Bild erscheint,	Your image appears to me,

Dann, dann wünscht ich so gerne,	Then I will so gladly wish
Daß uns die Liebe vereint.	That love would unite us.
Ja, ja, ja, ja, daß uns die Liebe vereint.	Yes, that love would unite us.

Rollicking drinking songs (often accompanied by an oompah band and swaying locals) are an important part of German beer-hall culture. You'll likely hear this simple *Trinklied* (drinking song), especially during Oktoberfest in Munich:

Ein Prosit der Gemütlichkeit!   A Toast to Coziness!
–Traditional

Ein Prosit, ein Prosit	A toast, a toast
Der Gemütlichkeit!	To coziness!
Ein Prosit, ein Prosit	A toast, a toast
Der Gemütlichkeit!	To coziness!

And finally, here's a lovesong often played on Rhine cruises passing the infamous Loreley. This huge hulking cliff is steeped in the legend of a beautiful siren who lured sailors to their deaths.

Die Lorelei   The Loreley
–Lyrics by Heinrich Heine, music by Friedrich Silcher, 1827

Ich weiß nicht, was soll es bedeuten, daß ich so traurig bin;	I don't know what it should mean that I'm so sad;
ein Märchen aus alten Zeiten, das mir nicht aus dem Sinn.	a tale from the olden times, kommt which does not come to me from reason.
Die Luft ist kühl, es dunkelt, und ruhig fließt der Rhein;	The air is cool, it gets dark, and gently flows the Rhine;
der Gipfel des Berges funkelt im Abendsonnenschein.	the peak of the mountain glistens in afternoon sunshine.

LANGUAGE TIPS

Die schönste Jungfrau sitzet
  dort oben wunderbar;
ihr goldnes Geschmeide blitzet,
  sie kämmt ihr goldnes Haar.
Sie kämmt es mit goldnem
  Kamme und singt ein Lied
dabei; das hat eine wunder-
  same, gewaltige Melodei.
	The prettiest maiden sits
	  up there wonderfully;
	her golden jewelry twinkles,
	  she combs her golden hair.
	She combs it with a golden comb
	  while she sings a song,
	which has a wondrous,
	  overwhelming melody.

Den Schiffer im kleinen Schiffe
  ergreift es mit wildem Weh;
er schaut nicht die Felsenriffe,
  er schaut nur hinauf in die Höh'.
Ich glaube, die Wellen
  verschlingen am Ende Schiffer
und Kahn;
und das hat mir ihrem
  Singen die Lorelei getan.
	The boatman in the small rowboat
	  seizes the song with a wild ache;
	he looks not at the cliff's reef,
	  but only above to the sky.
	I believe in the end the waves
	  will engulf the boatman and
	  his boat;
	and the Loreley has
	  done this with her singing.

Numbers and Stumblers

- Europeans write a few of their numbers differently than we do.
  1=*1*, 4=*4*, 7=*7*. Learn the difference or miss your train.
- Europeans write the date in this order: day/month/year.
- Commas are decimal points, and decimals are commas. A dollar
  and a half is 1,50, and there are 5.280 feet in a mile.
- The European "first floor" isn't the ground floor but the first
  floor up.
- When counting with your fingers, start with your thumb. If you
  hold up only your first finger, you'll probably get two of
  something.

APPENDIX

LET'S TALK TELEPHONES

Making Calls within a European Country: About half of all European countries use area codes (like we do); the other half uses a direct-dial system without area codes.

To make calls within a country that uses a direct-dial system (Belgium, Czech Republic, Denmark, France, Greece, Italy, Norway, Poland, Portugal, Spain, and Switzerland), you dial the same number whether you're calling across the country or across the street.

In countries that use area codes (such as Austria, Britain, Croatia, Finland, Germany, Ireland, Netherlands, Slovakia, Slovenia, and Sweden), you dial the local number when calling within a city and you add the area code if calling long-distance within the country.

Making International Calls: You always start with the international access code (011 if you're calling from America or Canada, or 00 from Europe), then dial the country code of the country you're calling (see codes on the next page).

What you dial next depends on the phone system of the country you're calling. If the country uses area codes, drop the initial zero of the area code, then dial the rest of the number.

Countries that use direct-dial systems (no area codes) vary in how they're accessed internationally by phone. You always start by dialing the international access code, followed by the country code. Then, if you're calling the Czech Republic, Denmark, Italy, Norway, Portugal, or Spain, simply dial the phone number in its entirety. But if you're calling Belgium, France, Poland, or Switzerland, drop the initial zero of the phone number.

Country Codes
After you've dialed the international access code, dial the code of the country you're calling.

Austria—43	France—33	Poland—48
Belgium—32	Germany—49	Portugal—351
Bosnia-	Gibraltar—350	Slovakia—421
Herzegovina—387	Greece—30	Slovenia—386
Britain—44	Hungary—36	Spain—34
Canada—1	Ireland—353	Sweden—46
Croatia—385	Italy—39	Switzerland—41
Czech Rep.—420	Montenegro—382	Turkey—90
Denmark—45	Morocco—212	United States—1
Estonia—372	Netherlands—31	
Finland—358	Norway—47	

Directory Assistance

	National	International	Train Information
Austria:	16	08	051717
Germany:	11833	11834	11861
German tourist offices—dial area code, then 19433			
Switzerland:	111	191	0900-300-3004

US Embassies
Austria (in Vienna)
• Tel. 01/313-390
• Boltzmanngasse 16
• www.usembassy.at

Germany
Embassy **(Berlin)**
- Tel. 030/83050, consular services tel. 030/832-9233
- Neustädtische Kirchstraße 4-5, consular services at
  Clayallee 170
- www.usembassy.de

Munich Consulate
- Tel. 089/28880
- Königinstraße 5

Switzerland (in Bern)
- Tel. 031-357-7234
- Jubilaeumsstraße 93
- http://bern.usembassy.gov

Tear-Out Cheat Sheet

Keep this sheet of German survival phrases in your pocket, handy to memorize or use if you're caught without your phrase book.

Good day.	*Guten Tag.*	**goo**-tehn tahg
Do you speak English?	*Sprechen Sie Englisch?*	**shprehkh**-ehn zee **ehng**-lish
Yes. / No.	*Ja. / Nein.*	yah / nīn
I don't understand.	*Ich verstehe nicht.*	ikh fehr-**shtay**-heh nikht
Please.	*Bitte.*	**bit**-teh
Thank you.	*Danke.*	**dahng**-keh
You're welcome.	*Bitte.*	**bit**-teh
I'm sorry.	*Es tut mir leid.*	ehs toot meer līt
Excuse me. (to pass or to get attention)	*Entschuldigung.*	ehnt-**shool**-dig-oong
No problem.	*Kein Problem.*	kīn proh-**blaym**
Very good.	*Sehr gut.*	zehr goot
Goodbye.	*Auf Wiedersehen.*	owf **vee**-der-zayn
How much is it?	*Wie viel kostet das?*	vee feel **kohs**-teht dahs
Write it down?	*Aufschreiben?*	**owf**-shrī-behn
euro (€)	*Euro*	**oy**-roh
one / two	*eins / zwei*	īns / tsvī
three / four	*drei / vier*	drī / feer
five / six	*fünf / sechs*	fewnf / zehkhs
seven / eight	*sieben / acht*	**zee**-behn / ahkht
nine / ten	*neun / zehn*	noyn / tsayn
20	*zwanzig*	**tsvahn**-tsig
30	*dreißig*	**drī**-sig
40	*vierzig*	**feer**-tsig
50	*fünfzig*	**fewnf**-tsig
60	*sechzig*	**zehkh**-tsig
70	*siebzig*	**zeeb**-tsig
80	*achtzig*	**ahkht**-tsig
90	*neunzig*	**noyn**-tsig
100	*hundert*	**hoon**-dert
I'd like...	*Ich hätte gern...*	ikh **heh**-teh gehrn

We'd like...	*Wir hätten gern...*	veer **heh**-tehn gehrn
...this.	*...dies.*	deez
...more.	*...mehr.*	mehr
...a ticket.	*...eine Fahrkarte.*	**ī**-neh **far**-kar-teh
...a room.	*...ein Zimmer.*	īn **tsim**-mer
...the bill.	*...die Rechnung.*	dee **rehkh**-noong
Is it possible?	*Ist es möglich?*	ist ehs **mur**-glikh
Where is the toilet?	*Wo ist die Toilette?*	voh ist dee toh-**leh**-teh
men / women	*Herren / Damen*	**hehr**-ehn / **dah**-mehn
entrance / exit	*Eingang / Ausgang*	**īn**-gahng / **ows**-gahng
no entry	*kein Zugang*	kīn **tsoo**-gahng
open / closed	*geöffnet / geschlossen*	geh-**urf**-neht / geh-**shloh**-sehn
When does this open / close?	*Wann ist hier geöffnet / geschlossen?*	vahn ist heer geh-**urf**-neht / geh-**shloh**-sehn
Now.	*Jetzt.*	yehtzt
Soon.	*Bald.*	bahlt
Later.	*Später.*	**shpay**-ter
Today.	*Heute.*	hoy-teh
Tomorrow.	*Morgen.*	**mor**-gehn
Monday	*Montag*	**mohn**-tahg
Tuesday	*Dienstag*	**deen**-stahg
Wednesday	*Mittwoch*	**mit**-vohkh
Thursday	*Donnerstag*	**doh**-ner-stahg
Friday	*Freitag*	**frī**-tahg
Saturday	*Samstag*	**zahm**-stahg
Sunday	*Sonntag*	**zohn**-tahg

Making Your Hotel Reservation

Most hotel managers know basic "hotel English." Emailing or faxing are the preferred methods for reserving a room. They're clearer and more foolproof than telephoning. Photocopy and enlarge this form, or find it online at www.ricksteves.com/reservation.

One-Page Fax

To: _____   _____
             hotel   *email or fax*

From: _____   _____
              name   *email or fax*

Today's date: _____/_____/_____
             day *month* *year*

Dear Hotel _____

Please make this reservation for me:

Name: _____

Total # of people: _____ # of rooms: _____ # of nights: _____

Arriving: _____/_____/_____ Arrival time: (24-hr clock): _____
        day *month* *year*   (I will telephone if I will be late)

Departing: _____/_____/_____
          day *month* *year*

Room(s): Single___ Double ___ Twin___ Triple___ Quad___ Quint ___

With: Toilet ___ Shower___ Bathtub___ Sink only___

Special needs: View ___ Quiet___ Cheapest ___ Ground floor ___

Please email or fax me confirmation of my reservation, along with the type of room reserved and the price. Please also inform me of your cancellation policy. After I hear from you, I will quickly send my credit-card information as a deposit to hold the room. Thank you.

Name _____

Address _____

City _____ State____ Zip Code_____ Country_____

Email address _____

NOTES

Rick Steves®
EUROPEAN TOURS
Experience Europe the Rick Steves
way, with great guides,
small groups...and no grumps!
See 30 itineraries at ricksteves.com

Start your trip at

Free information and great gear to

▶ Plan Your Trip

Browse thousands of articles and a wealth of money-saving tips for planning your dream trip. You'll find up-to-date information on Europe's best destinations, packing smart, getting around, finding rooms, staying healthy, avoiding scams and more.

▶ Eurail Passes

Find out, step-by-step, if a railpass makes sense for your trip—and how to avoid buying more than you need. Get a bunch of free extras!

▶ Graffiti Wall & Travelers' Helpline

Learn, ask, share— our online community of savvy travelers is a great resource for first-time travelers to Europe, as well as seasoned pros.

Rick Steves' Europe Through the Back Door, Inc.

The perfect complement
to your phrase book

Travel with Rick Steves' candid, up-to-date advice on the best places to eat and sleep, the must-see sights, getting off the beaten path—and getting the most out of every day and every dollar while you're in Europe.